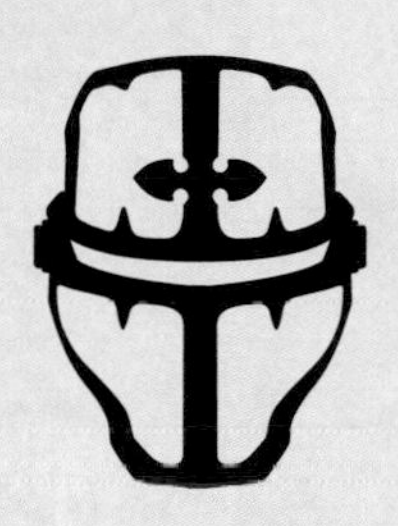

IMPERIAL KNIGHTS

'Let the power of your Knight flow through your veins. Let the ghosts of your Throne whisper wisdom into your mind. Let steel be your sinews and fire be your fists. Become your Knight, as it becomes you, and through symbiosis ascend. So shall you Become. So shall you protect your people and slaughter your foes.'

- Sixth Canticle of the Ritual of Becoming

PRODUCED BY THE WARHAMMER STUDIO

With thanks to the Mournival and the Infinity Circuit for their additional playtesting services.

British Cataloguing-in-Publication Data. A catalogue record for this book is available from the British Library.

Games Workshop Ltd, Willow Rd, Lenton, Nottingham, NG7 2WS

WARHAMMER.COM

INTRODUCTION

Hail, Noble pilot! You hold now *Codex: Imperial Knights*. No volume explores the storied history, glorious heraldry and implacable machines of the Questor Imperialis and Questor Mechanicus in greater detail. Every page is packed full of detail on the Imperial Knights' organisation, ways of war, iconography and how to collect a mighty host of these formidable war engines.

Armies of Imperial Knights invariably include only a handful of models – but what models they are! Each is a towering, heavily armed and armoured, bipedal war engine. Even the smallest of their number is a serious threat to entire enemy squads. A host of Knights on the battlefield is an awe-inspiring – or terror-inducing – sight.

Besides the sheer excitement of commanding an army of ironclad giants, there is much to be gained from collecting this army. Every Knight is a superb modelling project in its own right. The large and detailed Knight kits include a large number of flat panels, which are perfect for you to emblazon with iconography and heraldry. Most Knights belong to a noble household, a mighty organisation with beloved traditions, a great tally of victories going back thousands of years and its own colour scheme. This volume showcases many examples that you might want to collect, or serve as inspiration for you to invent your own. In addition to the background of these households, the beautiful artwork and photography that adorns every page of this book provides further evocative examples for you. With so few models in your collection, you can lavish each one with a great deal of care and attention if you so wish, and still produce an army you can be proud of quickly. You can easily take this a step further if you desire – not every Knight belongs to a household. Some are Freeblades – warriors who for one reason or another operate as individuals. Each has a unique colour scheme, character and history. With an army of Freeblades you can have a collection where every single Knight looks completely different, perfect for those who love to delve into the background of their army as well as want a range of different painting challenges – or those who can't decide on a single colour scheme.

Finally, this book contains all of the exciting rules you need to take your collection and make it a force to be truly terrifying on the battlefield. Datasheets for every unit in the range, Warlord Traits, Stratagems, household rules and Relics – all are here. For those who love narrative play, there are also the Crusade rules. These provide you with everything you need to develop your army over the course of many battles as your Knights gain experience, win victories and suffer defeats. These are bespoke to this Codex, unique to Imperial Knights, and are additions to the Crusade rules found in the Warhammer 40,000 Core Book.

Through the smoke and fires and battle do the Knights stride, pistons and servo-motors groaning and thumping with every thunderous step. They stand tall and proud in the face of any enemy, the magnificent designs of their heraldry emblazoned over armour painted in shining bright colours for all to see.

Their ion fields shimmer as enemy fire blasts ineffectively against them, creating a halo of holy light around these towering war engines. Shell, rocket and lasbeam ricochet harmlessly from their ionic barriers, and the Knights march through it all without fear. Victory is what they seek: for themselves, for their household, for their Emperor. And they shall have it.

Within the mighty armoured shell, the Noble pilot – a scion of a long bloodline whose members have mastered the use of their gigantic mechanical steeds over millennia – sits upon their Throne Mechanicum. Men and women of honour, chivalry, pride as well as formidable warriors, by them are the Knight's fearsome weapons directed. Just one of their number can annihilate countless foes and turn the tide of battle, and entire hosts can conquer star systems.

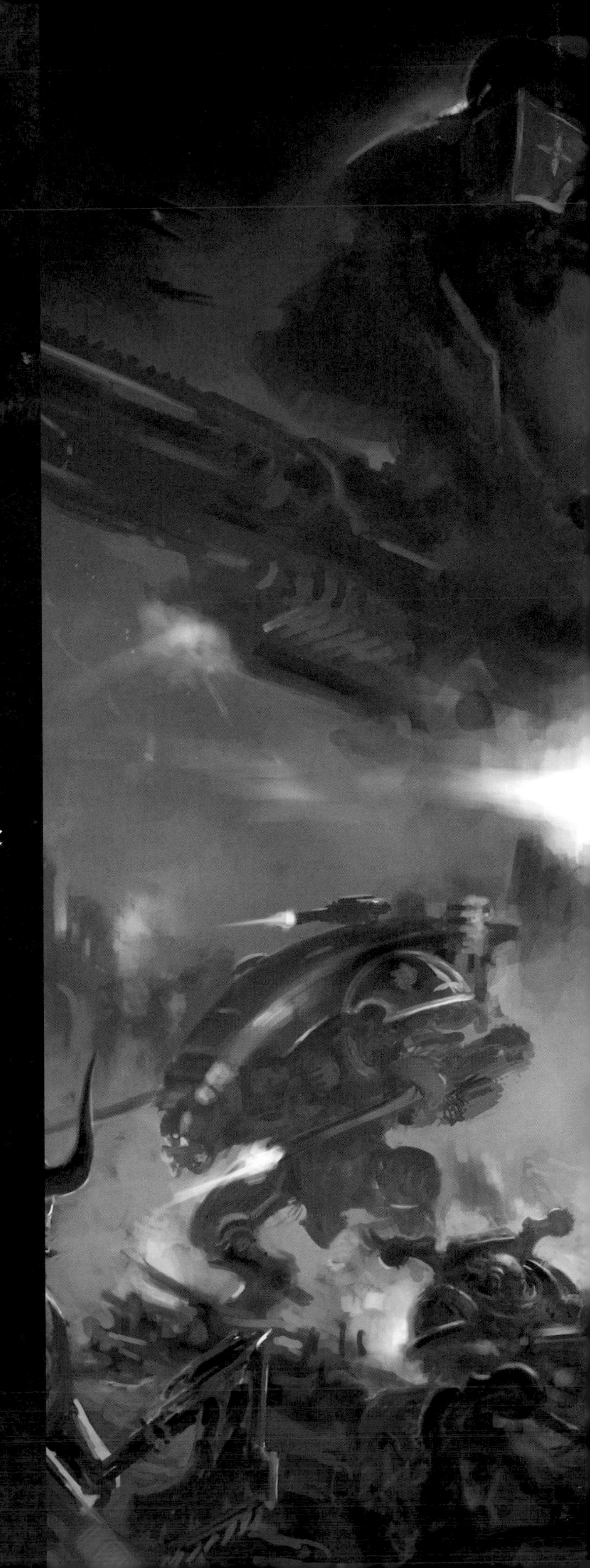

For a Noble to sit upon a Throne Mechanicum is to become not only one with their Knight suit, but also to commune with the spirits of those who have piloted this mechanical steed in the past. This is privilege and honour both, and fills Nobles with a righteous pride that fuels them across horrific war zone after horrific war zone.

A LEGACY OF HONOUR

The origins of the Imperial Knights go back further in time than the rise of the Emperor on Holy Terra. The first Knight worlds were settled during Mankind's earliest expansion into the stars and most have weathered through all of Humanity's great trials and tribulations. They remain to this day great bastions against the dark.

Fragments of ancient dataslates suggest that many of the earliest Human colonists to planets outside the Sol System encountered all manner of lethal flora and fauna, freak meteorological events, near-inhospitable environments, hostile alien species and viral outbreaks. Given that the raw materials they needed to found their colonies came from cannibalising their own Long March ships, the settlers had no choice but to endure whatever challenges they faced. They did so thanks to their pioneering Human spirit as well as Standard Template Construction technology. STC machines can each replicate a specific device perfectly. With them the colonists fashioned tools, shelter, power generators, transport and more. Some settlers used them to create towering constructs called Knight suits. These formidable armoured walkers could traverse dangerous terrain, prevail through horrific climatic conditions and be used by their pilots to defend their settlements against attack. Many colonies produced them in great numbers. Piloted by the most skilled and charismatic of colonists they became the mailed fist of Human expansionism, smashing aside any all threats.

None were aware that while the Knight suits served the colonists, those piloting them were being irrevocably changed by them. To operate a Knight suit, its pilot uses a technological marvel known as the Throne Mechanicum. These mount neural jacks and cerebral uplinks that directly connect Knight and pilot. Though no one knows how, or why, the longer they fought in their suits, the more authoritarian the pilots became. Over a few generations, notions of chivalric conduct, ritual observance, loyalty and fealty became completely embedded among the pilots and changed the dynamic of their colonies. These pilots became the first Nobles of the original houses, and those they protected became akin to feudal serfs.

In a surprisingly short time, their worlds became socially conservative and inward-looking in comparison to other colony worlds, and were seen as culturally and technologically backward. This, however, ultimately protected them from the apocalypse Mankind later endured in what was to become known as Old Night.

In that horrific time, Humanity was almost wiped out. Rampant, uncontrolled psykers drowned worlds in warp storms and daemonic incursions. Thinking machines carried out sector-wide purges and megalomaniacal overlords conducted devastating gene-wars. The Knight worlds had few of these problems. Most killed any psykers they found among their population as witches. They forbade the creation of thinking machines, emphasising the value of hard labour, and refused to dabble with their own genetics. As Humanity appeared to collapse all around them, the Knights fortified their holdings, patrolled their borders and hoarded resources. For thousands of years they persisted in this way. Though the cultures on some Knight worlds regressed, and their technologies were slowly worn down, a surprisingly large number emerged from Old Night intact.

It was only much later, when the Emperor sought to unite Humanity with the Great Crusade, that Humanity rediscovered the Knight worlds, which were found slowly by Rogue Traders and vanguard battle groups. Over a period of decades, hundreds were brought into the Imperial fold. Tens of thousands of Knights strode the battlefields of the Great Crusade, slaughtering xenos in droves and crushing those Human worlds that refused the Emperor's rule.

Both the Imperial Administratum and the Mechanicum of Mars recognised the formidable power of the Knight worlds. Not only were they bastions of military power, but they also held ancient technology that many believed had been lost forever. Many Knight worlds chose to follow Mars, or had little choice but to join with the Mechanicum through their deep need of the technological expertise of the Martian Magi to maintain the functionality of their Knight suits, becoming Questor Mechanicus. Others however pledged themselves to the Emperor and Terra, becoming Questor Imperialis.

When the disastrous Horus Heresy embroiled the Emperor's realm in civil war, a large number of Knight worlds turned traitor. Yet many more – shielded from spiritual corruption by the conditioning of their Thrones – joined the battle on the side of the loyalists. They proved their honour then and have ever since. To this day, the surviving Knight worlds are vital linchpins of the Imperial defence, protecting their allies from invaders. All the while, their crusading armies take the fight to the enemy, crushing them wherever they are found.

THE OMNISSIAH'S BOON

Imperial Knights maintain and use all manner of ancient technologies that no other element of the Imperium are known to have access to. It is largely thanks to the Tech-Priests of the Omnissiah, based on their mighty forge worlds, however, that the Nobles can continue to take their Knight suits to war.

FORGE WORLDS

These planets are controlled by the Adeptus Mechanicus and are places of endless industry and rampant pollution. Upon these worlds the priests of the Omnissiah, the Machine God, jealously hoard all their accumulated secrets and lore. Forge worlds are also nigh-impregnable military strongholds, boasting immense garrisons of cyborg, lobotomised and robot soldiers and a vast array of bizarre vehicles armed with all manner of devastating weapons. These armies are frequently bolstered by Knightly households. A majority of noble houses are associated with a forge world, because deep in the past the priests of the Omnissiah won a Machiavellian political contest among different arms of the Great Crusade to exploit, control and influence the Knight worlds. The tech-magi wanted the Nobles' archeotech and military might, and succeeded in making many of them dependent on the forge worlds for vital technology and knowledge.

In the past, the Adeptus Mechanicus settled many of the Knight worlds and trained the Nobles' feudal orders of technicians in the ways of maintaining their Knight suits. As a result, now virtually all Knights bear a sign of the Cult Mechanicus somewhere on their immense armoured forms, as a reminder of the debt they owe Mars. Many Knight worlds and forge worlds maintain extremely strong trade relations, with Adeptus Mechanicus vessels bringing armaments, new Knight suits, tools and mining machinery to the houses and leaving with holds packed with ores and food. Now, many Knight worlds are bastions of technological sophistication defended by mighty fortresses and elite warriors. However, relations between Knight and forge worlds vary greatly from planet to planet, Noble to Tech-Priest. Even those households that swear fealty to Mars are strong-willed warriors, with codes of honour that prevent them from following the command of the Adeptus Mechanicus without question.

THRONE MECHANICUM

These devices are testaments to the accomplishments of the Age of Technology, and are a pinnacle of creation from that forgotten era. Thrones Mechanicum allow a Knight suit to become an extension of the pilot's own body through the neural jacks connected directly to their cranial sockets. To

pilot a Knight suit is for the machine's mechanical senses to become the driver's own. For an unprepared mind, such an experience would almost certainly cause madness. Thus, household Nobles are conditioned from birth as well as cerebrally augmented to endure it. When they come of age, or when a Knight suit is available, eligible young Nobles undergo the Ritual of Becoming. In this rite, they are led to their house's sanctuary, a vast fortified structure within their ancestral stronghold that contains the Chamber of Echoes. There, they are connected to one of their house's dormant Thrones and are left for a full night. Thrones Mechanicum contain behavioural subroutines that weed out those not strong enough to control them and fight the young Noble for control. It is the task of the aspirant to wrestle with the Throne's energies, withstand the receipt of its cerebral engrams and imprint their own psyche upon it. The Ritual of Becoming has been known to drive aspirants mad, and even kill them. Those who emerge victorious leave childhood behind and are ennobled with the mantle of Knighthood.

One of the most unusual elements of the Thrones Mechanicum is that, beyond their interface and control circuits, they also contain mnemic engram reliquaries and spectronionic foci that let them store synaptic echoes of the pilots they have bonded with before. Therefore, every Throne is haunted by the ghosts of their former controllers, which communicate with a Knight's pilot. Nobles speak of whispering voices, visions and other strange manifestations that provide them with guidance, wisdom and advice.

HELM MECHANICUM

Armigers – among the smallest class of Knight – do not use Thrones Mechanicum, instead their pilots use a Helm Mechanicum. These are placed upon their heads and connected to the pilot's cerebrum via pre-frontal sockets, and do not require a full Becoming ritual for the neural interfacing to work. As a result, there is less prestige in piloting an Armiger, compounded by the fact that some Helms Mechanicum are neurally slaved to the command impulses of a larger Knight. Accepting this mental serfdom gives a pilot the rank of Bondsman, and while it is not as glorious as full Knighthood, is not seen as dishonourable. Typically, these pilots hail from lower-status Noble houses, minor offshoots of distant bloodlines or even survivors of other households fallen on hard times. Others are even from the finest troops of a Knight world's peasantry. Some belong to specialist sub-orders established by Knightly houses and are experts, fated from birth, in piloting Armigers.

SACRISTANS

Sacristans are skilled artisans responsible for maintaining their household's Knight suits. They learn their skills in the tech-shrines of the Adeptus Mechanicus as well as their house's unique knowledge and specialist skills from master Sacristans. As a result they tend to be insular and exhibit many similar traits to those of Tech-Priests. Their appearance, customs, traditions and organisation are influenced by their world's culture. Equally the attitudes of Nobles to their Sacristans varies across the households – they can be regarded as wise servants, hidebound engineers or even as suspiciously secretive spies of the Adeptus Mechanicus.

Sacristans are expected to follow their masters to war, working between battles or riding out in armoured crawlers, forge landers or servitor-striders to perform battlefield repairs. Some operate from devotional structures deployed in the midst of a war zone. Forge-shrines are the most common of these, armoured refuelling depots with servo-armatures which can be used to carry out rapid repairs which can even be remotely operated by the Sacristans.

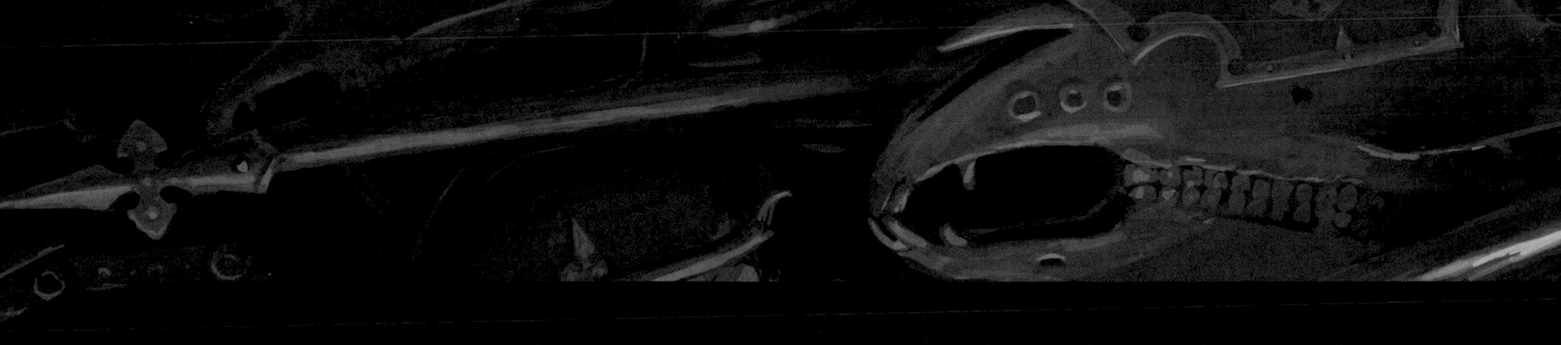

Baronette Sciera Tors, Heir-ward of House Winterveil, walked to the battlements of the Glakium Magna, principal fortress of her house on the world of Icefall. Servos whirred as her bionic left leg moved. The metal of the artificial limb tapped the frost-coated stone floors along with the tip of her long, dark elm cane. Her entire left side was made of metal. Where the replacement body parts met flesh, Tor's remaining skin was marked with hideous burn marks. Beside her walked a boy of ten. He had to jog to keep up with her and shivered as a light snow fell down on them. When the pair reached the battlements, he could not see over them. He placed a specially made platform up against the walls and stood upon it.

'Why do we come here each day?' asked Tors.

'So I can see and appreciate what will one day be mine to lead and rule,' the boy, Scion Tormun Winterveil, recited.

'Good. As it is now your mother's, so it will one day be yours. When you ascend to the throne of House Winterveil, you must know the world of Icefall better than any soul who dwells here. Your title will demand deference from your subjects, but you must earn their respect and devotion. A house is only as strong as its leader. The High Monarch is the keystone around which everything is held together. Weakness begets weakness. Weakness breeds politicking and disunity.'

Tors pointed at a crop of snow-coated mountains on the horizon. 'What are they?' she asked.

'The Whitemons, home of House Peak,' said Tormun. 'Our vassals, masters of the quarries and the salt mines.'

'Correct,' Tors said, nodding. 'They will owe their allegiance to you, as they have owed their allegiance to your family for thirteen thousand years. They are a tough and proud dynasty. But remember, though they are your vassals when we discuss them behind these walls, when we meet them they are our allies. Their numbers represent fifteen percent of the Knights you can call upon for war; needlessly upsetting them will do nothing for your cause.'

'Yes, Heir-ward.'

'That is not the only region you must consider, nor are the Nobles of House Peak the only people you must think of. Your duties will be to this entire world, once you are of age, and passed through the Ritual of Becoming. What is the chief output of the Band of Emerald? And of the Briarcopse, Ashcluster, Felwood and Oaktangle? And of all they provide, what is the most important resource of all?'

'Meat and grain from the equatorial grasslands,' the boy said. 'Lumber and game from the great forests.' He did not answer the third question, his face contorted with thought as he tried to find the answer.

'People, boy, people,' Tors said. She addressed him by no title, to teach him humility. 'Your farmers, trappers, woodspeople and herders are what make Icefall function. Without them, your house would collapse. Our means of trade with other planets would be lost, and our alliance with the tech-magi of Antax would fail. Not only that, but our Iceguard militia would be devoid of troops. All of them will follow your laws and look to you for guidance, strength, wisdom and example. They give their all, day and night, in exchange for your protection. There are no Knights without the toiling masses, and the toiling masses know they would not exist without the Knights. You must earn their respect as much as you must earn that of your Barons and vassals. Tell me our mantra.'

'To be like winter, harsh but fair.'

'Correct, Tormun.'

The boy fidgeted, as if he was about to say something but stopped himself. Most of what he was hearing he had heard before. He wore robes coloured with the black and silver of his house and a thick, fur-lined cloak hung over his shoulders. At his hip he carried the Heirsword, a blade designed to be carried by the next in line to the throne of House Winterveil. It was both a symbol of status and served as a reminder to the heir of their future role as a leader of warriors in battle.

'Are you bored of this, boy?' Tors asked.

'No, Heir-ward.'

'Do not lie to me. What do you wish to speak of?' She knew the answer. He was a young, bright, future warrior of a mighty household who spent every moment of his free time running around playing at sword-fighting with the heirs of the barons.

'I want to... know about battles, Heir-ward, please,' said Tormun sheepishly. He had learned long ago that his

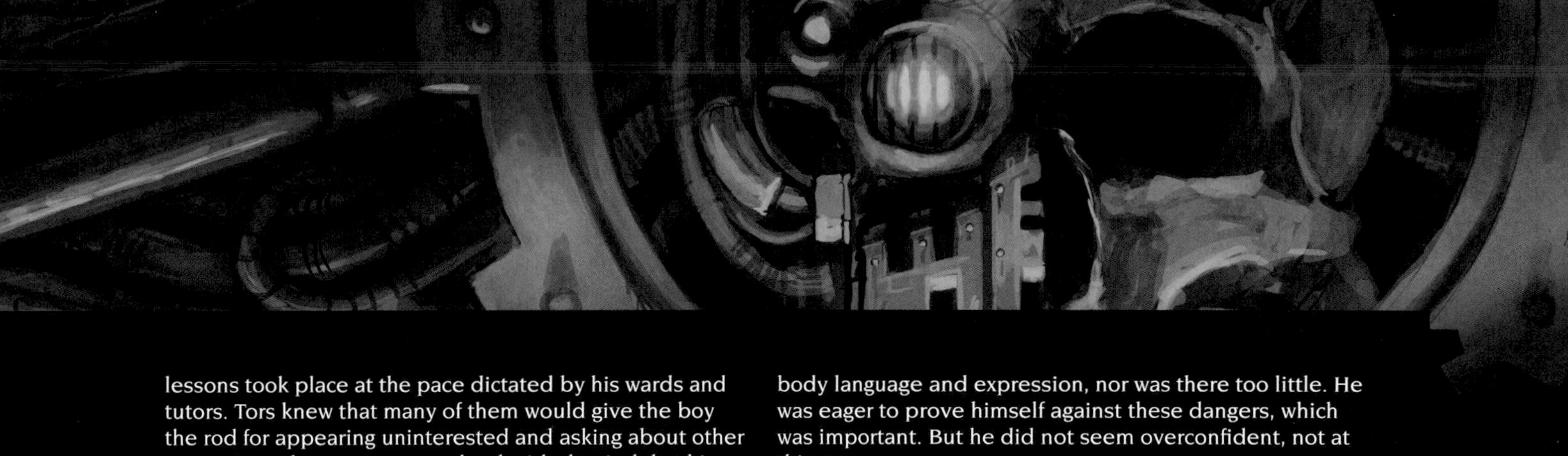

lessons took place at the pace dictated by his wards and tutors. Tors knew that many of them would give the boy the rod for appearing uninterested and asking about other topics. For whatever reason, she decided to indulge him this time. Sooner or later he would have to learn the harsh truths about what war in the galaxy was like. Tors could also not blame his intrigue when she herself was half-machine thanks to her injuries. She was a walking curiosity, and that was something she could not avoid. There was no shame to her from having suffered in battle. There was little greater proof of one's willingness to put oneself in danger than that.

'What would you wish to know?' she asked.

Tormun looked to the ground. 'What battles have you been in, Heir-ward?'

'No one follows a leader who looks at his feet when he asks a question,' she said. 'Look me in the eye when you ask me, as you will have to look all of those you rule.' It was not an easy request for the boy. One of her eyes was an ugly bionic implant that glowed blood red. Nonetheless, Tormun did as instructed. He was not without courage. He would be a strong king, one day. He asked again.

'Good,' Tors said. 'I will tell you. I have served your family for over a century now, and your mother the High Queen for half of that. We bled together defending Kobeobis from the greenskins besieging that world. Forty-five of our number went with us, and eight did not return, slain by the brutes, though we claimed many thousands of the xenos. We intercepted Dvorgite blood-hunters at Lariny VIII before they ravaged the world's subsistence farmers. My Knight, Helm of Winter, was slick with the blood of the xenos, and its reaper blade arm severed. A dozen of this house, and four of those of Peak, fell in that battle, half of those of us who went. Truly, the memory of the aliens' blood-cries even now haunts me. I tell you this because though each of us will answer the call to war whenever it is made, battle is no light affair. It is no jest, no game of rough and tumble. You must know what you are doing when you commit men and women who follow you to it. You must know what you are asking of them, and you must be prepared to carry out any order you issue. Anything less is cowardice, and your Nobles will smell its reek upon you as a hound can detect the scent of a gorebear.'

Baronette Tors could tell that Tormun was gripped by what she said. There was not too much excitement in his body language and expression, nor was there too little. He was eager to prove himself against these dangers, which was important. But he did not seem overconfident, not at this stage.

'You want to know more?' she asked.

'What happened to you, Heir-ward?'

Tors smiled. The question was inevitable. 'We were fighting our most hated enemies, the Drukhari. Once again they dared to trespass on the world of Langzide. Your mother mobilised fifty Nobles, I among them. When we arrived, anarchy had already descended. Dozens of villages had already been razed, their peoples murdered or taken. People fled from the settlements into the major cities, pursued by the xenos' wicked grav-vehicles. They must have been led by a particularly vicious member of their foul breed, for they only attacked more aggressively when we arrived. Normally many would withdraw at the sight of us, for they are cowards who refuse a fair fight more often than not. But these xenos stood against us. Though we destroyed many of their darting barges, the xenos were much faster than us. One by one, our fellows were brought down by beams of black energy that punched through shields and armour. Eventually, one struck Helm of Winter in its fuel cells, setting my brave steed alight. I was caught in the flames. I remember being pulled free, then I awoke in the medicae facility on one of our ships. The results of all this, you can see before you. Now I have answered your questions, you must answer mine. You wish to speak of war. Tell me of Icefall's primary keeps.'

'We stand within Glakium Magna, which watches over the northern marches. Glakium Minor guards the southern reaches and is commanded by Baron Iphanzor Winterveil. The Greenfort is commanded by Baronette Herenzah Argus. The Blackmoat is commanded by Baron Fegrin Pars, known as the Raidbreaker. Tripon is commanded by Duke Pifranzil and Duchess Tigranzel Regattis. The Oakwall garrison, guardians of the Branchtwyst Forest who hold back its denizens, is led by Crenel-Captain Iarn Gelt, the Iceget.'

Sciera struck the boy with her cane. 'Do not use that slur. He may be of low birth, but he has earned his position as a pilot on a dozen battlefields. It was he who pulled me free on Langzide. And remember, before you ever sit in a Throne Mechanicum you will learn to fight on foot from him. You will give him your fullest attention.'

QUESTOR IMPERIALIS

Imperial Knight worlds are typically ruled over by one or more Noble houses, each with their own heraldry, insignia, traditions and character. Though often hidebound and intractable on matters of honour, the Noble houses make for powerful allies, and when they send their Imperial Knights to war, the enemies of the Emperor tremble.

Questor Imperialis Knight worlds are those who have sworn allegiance to the Emperor and Terra rather than Mars. Like any Knight worlds their home planets are immensely varied. Bleak, mountainous wastelands, hard-edged idylls of deep forests and rolling plains, airless deserts dotted with hab-domes, primordial wildernesses of volcanic jungle, ocean-locked island worlds and countless others all support Knightly civilisations. Yet as much as each of these worlds differ, and as much as those differences have done to shape the societies that inhabit them, certain similarities hold true across virtually every Questor Imperialis Knight world in the Emperor's realm.

Most Questor Imperialis worlds organise their populations on a feudal structure, dividing lands into fiefdoms – or whatever local term is used. Each of these territories is ruled by one or more Nobles, with the population they are responsible for toiling, farming, herding, mining, quarrying or producing in their liege's name. In exchange for loyal service, the Nobles protect their people from off-world invaders or from native dangers. In turn, every Knight owes their allegiance to a high-ranking local leader. These are most commonly called Barons, though this term varies from world to world. Other examples include Marshal, Countess, Seneschal or Marchioness. Each of these leaders then bows the knee to their world's High Monarch. Depending on the world, a Baron may be the head of their own Noble house. On some, a single Noble house may rule the entire planet – these immensely powerful entities are known at the Great Houses, and include renowned institutions such as Griffith, Cadmus, Terryn, and Hawkshroud.

The cultures of the Questor Imperialis worlds vary greatly, though most households feature veneration of the Emperor in their traditions, architecture, iconography, heraldry and rituals. Each planet has an enormously long history, unique heroes as well as geographical features which over time have moulded the mindset and practises of the Nobles of the 41st Millennium. Some Questor Imperialis worlds are run by repressive patriarchies or matriarchies. Others operate martial meritocracies where skill in battle is more important than lineage. A handful follow restricted democratic procedures, with certain Nobles enfranchised to cast a vote on who should be their world's leaders for a period of time, whether that be for life or a number of years.

Most Knight worlds have significant operations dedicated to sourcing raw materials, which they require to support their own populations as well as trade with other worlds. Few Questor Imperialis worlds have large-scale industrial centres due to their long history of isolation and cultural backwardness, and most have low population densities. This has resulted in many being surprisingly unspoilt in comparison to many other Imperial worlds. However, many over the millennia have faced invasion and war, and some harbour mutation, sedition or madness as a result. These are dangers the rulers of a Knight world must forever watch for, and be ready to suppress the moment they are discovered. Fighting these evils serves as good practice.

Regardless of how they come to hold the title, on a Questor Imperialis world the word of its ruling High Monarch is law. Of course there will be times when at least a small number of Nobles are engaged in some form of politicking, or involved in disputes that may demand honour duels or Knightly jousts to settle. Yet should the High Monarch issue the summons for war, these issues must be put to one side. To reject the order, or to be seen to be undermining the High Monarch's efforts in favour of personal gain or to achieve a petty victory over a rival, is to bring much dishonour upon a Noble's name and house.

It takes little provocation, however, for a Noble to mount their Throne. The rush of power given to an individual in control of a weapon as powerful as a Knight suit is an intoxicant in its own right. Battle and war are also seen as escapes from the tedium of courtly life. In times of peace, a Noble spends much of their time attending to the needs of their serfs, dealing with administrative matters of state or conducting long, esoteric rituals that have grown both in length and complexity over the millennia. Whilst any Noble conducts their duties with all the stoicism expected of a person of their standing, they will go to war as often as the opportunity presents itself. When they do so, it is with much pomp, ceremony and fanfare, their heraldry gleaming and their banners fluttering in the wind.

Regardless of whether they go to war in response to a call for aid from an embattled Imperial commander, racing to save a beleaguered planet in the grip

of alien invasion or setting off on a grand crusade to avenge a perceived slight, the Knights go to war in formations known as lances. Most often, groups of these detachments will go to battle, each led by a sufficiently powerful Baron. Though they may travel in groups, it is not unheard of for Knights to operate alone once they have reached the battlefield, each Noble bringing death to the foe in whichever way they see fit. High Monarchs lead the march against the greatest threats. They do so often at the head of their Exalted Court, a body of the highest-ranking Knights of their house. Some of these warriors are close relatives of the High Monarch, lesser rulers from the home world, the Monarch's finest warriors or their closest friends. Regardless, they are sublime commanders and warriors, capable of defeating almost any opposition they might encounter.

TO SAIL THE VOID

When fighting to defend their own worlds, the speed and manoeuvrability of Knights is usually sufficient to get them to where they are needed, but when they take the fight to foes on other planets the Nobles must use transports to reach their designated war zone. Some Knight worlds, especially those ruled by houses pledged to Terra, maintain their own fleets of transport and combat cruisers, often former Imperial Navy craft. Others – including the vast majority of Questor Mechanicus Knight worlds – instead utilise Explorator craft and mass-conveyance barges provided by an allied forge world. These ships ferry Nobles, Knight suits, Sacristans, attendant household servants, courtiers and bondsmilitia to war, often alongside the towering engines of the Legios Titanicus or massed maniples of cyborg Skitarii. Different Knight worlds also approach combat drops in different ways. Though most Noble houses deploy their Knights using heavy haulers and mass transporters, there are some that employ armoured drop-keeps for the task, using auxiliary air forces of Lightning and Thunderbolt fighters to clear landing zones, or – in the case of the Mechanicus-aligned House Faustiaris – make use of huge and ancient teleportariums that translocate their Knight suits straight into battle amidst coronae of crackling warplight.

By the Grace of Mars were we brought out from the oldest and longest of darks. By the Might of Mars was our strength restored. By the Will of the Omnissiah do we now purge the stars in Its Name.

QUESTOR MECHANICUS

Through mutual and binding oaths, the Adeptus Mechanicus have forged alliances with many Knight worlds. In return for technical aid and reciprocal protection, these Questor Mechanicus houses send forth their adamantine Knight suits to honour any request made by their allies.

The Knights of Questor Mechanicus houses are regularly expected to uphold their ancient pacts with whichever forge world they are bonded. This may be to defend against an invasion of the forge world, accompany a mission to recover lost technology, quash an outbreak of tech-heresy, defend a mining world supplying essential natural resources or to join an explorator fleet. In battle, Questor Mechanicus Knights are frequently tasked with supporting the Titan Legions, either fighting in battle alongside them or serving as scouts or flank guards. The commitments expected from a Questor Mechanicus house may well be as little as a single Knight, up to an entire Great House. It is not unheard of for a detachment of Knights to be seconded to a Titan Legion on a permanent basis. Should they do this then those Knights change their vows of allegiance as well as their heraldry to reflect the Legio they now serve. To fight beside such mighty engines of war as the Titans is considered a great honour indeed, for there are few greater symbols of the Omnissiah's power.

Some Questor Mechanicus worlds are based on forge worlds. Those who control their own planets operate them on a feudal basis similar to the Questor Imperialis, and they are different in many ways. They have considerably less cultural and martial autonomy due to vows they have made to their patron forge world. They are regularly visited by conclaves of tech-magi, who while on the one hand bring resources and expertise, also bring scrutinising eyes and watch the household's rituals carefully. The Nobles of a Questor Mechanicus household are also more bound to the worship of the

Omnissiah. They wear robes in the hues of their patron forge world, exhibit the Adeptus Mechanicus cog on their armour and as tattoos, have electoo designs inlaid into their flesh and sport mechanical augmetics and bionics that aid them to mesh more closely with the systems of their Knight suits.

Their domains also bear signs of the close involvement of the Adeptus Mechanicus. Unlike many Questor Imperialis worlds, Questor Mechanicus planets feature vast strip mines, manufactorums that rumble with the sounds of industry day and night, and continent-sized agri-plexes, all there to efficiently extract natural resources. Whilst this means that pollution is rife on many of these worlds, the Knights benefit from easy replenishment of stocks of armoured suits, weapons and munitions. Thus they are almost always very-well equipped, can replace losses more quickly and mount fresh crusades at a much more rapid rate. For many Questor Mechanicus worlds, even with these advantages it is all but impossible for them to keep up with the relentless demands of the forge world they are allied with.

For all of this, the Nobles of such a world are no less proud, honourable or strong-willed. They still rule their vast domains, march out to protect their borders, and owe ultimate fealty to their world's supreme ruler, who most often takes the revered title of Princeps. The appearance of Questor Mechanicus Nobles is generally more sombre than that of their counterparts in the Imperial-aligned noble houses, and they are often less unruly and wilful. Their ties to the Sacristan orders are strong, untroubled by suspicions of divided loyalties. Their battle doctrines are bellicose and expertly cogitated, while the bond that each Noble forges with their Throne Mechanicum and the machine spirit of their Knight suit is nigh symbiotic. When the lances of the Questor Mechanicus Knights go to battle, they do so with devastating efficiency and absolute, unified conviction.

HOUSE RIVALRIES

The Cult Mechanicus venerates the Omnissiah as the god of machines, or Deus Mechanicus. Its adherents see the Machine God as the source of all technology, and believe in the complete superiority of the machine over flesh. Those Knight worlds with the closest ties to the forge worlds often share their beliefs, but this is far from a universal trend – many other Knightly houses choose to venerate the divine Emperor instead. This has led to many rivalries between houses of differing beliefs over the long millennia. Even since the Horus Heresy, some have even come to blows due to disputes, though most are settled honourably through duels and contests mediated by another, neutral, party.

Some Imperial scholars believe that the Omnissiah and the Emperor are one and the same, or just different aspects of the same divine force. It is said that the Emperor, when he arrived on Mars before the start of the Great Crusade, channelled the power of the Omnissiah to heal the irreparably damaged leg of one Knight's suit, fulfilling an ancient prophecy of the Cult Mechanicus and thus proving his machine divinity. Whatever the truth of the matter, the Emperor was able to forge a pact between Mars and Terra that still exists today.

'Awaken, oh plasma generator, and pump thine blood of fire.

Awaken, oh cannons, oh rockets, oh blades and fists, and prepare to smite the foe.

Awaken, oh ion shield, and muster thine bastion of light.

Awaken, oh Throne Mechanicum. The time for war has come.'

– *The Sacristans' Chant of Awakening*

'The Omnissiah gifts us with his wrath made manifest, that we may turn it upon his foes with fulsome vengeance.'

– *Sacristan Nymax Dar Mechanicus*

'Deeds of heroism and glory bring renown to your house, but zeal, faith and chivalry in the Omnissiah's name – these things will see your legacy last eternal.'

– *Baron Dasorakis Gau-Taranis*

KNIGHT WORLDS OF THE IMPERIUM

There are hundreds of Knight worlds in the galaxy. Though some lords of Terra believe that many have been brought into the Imperial fold, the galaxy is a huge place, with much of it unexplored by the Imperium and shrouded in mystery. Many more may still be unaccounted for, fighting alone, their Nobles guarding walls, mounting patrols and being ever watchful.

1 WAR ZONE NACHMUND

The Nachmund Gauntlet is one of the most strategically vital locations in all the Imperium – a channel through the Great Rift that is relatively stable. Conflict rages throughout the region as the forces of Chaos and those of the Imperium fight hard to control the region. Knights from dozens of houses stride over battlefields on countless worlds as a part of the Imperial effort. They clash with Heretic Astartes from every Traitor Legion and countless other renegade forces. They cross blades with traitorous Knights, fury and hatred for them coursing through their veins. Wave upon wave of heretic hordes throws itself upon the Imperial Knights, who weather the storm.

2 SAVAGE WARS OF STEEL

These conflicts eclipse the Knight worlds of Vorinth and Dragon's End. As the Necron Novokh Dynasty's bloodthirsty assaults gather pace, Knight Houses Griffith and Neo-Ilius are drawn in to the escalating fighting, both determined to put an end to the Necron advances. The High Monarchs of both houses have forged a strong bond, their Knights fighting, killing and dying side by side on battlefield after battlefield. The sight of them striding the landscape fills the hearts of other Imperial defenders with hope, and wherever they stand even battered Imperial defences hold firm. But the Necrons are unrelenting, and the Knights' ranks are thinning...

3 WAR ZONE OCTARIUS

Many Imperial observers feared the worst when Inquisitor Kryptman lured a tendril of Hive Fleet Leviathan into the Orkoid Octarian Empire. They were right to. Despite the efforts of Imperial forces, and particularly those of Inquisitor Nashir Sahansun, Orks and Tyranids alike batter at Imperial defences in the region with a new strength and power. Imperial Knights respond to this new, immense threat in considerable numbers. Houses Xiphos, Feurus, Adamant, Miranor, Terryn, Vulker and Cadmus are a few among many houses to partake in the fighting, thousands of Knights in all, with scores of Freeblades. Despite even this incredible strength, victory is far from certain.

4 WAR ZONE CHALNATH

The mysterious arrival of the T'au in the Chalnath Expanse has caused immense upheaval in the region. Many Imperial worlds have come under attack, and the T'au's actions have stirred up numerous Genestealer Cults. Knights of Houses Beaumaris, Winterveil, Kamata and Hasburg have all despatched lances to the region. The fighting in the Riatov System is amongst the fiercest many of even the experienced Nobles have experienced. They attempt to counter the rapid, fleeting strikes of the fast-moving T'au forces and the incessant guerrilla tactics of Genestealer Cultists that forever threaten supply lines and the Sacristans.

WAR ZONE: ARANAE

The world of Aranae was home to the Chaos Knights Iconoclast Houses of Araknis and Skorpiod. Long had they plagued the regions of the Latrodek Cluster, raiding worlds, slaughtering troops and enslaving Imperial citizens. Eventually, a great host was assembled to force the traitor Knights back to their home world and wipe them out.

The Imperial coalition was spearheaded by Knights from no fewer than five Houses: Terryn, Winterveil, Faustiaris, Beaumaris and Hawkwood. In addition to several hundred Knights, the Houses brought with them thousands of Sacristans and even more household troops. Joining the Questor Imperialis and Questor Mechanicus forces were scores of Astra Militarum regiments, Space Marines of the Deathdealers and Ashen Conquerors Chapters and Battle Sisters of the Orders of the Argent Shroud, Ebon Chalice and Grey Spear.

It took many months of campaigning over many planets to drive the traitor Knights fully back to their home world of Aranae. Imperial forces fought through the desolated ruins of Imperial cities. They battled across ice-capped mountains and snow-laden forests. They battered down keeps and outposts garrisoned by corrupted soldiery in thrall to the Chaos Knights. It was a bloody effort, but with each victory Araknis and Skorpiod grew weaker.

As for Aranae itself, its landmasses were dominated by rocky deserts and bushland, and populated by hundreds of millions of slaves. Though some were of the world's native population, most had been brought from elsewhere to toil. They laboured upon agri-fields while the baking heat of the planet's two suns beat down upon them, within perilous mine shafts or on fast-moving production lines where munitions were manufactured.

When armies of Imperial Knights take to the battlefield, they employ the time-honoured strategies and tactics that have brought them victory for thousands upon thousands of years. Regardless of whether they are Questor Mechanicus or Questor Imperialis they adhere strictly to the tenets of the Code Chivalric and to the martial structure of their own worlds. These methods of fighting are invariably dynamic, high impact and utterly destructive. So it was on Aranae. Armiger-class Knights, smaller suits piloted by bondsmen or lesser Nobles, performed swift flanking attacks, and scouting operations. The core of the Knightly hosts were of the Questoris-class, a mid-size suit and versatile chassis. Lances of these suits, three to six Knights strong, strode over Aranae's surface, duelling with traitor Knights, knocking out bunkers and crushing foes underfoot. Among the largest Knights to fight were the Dominus-class suits. These indomitable war-engines can mount an intimidating array of heavy weaponry, powered by dual plasma cores. They provided overwhelming supporting fire to Imperial forces they fought beside, cracking open bastion walls with volcano lances or flooding enemy-held ground with fire from their conflagration cannons.

001 HUNTMAN'S PASS
Huntsman's Pass was finally taken after Knights from House Faustiaris teleported dozens of their number behind House Araknis' positions, wiping out hundreds of the house's Idolators before smashing into the Chaos Knights' rear.

002 BLACK WIDOW PEAK
Black Widow Peak dominated a huge open landscape, and the cannons House Araknis deployed there could decimate any Imperial forces moving around for scores of kilometres. House Faustiaris led the attack against the Peak, which was held entirely by traitor slave troops, aided by Battle Sisters of the Order of the Grey Spear and Astra Militarum from the Cthonol Nineguards. The bloody fighting claimed more than two-thirds of the Imperial troops before it was done.

003 THE CRIMSON BARB
House Winterveil deployed close to the Crimson Barb – a peninsula pointing out into the Silkvenom Ocean – using armoured drop keeps. They came under fire from the moment they broke through Aranae's atmosphere, their fortified landing craft protecting them. For weeks every breakout attempt from their own landing zone was driven back by House Araknis, until eventually a suicidal charge by a lance of Knights Gallant finally achieved a breakthrough.

004 THE GREY PINCER
The dried lake bed, known as the Grey Pincer for its shape, was a nightmarish tangle of rocky outcrops, ravines and the petrified skeletons of long-dead sea creatures. House Skorpiod ran a guerrilla campaign within it, holding out for months against House Hawkwood, Aeronautica Imperialis bomber groups and regiments of Indigan Praefects, despite being hugely outnumbered.

005 STING
The primary household keep of House Skorpiod, Sting was an immense bastion. Houses Beaumaris and Terryn combined their strength for the siege of the fortress, and were joined by Space Marines of the Ashen Conquerors. In the fighting that followed, every nook and cranny of the fortification had to be purged one by one. Each was defended by rampaging Knights and fanatical militia. Knights Errant, Valiant and Armiger Warglaives came into their own, burning out their foes or reducing walls to slag at extremely close ranges.

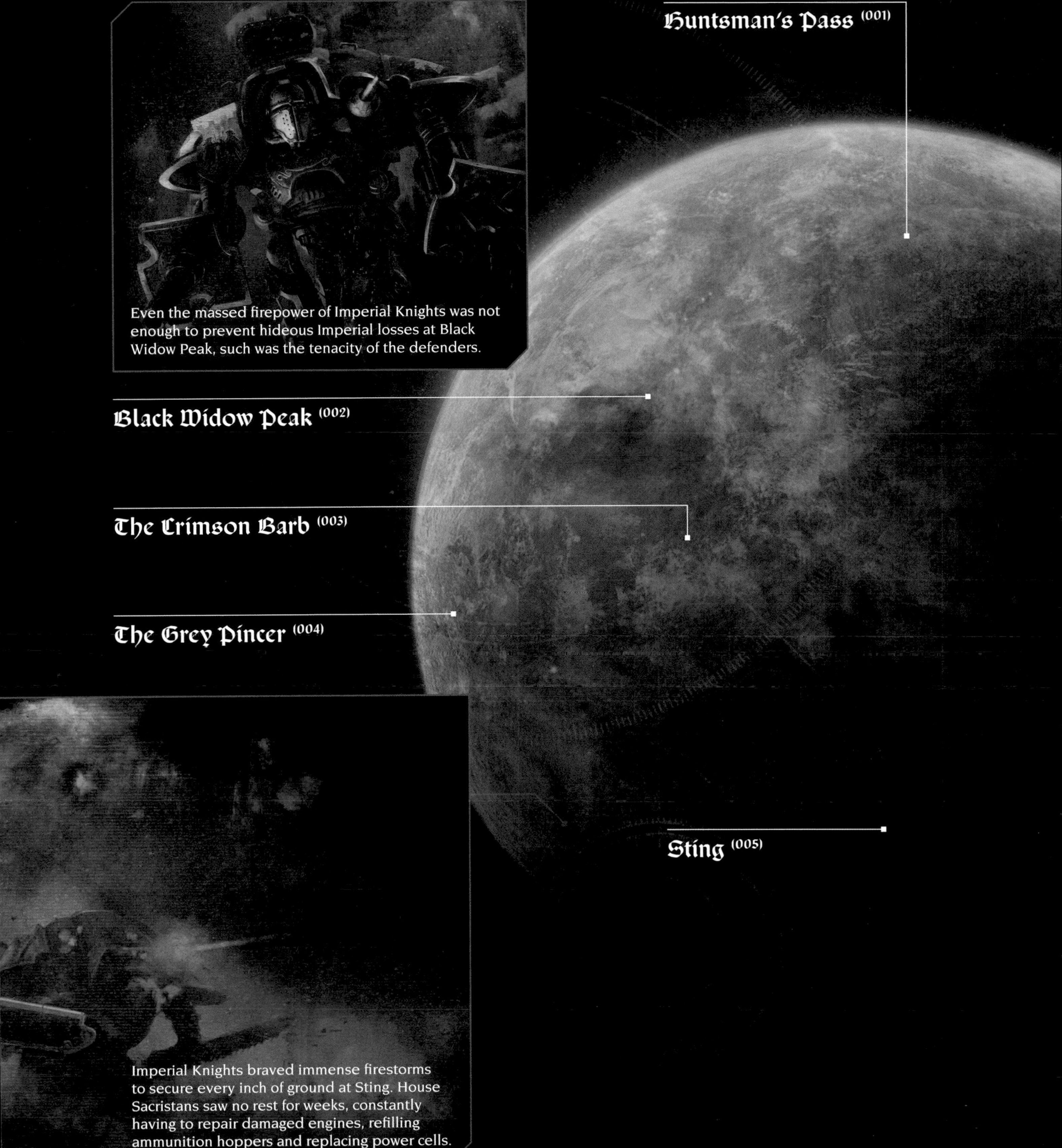

Even the massed firepower of Imperial Knights was not enough to prevent hideous Imperial losses at Black Widow Peak, such was the tenacity of the defenders.

Imperial Knights braved immense firestorms to secure every inch of ground at Sting. House Sacristans saw no rest for weeks, constantly having to repair damaged engines, refilling ammunition hoppers and replacing power cells.

STRUCTURE OF A QUESTOR IMPERIALIS GREAT HOUSE

HIGH MONARCH

BARON/ESS MONARCHSWARD	**BARON/ESS** HERALD	**BARON/ESS** MASTER OF JUSTICE	**BARON/ESS** GATEKEEPER	**BARON/ESS**
KNIGHTLY VASSALS	**KNIGHTLY VASSALS**	**KNIGHTLY VASSALS**	**KNIGHTLY VASSALS**	**KNIGHTLY VASSALS**

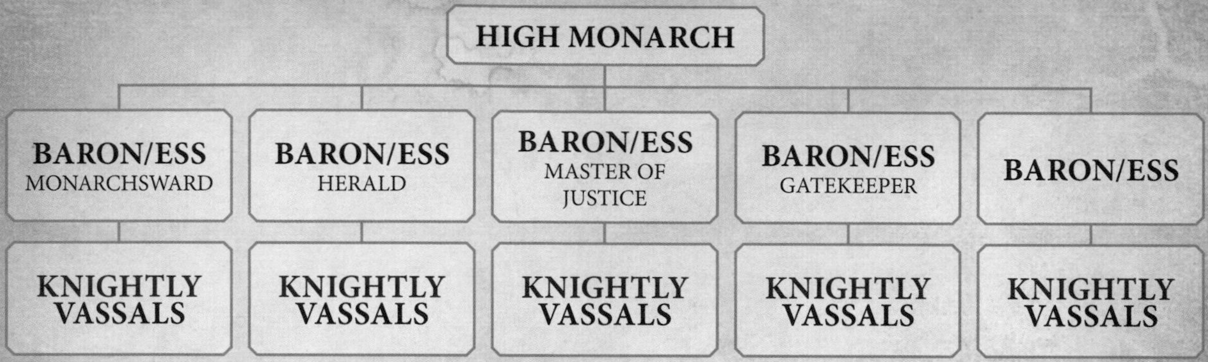

At the head of every Questor Imperialis Great House is a High Monarch. Directly beneath them in rank are their Barons, each a land-owning commander in their own right. All owe allegiance to their High Monarch, but are not all equal. The highest ranking Barons are usually those the High Monarch has selected to join their Exalted Court. These are the most loyal and veteran Nobles, and typically rule the largest swathes of territory. Those Nobles beneath the Baron are their vassals; at their lord's call these Knights will assemble for war, and can also be called upon directly by their High Monarch or members of the Exalted Court.

The Knights themselves fight individually or in formations called lances. These are often made up of the vassal Knights of different Barons, constructed according to each member's individual talents, renown and determination.

STRUCTURE OF A QUESTOR MECHANICUS GREAT HOUSE

PRINCEPS

BARON/ESS MASTER TACTICIAN	**BARON/ESS** MASTER OF VOX	**BARON/ESS** MASTER OF LORE	**BARON/ESS** FORGE MASTER	**BARON/ESS**
KNIGHTLY VASSALS	**KNIGHTLY VASSALS**	**KNIGHTLY VASSALS**	**KNIGHTLY VASSALS**	**KNIGHTLY VASSALS**

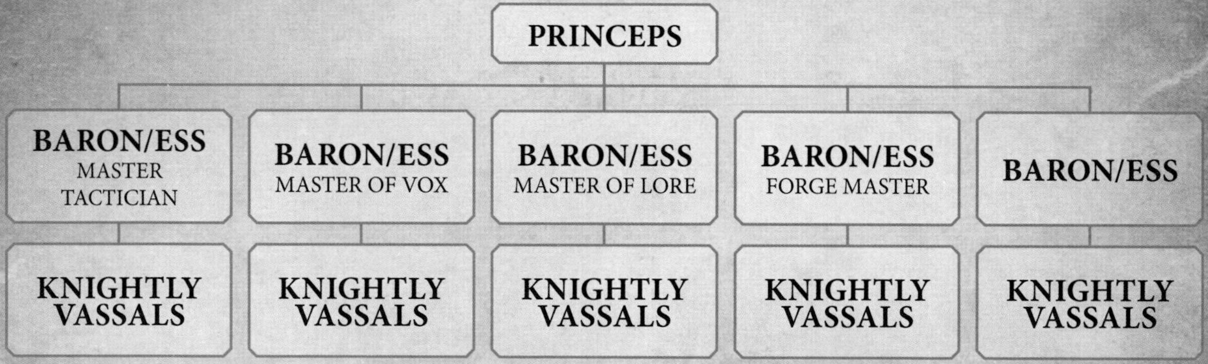

Questor Mechanicus houses are organised similarly to their Imperialis cousins. The ruler of the Great House is known as a Princeps, and they command numerous Barons who are ranked in terms of their experience and influence. For a Questor Mechanicus Great House's ruling council – also called an Exalted Court – the Princeps will promote four Barons. Known as Barons Prime, these individuals are second in power only to the Princeps. Each Baron will have vassals beneath them, who are duty-bound to muster should they be called to battle. The exact number and organisation of these vassals varies wildly, depending upon the size and power of the Knightly Great House in question. Regardless, when the summons to war is received, groups of oath-sworn Knights and entire detachments will be drawn from the Great House's strength. Only in unusual circumstances will the Princeps, or one acting in their stead, choose to select only from a single Baron's vassals.

KNIGHT HERALDRY

Imperial Knight houses are proud organisations that place enormous importance on tradition and lineage. Knights go to war in the colours of their houses, armour and banners adorned with myriad storied symbols.

Almost every noble household has a crest or emblem, which Nobles sport on their armour. These heraldic symbols can be traced back to a house's very beginning. Regardless of a crest's history, Knights wear it with pride – it connects them with their past and establishes them as inheritors of a legacy which very often predates the Imperium itself. When the allies of a Knight house look upon the towering war engines, they are in effect taking a glimpse into a deep part of Humanity's past.

Beyond their house's crest, Knights bear a huge variety of campaign badges, battle honours, family iconography, oathmarks, rank idents and more. Some of these markings celebrate feats of glory, others represent personal shames that the Knight will fight furiously to seek redemption from. Many symbols they use represent ideals that mean much to the house, such as integrity, loyalty, honour, swordsmanship, marksmanship, courage and so on. It is far from unheard of for a Knight suit to have former pilots recognised upon its armour. This might take the form of a scroll bearing the fallen Noble's name or a small representation of their personal heraldry. For many Nobles, having this constant reminder of those who came before them spurs them on to ever greater acts of martial greatness and bravery. How Nobles display all of these symbols and markings depends on their house's culture, and greater variance can be found between Questor Imperialis and Questor Mechanicus houses.

Aside from iconography, many Knight houses use a wide variety of archaic and elaborate forms of address. Not only does every Knight world have its own conventions, but even within the households of a single planet there may be multiple prefixes, suffixes and derivations that date back thousands of years. In many Knightly cultures it is considered deeply offensive to address a Noble incorrectly and Imperial authorities persist in their attempts to learn these systems of name and title as they are a vital part of communicating with the Knight pilots in battle.

The majority of Knight worlds tend towards sir or lady as a standard honour-prefix, although variations such as sire, sor and sirrah are not uncommon. Other worlds attach terms such as 'most honoured' or 'Become' after the Noble's name, or else a derivation of their home world such as 'ap Kostonor' or 'fon Medusar'. Multiple terms denoting standing within a world's Knightly houses are not uncommon: a Knight of a ruling household might be Lady Eleanora Uhl Tassos, while a lesser Noble of the same world might be Sir Geralt Lor Tassos. There are as many of these complex honorifics as there are stars in Imperial skies, and all are of grave import to the Nobles who use them.

'Your crest is your honour. It is the visual expression of heroic deeds and selfless sacrifices beyond count. It is the soul of your house worn proud for all to see. Protect it wherever you can. Shield it from the fire and fury of battle and see to it that, should the crest come to harm, it is the first thing your Sacristans restore.'

- Tenets of the Code Chivalric, 46th Vol

THE RAVEN CREST

As with the principal heraldry of other Knight houses, that of House Raven has evolved over time. In its first incarnation, it was no more than a tilting shield with the symbol of a stylised black fortress representing the Keep Inviolate. Millennia later, the crossed blades symbol of the house's Order of Companions was added. The latest version of the crest was formed in M31, when House Raven Knights met with the first emissaries from the forge world of Metalica and swore oaths to fight for it.

QUESTOR MECHANICUS HERALDRY

Heraldic Principles

Typically, the heraldry displayed by members of a Questor Mechanicus household is identical across each Knight.

- 1 Full house crest
- 2 House emblem
- ■ Major Adeptus Mechanicus livery (typically red, silver or white)
- ■ Minor Adeptus Mechanicus livery (typically yellow or black)

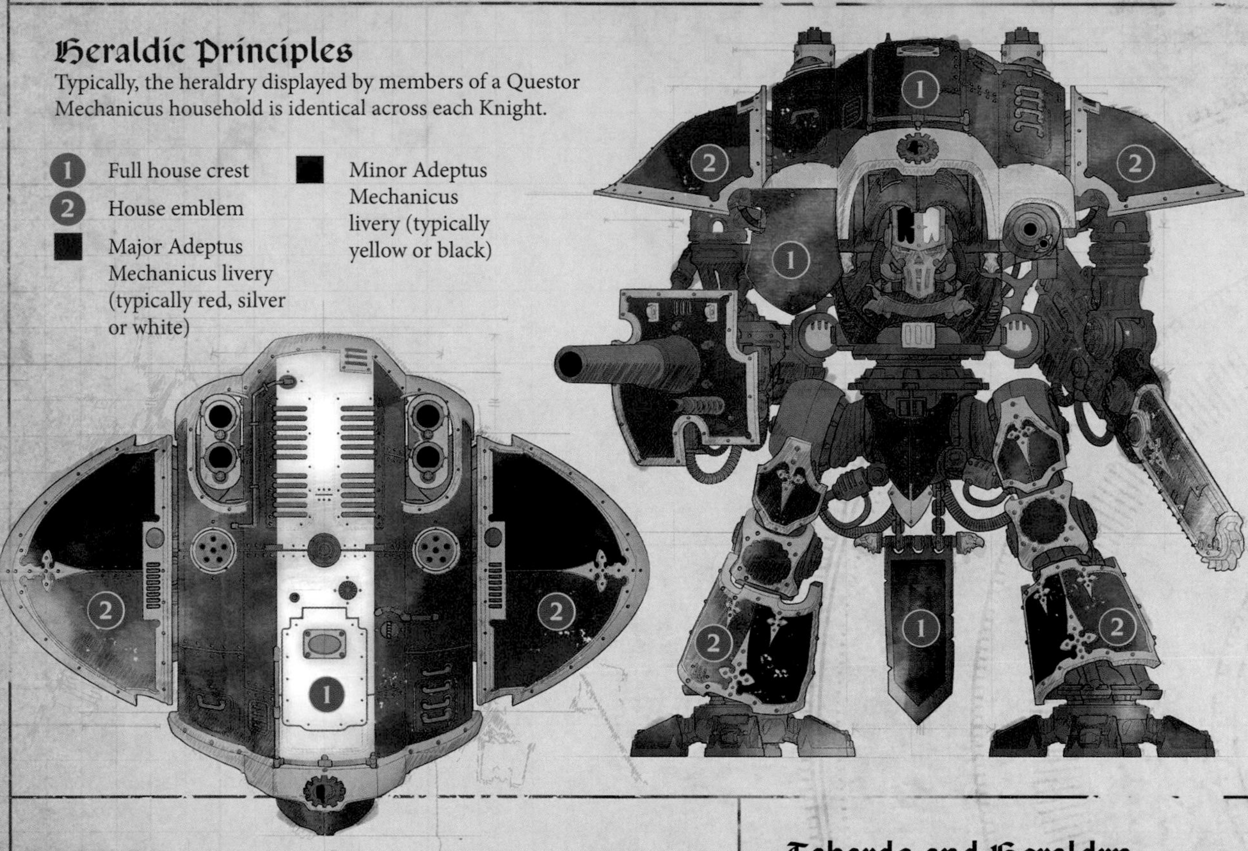

Questor Mechanicus houses follow several conventions in the markings on their banners; usually, these designs are black and white, and display the cog symbol of their allies above their battle honours.

Tabards and Heraldry

Tabards are a place for Imperial Knights to display their house crest or emblem, as well as other badges and symbols of importance. These can vary widely in style and acknowledge the wearer's battle honours and celebrate their role in famous campaigns or alliances.

While houses dedicated to the Machine God are less predisposed to tolerate personal heraldry, this does not, however, preclude individual differences.

The designs of this carapace specify the Knight holds the rank of Princeps.

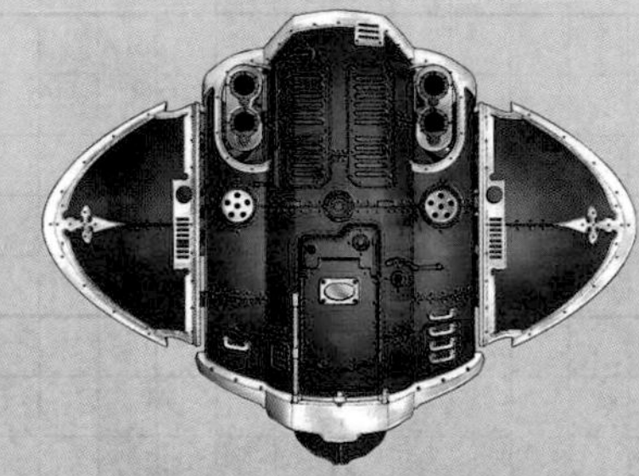

The designs of this carapace specify the Knight holds the rank of Knight.

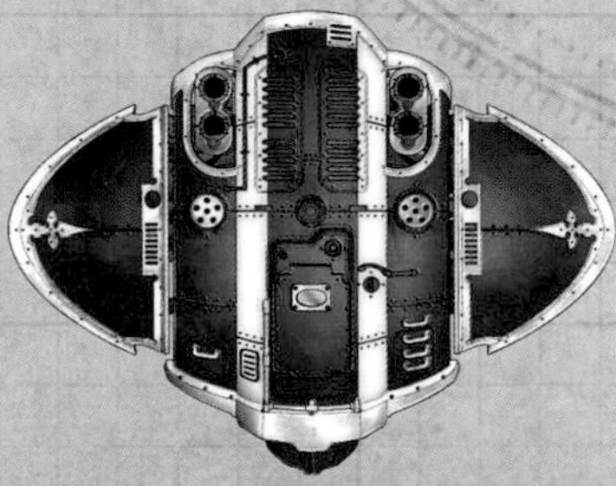

The designs of this carapace specify the Knight holds the rank of Baron.

QUESTOR IMPERIALIS HERALDRY

Senior Nobles

The honoured members of a house's Exalted Court typically each bear a specific design on their tilting plate, on top of which their house's icon is emblazoned. From left to right, the designs above indicate the Herald, Gatekeeper, Master of Justice and Monarchsward. Symbols, colouration and pattern varies greatly between households, and are decided by traditions often dating back millennia. For any Knight of a household, to bear one or more of these designs in their lifetime is an immense honour for them and their bloodline.

Battle Honours

Almost all Imperial Knight houses go to great lengths to recognise and commemorate impressive kills and heroic actions performed on the battlefield. Young Nobles are told stories of their forebears' formidable achievements and glorious victories so as to inspire them, and many families place the awards won by their ancestors on full display in feasting halls and primary courts for every visitor to see. Whilst some awards can be seen across multiple houses, perhaps granted to them from other organisations, such as the Holy Ordos Alliance Icon, most are bespoke. Such examples include the Emerald Cross of House Terryn, the Flaming Falcon of House Hawkshroud and the Iron Deathcog of House Taranis.

Elements of a Knight's panoply are the same for all their household, or unique to them.

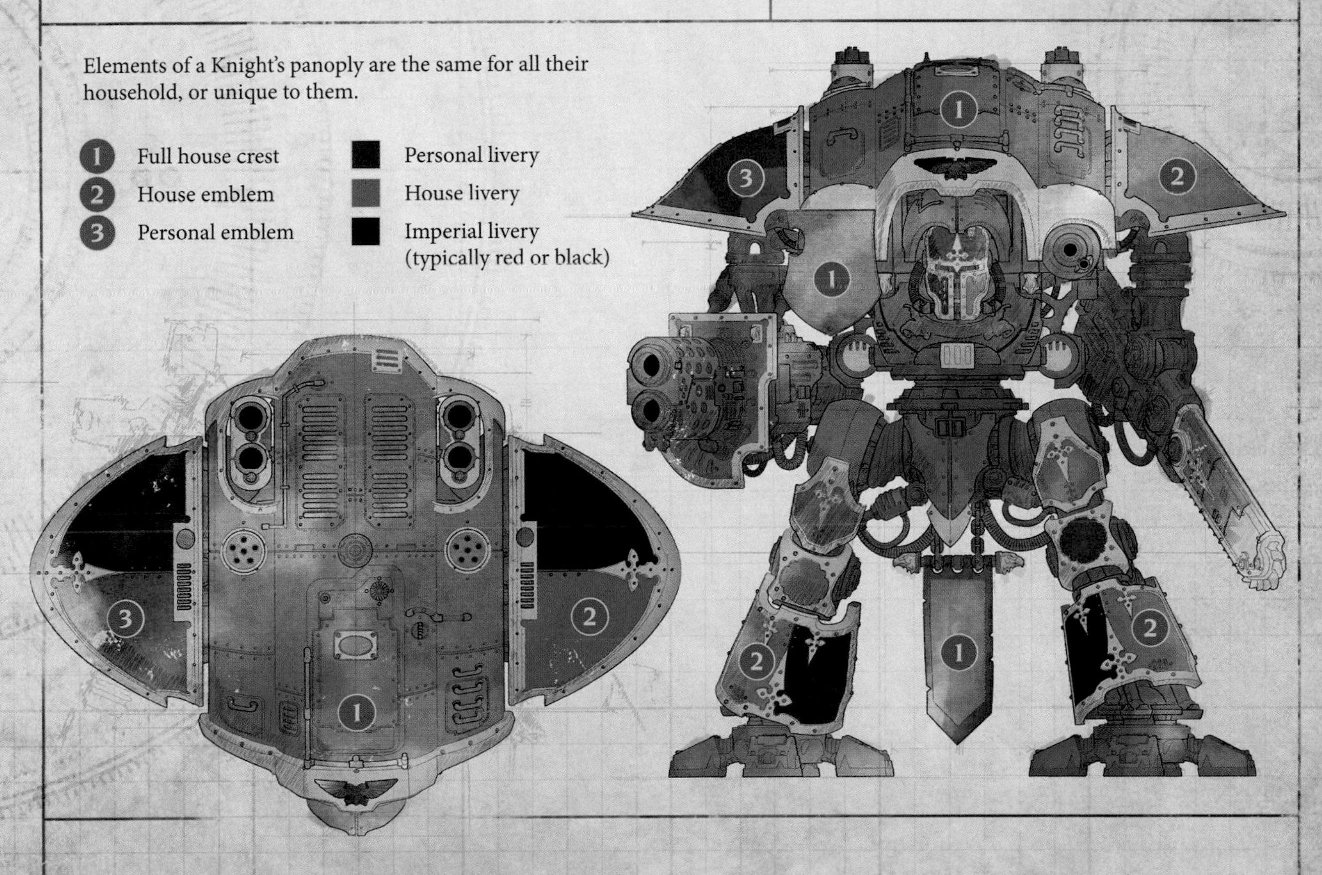

Upon my suit are the marks of a three-score campaigns and crusades and more. Battlefields where I have reduced my foes to ash, crushed them beneath my tread and routed all before me. I proclaim my past victories to the foes of today, so they might know who I am, and to know their defeat and destruction are inevitable.

HOUSE TARANIS

'HONOUR THE FORGE, HONOUR THE PRIMUS ORDINUS'

The Knights of House Taranis are true servants of the Machine God and bear the honour of being the first of the Knightly houses, for they were founded upon Mars itself centuries before any other. They knelt before the Emperor at the same time the Martian tech-magi signed the Treaty of Olympus Mons, which unified the Red Planet and Terra.

The Nobles of House Taranis piloted the very first Knight suit prototypes developed on Mars during the Age of Technology. Having always been based upon the Red Planet, they have never been forced to survive alone on a frontier, sheltering behind high fortress walls against the perils of the outer dark. Thus, their culture has not been shaped by a necessary isolation.

Uniquely among all the households, the subtle mind-altering technology that over time turned the Nobles of other houses into feudal overlords is not present in the Knights piloted by the Nobles of House Taranis. As a result they do not operate on a feudal structure. They refuse to share how their Thrones Mechanicum operate. The reasons as to why most Thrones Mechanicum bear this technology and why those of House Taranis do not incorporate it are now lost to time. That has not prevented high-powered observers from suggesting that the first Nobles were already fiercely loyal to the Mechanicum and that they were an integral part of Mars' defensive infrastructure.

House Taranis' crest bears the crimson and stylised cog of Mars, showing their eternal devotion to the Red Planet and the Martian priesthood. Though many other households aligned with the Adeptus Mechanicus have adopted the same colour, Taranis was the first. The sword that bisects the household's crest is claimed to have been added after the Horus Heresy. During that terrible time, House Taranis suffered horrific losses in the internecine fighting. Legends tell that only two Knights remained. One of these, Raf Maven, insisted on adding the emblem in honour of his fallen kinsmen. In the years that followed, Maven committed himself to rebuilding his house. Thanks to his tireless efforts, and the skill of Mars' Tech-Adepts, House Taranis survived its darkest hour and grew into the formidable host it is in the Era Indomitus. This recovery from almost total annihilation has convinced the Nobles of House Taranis that the Omnissiah will always protect them, no matter the circumstances. This deep, unshakeable faith has served them very well on countless battlefields. House Taranis strives to fight harder than any other Knight house to demonstrate they are worthy of their pre-eminence. They have been put to the test in recent years defending routes to the Sol System from heretic incursions aided by the powerful relics their alliance with the Adeptus Mechanicus afford them.

WARS OF HOUSE TARANIS

House Taranis has fought countless wars over ten millennia, ranging from the fabled War of the Beast against the Orks to the colossal, ongoing campaigns of the Indomitus Crusade. On Tarsok V, Knights of the house battled a daemonic invasion. Seneschal Halver's forces waded through a flood of Plaguebearers to kill the Great Unclean One at the incursion's head. They crushed Dark Mechanicum forces on the artificial world of Hyperior III, and annihilated pirate enclaves in the Cold Trade Wars alongside Houses Raven and Drakhs. They also fought in the War of Recovery alongside the Adeptus Mechanicus in the Mortuam Chain System, wresting much ancient Human technology from the xenos warlords there. In the later years of M41, House Taranis committed many of its number to the defence of Cadia, and many more to the Indomitus Crusade itself. The House roused many of its most ancient Knight suits from slumber and readied their greatest archeotech relics for these coming wars, which they knew would be like nothing the house had seen for millennia.

001

Terribly wounded by a Chaos Titan, Xantek is one of the few Nobles who have survived the Ritual of Becoming twice. He believes himself the embodiment of his house's ability to rise again from darkness, and his faith is fervent indeed.

002

Sir Thassor considers himself an exterminator of unclean engines. His Armiger Warglaive, Red Jackal, has a predatory machine spirit, and together the two of them run down and execute traitor tanks without mercy.

003

Soberan, like many Knights of House Taranis, accompanies explorator fleets, providing protection amongst alien stars. He has seen battle against the Dvorgites, Nicassar, Tyranids, Orks, Londaxi and Empothanes.

HOUSE KRAST

'CRUSH THE SERPENT'

House Krast legend tells that the Knight world of Chrysis, their world, was the first of its kind to be rediscovered at the outset of the Great Crusade. The Nobles of that planet showed no hesitation in joining the Emperor, making House Krast one of the longest-serving defenders of Mankind's realm. It is a fact of which they remain rightfully proud.

'Even the mightiest machine will fail if all of its component parts do not work in holy synchronicity. Never forget that each Noble pilot is just such a component part.'

- Precept Tenacia Krast

The Knights of House Krast are characterised by a deep bitterness, one they can trace back ten thousand years. They fought during the Great Crusade as many noble houses did, as new allies of the Mechanicum and clad in the red of Mars. A powerful military force even before their unification with the rest of Mankind, they were bolstered greatly thanks to their alliance with the Martian priesthood. While the Nobles of House Krast took cannon and blade to the foes of the Emperor, those of lesser houses remained on Chrysis to consolidate the world's new alliances. Supplies and technology were in constant supply there from nearby Mars.

Every young Noble of House Krast is taught that, when Horus rebelled against the Emperor, his treachery took a fearsome toll on Chrysis. Being close to the Sol System, it was caught in Horus' path as he carved a route to Terra. The traitor Titans of Legio Mortis – the Death's Heads – were the chief component of the invasion force that came to Chrysis. This was a most bitter reality for those of House Krast to accept, for they had fought alongside the Titans of that Legion over many battlefields. When the Nobles of the house returned to Chrysis in the wake of the Horus Heresy, they found their world in ruins. Once its vast oceans and woodlands teemed with life. The attack saw it reduced to a toxic wasteland, dotted with skeletal, petrified forests and huge open basins where seas were drained. Shorelines were reduced from wave-washed beaches to dry cliff faces, blasted islands rose above empty seas and the once mighty strongholds of the other houses were rendered as little more than blackened ruins. House Krast was the only house to survive the Horus Heresy, and a hatred burned in their hearts for the horrors which had been inflicted upon them that has not dimmed in ten thousand years.

The house's ties with the Adeptus Mechanicus only grew stronger after those events. The Nobles relied much on the generosity of Mars to replace their losses and to rebuild what they could of their home world, providing what resources they could to the Red Planet in exchange. They constructed shielded strongholds to replace the destroyed keeps and slowly recouped their numbers. Every Noble swore an oath to forever be the bane of traitors, and to be forever loyal to Mars. After the Horus Heresy, the house also changed its crest, replacing the lion rampant for an iron fist squeezing the life from a serpent that represented Chaos. Ever since, House Krast has been at the forefront of the wars against the Arch-enemy, maintaining their deep hatred for traitor Titans and the Legio Mortis especially. Knights of House Krast fought valiantly to defend Cadia, racing there once they heard the Death's Heads were present. After the Great Rift emerged, and the forces of the Arch-enemy were identified across the galaxy, House Krast launched six crusades of vengeance to the forge worlds of Voss, Phaeton, Urdesh, Stygies, Artemia Majoris and Graia, to link with Adeptus Mechanicus forces and bring the fight to the traitors.

The killing of a traitor Titan is a cause of great celebration for the Nobles of House Krast. Claiming one of the Legio Mortis leads to a great triumph in honour of the slayer, who henceforth is known as a 'Headtaker'. These mighty heroes are held in the highest esteem by all of their household as well as serfs, and are permitted to bear the symbol of the broken Death's Head on their Knight suit or tabard.

Krast

Skitarii Alliance Icon

Duelling Medal

Blessed Laurel-cog

Questor Mechanicus badges are normally displayed upon the tabard.

Lagos (001)

001

Baron Lagos is the pilot of the Knight Crusader known as the Redemption of Adamant. In House Krast, the rank of Baron is signified by twin yellow stripes atop the carapace. Over long years of service, the Redemption of Adamant has weathered the worst battle damage the enemies of Mankind could inflict, yet always the Sacristans have repaired its adamantine armour; if anything, Lagos and the myriad ancestral engrams within his Throne Mechanicum come back stronger each time, eager to exact revenge.

As a Baron, Lagos' duties are to maintain his stronghold, to lead the Knights under his service, and to answer the call of the Princeps should he summon members of House Krast to war. Depending upon his liege's needs, Baron Lagos might send a household detachment of his Knights, go into battle himself, or lead his own favoured escort – a Baronial Court – into battle.

002

Teros has displayed a special gift for finding witches on the battlefield and also a keen desire to destroy them. He pilots the Knight Errant suit Hexenhammer. With the growing number of psykers throughout the galaxy since the Great Rift's emergence, Teros has taken to the field as often as possible in pursuit of his malevolent quarry.

Teros (002)

001

Krewald and his Knight, Glory Unblemished, served with distinction alongside Legio Metalica's Titanicus, fighting in support of the Emperor-class Titan Hand of Judgement while it annihilated a turncoat city.

002

Walkorn and his Knight, Unyielding Iron, have been inducted into House Raven's revered Order of Companions. Like all the Companions, Unyielding Iron bears no mark to distinguish its elite status, for House Raven holds that such iconography only benefits their enemies. Despite this, House Raven are proud users of the chevron designs that mark the age and experience of its Nobles.

003

Sir Karstin, pilot of Hammerblow is a minor Noble who submits willingly to the mental dominance of Sir Krewald in return for greater standing.

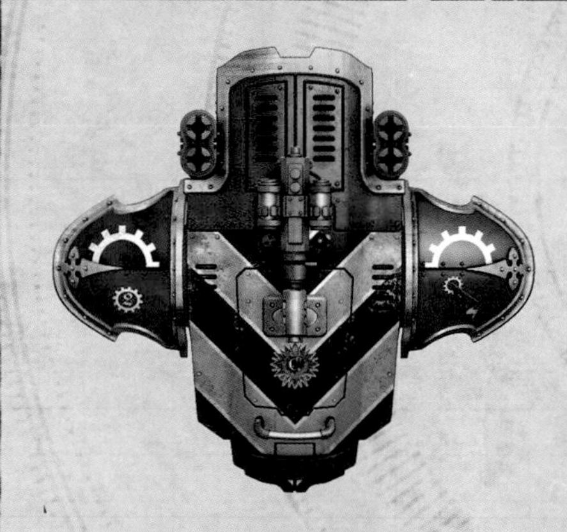

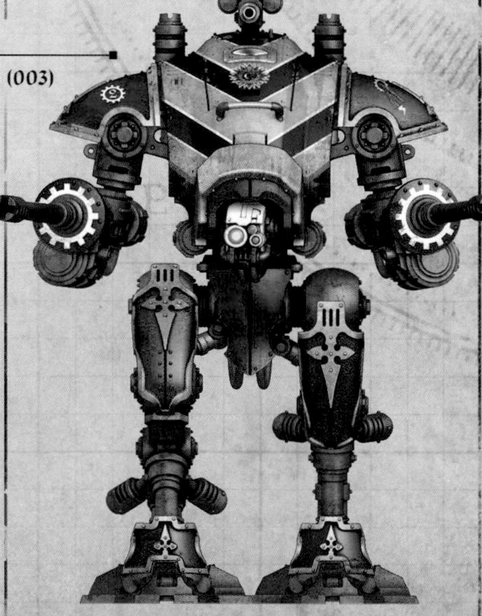

HOUSE RAVEN

'HONOUR INVIOLATE, KOLOSSI ETERNAL'

The Knights of House Raven seek vengeance above all else. Their numbers have been depleted. Their home world, Kolossi, has been stolen away by some malevolent power. Now they spend every waking moment seeking out news of it and those responsible for its fall and vanishing. House Raven will not rest until their quest is done.

In the recent past, House Raven not only boasted the greatest number of Knights of any house and the fealty of dozens of lesser households, but also one of the mightiest fortresses in the entire Imperium – the Keep Inviolate. So large was this immense stronghold that its tallest towers jutted into the void. Its walls were hundreds of feet thick and bristled with macro-cannon emplacements. It was a place of buttressed bastions and armoured towers. Even its roots stretched deep, its vaults full of ancient relics. Some observers believe that the Keep was comparable to the Fang, the fortress-monastery of the Space Wolves, or even the Imperial Palace, in size and strength. The Keep itself remains a featured part of the house's emblem, represented by a tall black tower. Kolossi, their home world, was a place of immense industry, its cities were islands of steel and smoke among deep-core shafts and strip-mine canyons. House Raven's power was maintained by its vast resources as well as its alliance with the forge world of Metalica. The Knight house's Sacristans, known collectively as the Iron Brotherhood, received exemplary training in their arts there, and the tech-magi of that world provided vital expertise. It was said that House Raven's power matched that of a Titan Legion.

Kolossi fell during the heretic invasion of the Charadon Sector, a vicious war that cost the Imperium thousands of ships and billions of lives. In keeping with their oath of allegiance, Princeps Grevan Raven led some eighty percent of his house's strength to the Obolis Sub-Sector to aid Metalica, leaving the defence of Kolossi in the hands of a faithful warrior called Sir Havlorn. A sizeable contingent of Knights remained, as well as a large garrison of other forces. Combined with the formidable strength of the Keep Inviolate itself, Kolossi could still hold against conventional forces for months or even years – plenty of time for Sir Havlorn to request the return of Raven's full strength should any invaders prove too mighty. But the enemy who had designs on their world was far from conventional. The Daemon Prince Be'lakor wanted Kolossi for his own.

The Dark Master began his campaign by sowing seeds of doubt and resentment amongst the population of Kolossi. He enslaved some to his will, who seeded cults and performed acts of sabotage. Be'lakor himself worked his power. Over time, these efforts affected a subtle change. At first this was put down to faulty instruments or organic error. But over time it became unquestionable. The nights on Kolossi were growing longer. Panic spread as malevolent entities seemed to stalk people in the shadows. Despite much effort on the part of Sir Havlorn's forces, such predators were never found. Still, the Noble sent out messages to the Princeps, explaining that a dire threat was growing. He ordered the shepherding of the people into the cities so that they could be better protected, yet, one by one, the fortified settlements dropped off the vox network. Soon, the Keep Inviolate stood alone.

Sir Havlorn had no idea that all this time some of the house's own Sacristans had been corrupted by Be'lakor. When he mobilised his warriors to arms after daemons attacked the Keep Inviolate in force, it became apparent that many Thrones Mechanicum had been tainted. Once-loyal Knights turned on their fellows. Be'lakor himself manifested to oversee the capture of the fortress.

What happened next was even stranger. After Kolossi fell, it vanished altogether, as though swallowed by the warp. When Princeps Grevan learned of the disappearance of his home world, he declared that his remaining Knights would not become Freeblades – such a choice would only further cement the victory of their enemies in his eyes. Instead, his house swore a new oath: to roam the stars, battle heretics wherever they found them and seek news of Kolossi's fate. They would hunt down whoever had wounded their house so mortally, and seek vengeance.

House Raven still fights in the manner it always did. Its Knights march forward like an endless wall of red metal, large numbers of Knights Crusader providing overwhelming support. At their head are the Companions, an inner circle of Knightly elite. These warriors maintain noospheric communication, working in close concert to crush the foe.

Word has reached the Inquisition of what might have happened to Kolossi. Mysterious reports speak of a fractured world in the Imperium Nihilus which emerged apparently from nowhere and is home to nightmarish horrors, monstrous machines and a body of deformed Chaos Knights who call themselves House Korvax.

We will leave no stone unturned. Vengeance will be ours.

HOUSE VULKER

'FOR THE GILDED GLORY OF THE OMNISSIAH'

House Vulker is regarded as one of the greater houses among those aligned with the Adeptus Mechanicus. Though its power is clearly visible whenever its Knights stride the battlefield, guns blazing, the house is seen as being particularly reclusive and mysterious. This is a reputation the Nobles of Vulker see no reason to amend, content to keep their ways, rituals and traditions out of the sight of outsiders.

'The Omnissiah has blessed us with gifts. It has not given us the right to reveal them.'

– Baron Golphytes

The home world of House Vulker is Aurous IV, a mineral-rich planet in a crowded star system. Its allied forge world, Bellus Prime, was established nearby for the very purpose of exploiting Aurous IV's natural resources, as well as that of surrounding asteroid belts. The bond between both planets is strong indeed, and golden-plated servitor creatures toil upon them day and night to extract raw materials. The gilded House Vulker crest proclaims their wealth. Beyond the central diadem with the cog-skull motif, none of the mysterious symbols are decipherable to any outside the learned, yet secretive servants of the Cult Mechanicus. Whether the house's reclusive nature is due to a desire to hide some deep shame from others, demonstrates lack of trust, or merely lack of interest in revealing much of their ways to others, is unclear even to more studied observers of the Knight houses.

House Vulker's courts are full of Tech-Priests and servitors that speak in coded machine language and number sequences. Unlike some other houses, House Vulker welcomes tech-magi into their bastions and upon their world without hesitation, seeing such beings not as outside interference but allies integral to their way of life. Both Nobles and Priests take part in the house's mechanical ceremonies. Such events would be, should an outsider ever see them, disturbing to look upon, and their meanings would be unclear yet appear deeply sinister. But outsiders are not welcome within the steel-clad fortresses of House Vulker, so few souls have even the slightest idea of what occurs there.

When not at war, the Nobles of House Vulker hide every inch of their flesh with robes in hues of crimson, silver, white, black and gold in various combinations and patterns, and sometimes will wear gold masks that have blank expressions. The colours a Noble wears is dictated by their rank, title, region of origin on Aurous IV as well as more esoteric reasons. However, when the call to war comes, they put aside many of their curious trappings and stride out with all the determination and wrath a Knight house is known for. They place a premium upon well-coordinated plans for both attack and defence, always engaging the enemy at the optimal distance by utilising carefully cogitated trajectories. This often results in Vulker's Knights waiting patiently for the enemy to draw close before annihilating them with searing barrages. It was they who first developed the Tripartite Lance, a formation later adopted by all other houses, in which the fire of a Knight Warden, Knight Crusader and Knight Gallant are combined.

In recent years war has come both to Bellus Prime and Aurous IV. From beneath Bellus Prime's surface, Necrons of the expansionist Sautekh Dynasty rise. On Aurous IV, many of the planet's most remote and inhospitable mountain ranges have proven to be immense Necron tomb structures encrusted with the rocky strata of past aeons. The bonds between the two worlds have been strengthened with each battle they have fought together against the xenos – both have stood firm against nigh endless legions of android warriors and metallic constructs. Forges have been fired day and night to produce weapons and munitions. Clade after clade of servitors have been worn through to keep production lines operating and mines open to find resources. Slowly but surely, however, the situation grows more desperate for House Vulker, driving them ever closer to desperate measures that might reveal their secrets.

Lady Luxious (001)

001

The display of bare adamantine armour plates is considered a deeply significant tribute by House Vulker. Lady Luxious earned this honour during fierce fighting on the death world of Tasmadar II, after Tyranid bio-horrors ambushed Baron Dyrok's lance. Surging from the overgrown slopes of the valley known simply as the Gullet, a pair of huge serpentine beasts crippled the Baron's Knight and toppled Sir Ulrecht's Gallant with a punishing body-blow. With icy calm, Luxious cogitated firing solutions and unleashed a punishing salvo of fire that ripped one beast apart before it could finish Ulrecht off. Unalloyed Victory went blade-to-chitinous-claw with the other Tyranid monster, sustaining heavy damage before finally bisecting the creature's head with its roaring chainsword. The Lady and her Knight stood guard over their damaged comrades for a further eight hours, seeing off predatory waves of beasts before relief finally reached them.

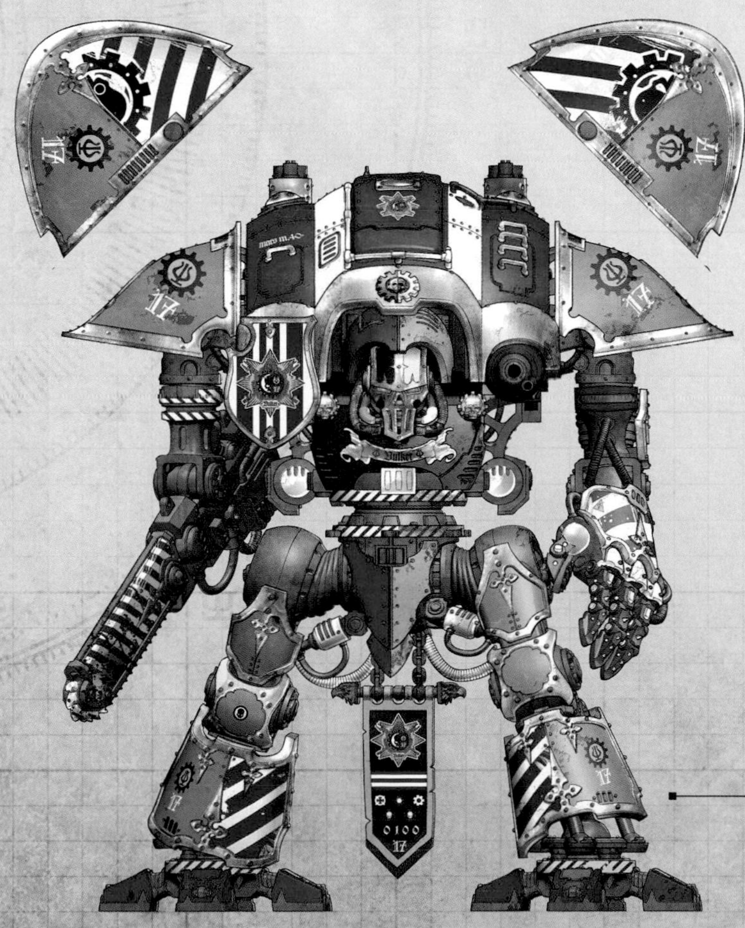

002

The twin stripes upon his Knight's carapace mark Vroth as a Baron, and the pattern upon his tilting plate denotes his position within the Exalted Court as Master of Vox. The Master of Vox, sometimes known as a Broadhailer, bears the internal comms equipment that can network together all the fighting detachments of House Vulker's Knights as well as broadcast vox hails to distant allies. In many Exalted Courts, the Master of Vox commands a rearguard position, focusing upon communications and lending supporting fire. Not so for Baron Vroth. In typical Knight Gallant fashion, Baron Vroth wades into the thickest of the fighting, crushing all before him. His Knight, the Gilded Conqueror, is one of House Vulker's eldest and most richly decorated suits. Only the most ancient of machines bear gilded armour burnished to a sheen, and the Gilded Conqueror boasts a full helm-plate made of precious metal.

Baron Vroth (002)

001

Bold to the point of recklessness, Sir William is the latest Noble to pilot the Knight Paladin Bloody Broadsword. He has performed superbly in the Cull on Raisa every time he has taken part, claiming many kills indeed and surpassing many Nobles with years more experience. Should he continue to survive his foolhardy actions in battle, and over time temper his manner in battle, many believe he has the potential to reach some of House Cadmus' highest ranks. For now, however, it seems that Sir William is satisfied excelling purely in combat, as opposed to mastering wider strategy or political nous. His actions have, up until this point, only been to the gain of House Cadmus, though Roland knows he may have to bring the maverick Noble into line if necessary.

002

Orlando is next in line to become one of the Twelve Barons of Raisa, a position that would ordinarily mark out its occupier as a potential rival to the ruler of House Cadmus. However, Orlando's disregard for the annual Cull, an event of great significance on Raisa, ensures that he could never claim kingship of his house. For Orlando, slaying the beasts is an everyday task, not a sporting event. Thus, Orlando is content as ruler of Patton Hall, a keep in the most isolated province of Raisa.

When called to war, Orlando pilots Coward's Bane, his Knight Crusader and one of the eldest of Raisa's Knight suits. Orlando's vassals all know well the thunderclap roar emitted when his Knight's gauntleted fist strikes home. It is a sound heard often enough, for Orlando is tasked with leading many campaigns – a tribute to his fighting prowess.

HOUSE CADMUS

'THEY WHO ARE NOT OUR ALLIES ARE OUR PREY'

Hailing from the heavily forested world of Raisa, the Nobles of House Cadmus are fiercely independent and peerless monster hunters. Once aligned with the forge world of Gryphonne IV, that planet's fall to the Tyranids of Hive Fleet Leviathan has freed the house from its obligations to the Tech-Priests and they have reasserted their identity.

House Cadmus legend tells that when the Imperium first made contact with the Nobles of Raisa they received a cold welcome, and it was many years before tentative alliances were formed. When Baron Godfrey swore fealty to the forge world of Gryphonne IV in exchange for Sacristans and technology, knowing his house needed it, his fellow Nobles were aghast, deeming the treaty a betrayal of all they stood for. Godfrey earned yet more ire when he changed the house's crest to incorporate the cog of the Adeptus Mechanicus. None opposed Godfrey openly however, for the might of the tech-magi of Gryphonne IV was behind him. For millennia, the Knights of House Cadmus upheld their part of the bargain, and suffered heavy losses in the defence of the forge world against a Tyranid invasion that saw its fall. Since then, Baron Roland, the current ruler of Raisa, has seized the opportunity to restore House Cadmus' ancient heraldry, replete with wings and crest of a slain mutant. His Sacristans were horrified by this sacrilege against the Omnissiah, but have no say in such a decision.

Raisa has always been troubled by high rates of mutation, the deformed creatures lurking within the world's forests and threatening its settlements. For thousands of years, the Knights of House Cadmus have gathered every midsummer's eve to prepare for the annual hunt of these creatures. This much-celebrated event is known as the Cull. Bio-reading cogitators are attached to their Knight suits before every event, enabling each Knight to track the number of monsters they have slain during the course of the hunt. The Knight who claims the greatest number of kills is the winner of this macabre tourney, and will rule the affairs of the house for the next year. The creatures are so numerous that only the vast plateaus that pierce Raisa's evergreen canopy are completely free from their touch, and it is on these highland plains that House Cadmus erect their fortresses, including their primary stronghold, Golem Keep. This monolithic edifice was named – or so myth tells – after the mighty elementals that once haunted the planet's wildernesses, before they were hunted to extinction by the first Imperial Knights to settle on Raisa many thousands of years ago. Now only tribes of mutants remain, and House Cadmus chooses not to fully wipe them out. This is not out of loyalty or pity, but rather to maintain the tradition of the Cull, which also gives more youthful Knights experience of combat before heading out to battles across the galaxy.

BARON ROLAND

Roland was born of an old and powerful baronial family and hails from Swinford Hall, a cavernous and luxurious wing of Golem Keep. An uncompromising man, he does not suffer fools and has demonstrated legendary courage in the face of the enemy by often leading from the front. He has an unbroken run of thirty two victories in the Cull. It is well that a leader of such experience rules, given the losses suffered by House Cadmus on Gryphonne IV and the increasing dangers presented by the emergence of the Great Rift.

The Cicatrix Maledictum caused a sudden explosion of mutant numbers on Raisa, and great hordes of the abominations destroyed agri-plexes and peasant settlements at will in vengeful rampages against House Cadmus. Roland ordered the Cull to end all Culls and marched at the head of the entire household. Weeks of slaughter followed and many lives were lost before the mutants were driven back. In the aftermath, Roland ordered the raising of new fortifications to overlook the deepest woodlands.

HOUSE GRIFFITH

'HONOUR AND FURY, COURAGE AND STRENGTH'

The Nobles of House Griffith are among the most skilled warriors of all their kind. Raised on tales of daring valour and heroic deeds, their traditions and practises yield consummate bladesmen. In battle, their aggression is legendary. They crave the thrill of melee and seek out the largest foes, bringing them down with thundering charges and precise blows.

The home world of House Griffith is the volcanic planet of Dragon's End, which derives its name from the winged drakes that dwelled there millennia ago. They soared on the world's thermals and hunted the megasaur herds that grazed in the valleys, before being hunted to extinction. It was the quick foundation of House Griffith that saw the irrevocable changes to the planet's primordial ecosystem.

Dragon's End's first Human settlers brought with them great herds of Terran horses, and in those days as now the Nobles were adept riders. As their colonies expanded they sought dominance over the megasaur herds, which brought them into conflict with the planet's great drakes. Before the colonists constructed the first Knight suits, they fought the drakes from horseback, wearing baroque armour made from locally mined obsidian. In order to defeat the monstrous creatures, the Nobles had to become superlative warriors and riders. Though many were killed, those who survived quickly became tough and strong. Nathaniel Griffith was among the very greatest of the Nobles, killing three dragons before becoming inaugural ruler of the newfound Knightly house. Once the colonists constructed Knight suits, it was only a matter of time before the dragons were exterminated, but despite the advent of this new technology, the Nobles never forgot their heritage.

To this day, the Nobles of House Griffith are told the tales of the wars against the dragons, and train on horses with traditional weapons such as lance and blade in one of the most stringent training regimes of any house. They are determined to maintain the legacy of their forebears' martial excellence and mental fortitude, and ever seek to demonstrate themselves as worthy inheritors of their ancestors' bloody reputation – to enemies, allies, as well as fellow members of their house. Disputes are regularly settled with duels or jousts and tournaments see families compete for standing and prestige. With some of their Thrones Mechanicum dating back to time when the Knights fought the drakes, even now members of House Griffith can commune with long-dead dragon slayers and hear the tales and stories of that fabled time directly from those there.

The heraldry of House Griffith owes much to Nathaniel Griffith. He chose

001

The ruler of House Griffith bears the honorific of Grand Master of the Lance, a title the current ruler, Bryce Griffith, has proven worthy of many times over. House Griffith is unusual in that its High King is not marked out by the traditional band upon his carapace, but Bryce's personal heraldry is instantly recognisable to all of his house's Knights regardless.

As has been the tradition upon Dragon's End for centuries, only a Knight who has slain an enemy High King can bear a red blade, gauntlet or lance. Exactly what qualifies a foe as a High King is a matter of conjecture amongst the Nobles, but all agree Byrce earned the honour fairly when he carved Warlord Grazzgha's Gargant to pieces, and again when he felled a Lord of Skulls with the thermal cannon of his Knight, Fires of Valour.

the crest, which depicts the great dragon Alvirax holding the broken lance with which Nathaniel slew him. The other half features a crimson demi-Aquila on a field of black, symbolising the house's loyalty to the Imperium.

The bone-coloured livery of House Griffith's Knights is in honour of the legendary lance that Nathaniel wielded in battle from horseback, which was intricately carved and made from the femur of a great drake the hero slew. To this day, the grand master of the House bears a stylised lance emblem on their Knight suit in honour of Nathaniel, and in the great jousting tournament in the Field of Adamantine, the Grand Master has the honour of wielding the very lance Nathaniel carried.

'Some say these are dark times for Mankind, for there is much darkness, and it is full of monsters. We of House Griffith are bred for such times.'

– *Baron Isak Griffith*

THE SAVIOUR'S HUNT

When the factory world of Drakkatoria was struck by a reality disjunction, tides of horrifying shadow-spawn from the nether-realm of Aelindrach in Commorragh infested all of its cities. The world fell into darkness. Murderous Mandrakes hunted the terrified populace, led by the fiendish Kheradruakh the Decapitator. Drakkatoria's Astropaths screamed their minds bloody in their cries for aid. Though it cost them their lives, their pleas were answered, with bastion ships of House Griffith arriving in orbit. Griffith Armigers swept through industrial ruins, banishing shadows with their hull-lumen and using their weapons to flush out xenos packs into the line of fire of larger Knights. Hissing Mandrakes emerged impossibly within the cockpits of Knight suits, knifing screaming Nobles to death in frenzies of violence. Victory was finally achieved when three Dominus-class Knights forged a path to the shattered webway spar that began the madness and bombarded it. Realising their link to their realm was threatened, the shadow creatures fled.

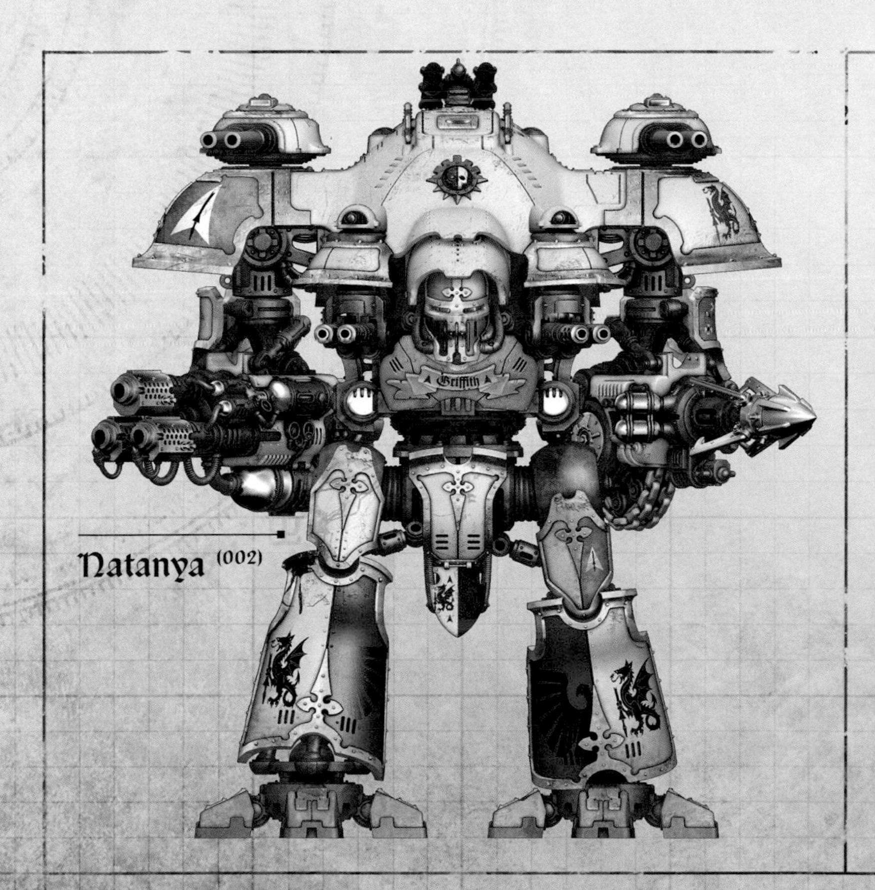

Natanya (002)

002

Lady Natanya pilots the immense Knight Valiant known as Bane of Iron, whose machine spirit is amongst the most aggressive of all House Griffith's hunting steeds. Natanya herself is strong-willed and courageous, the only Noble ever to fully break the unruly Bane of Iron to their command. Natanya has harnessed her war engine's natural ferocity and destructive power, and now specialises in providing devastating close-range fire support to her comrades in the field.

Griffith's fine tradition of monster hunting has found a worthy proponent in Lady Natanya, who excels in obliterating the Daemon Engines of the Heretic Astartes. She was amongst the Knights seconded to Guilliman's Indomitus Crusade, and soon proved her valour by protecting her Ultramarines allies with her Knight's crackling ion shield while annihilating heretical war machines one after another with pinpoint fire. Natanya has shared an honour-bond with the sons of Ultramar ever since.

HOUSE HAWKSHROUD

'NO REQUEST FOR AID SHALL BE DENIED'

No house is more loyal to the Imperium than House Hawkshroud. Its mighty Nobles always honour debts regardless of the cost or the odds. Valiant and steadfast all, they march out to war and lay down their lives to uphold past alliances, and their word is trusted to the end by those who fight beside them.

Scions of House Hawkshroud have a very disciplined and virtue-focused upbringing, taught from a very young age to honour and respect their fellows. A mantra of the house is to repay debts tenfold. This gives them a zealous sense of honour, such that they almost never turn down a request for aid. As a result, they are well-versed in fighting battles against the odds. This mentality stretches throughout every strata of society on their home world of Krastellan – even for the peasants their word is their bond.

The house's strict code of honour often results in many of its Knights being spread far and wide across the galaxy in support of those that have earned their loyalty and respect. Unlike many of the other Knightly houses, Hawkshroud's Knights often sport campaign markings, army badges, Space Marine Chapter symbols, regimental crests and other such emblems as a sign of respect for those they have sworn to aid in battle. This not only serves as a sign of dedication to the cause of their allies, but acts to strengthen the bonds of brotherhood between the Knights and those that they fight alongside.

Krastellan itself is an eerie, haunted place, with desolate moors and black hills that stretch in all directions under skies often heavy with ice-cold rain. Where most Knight worlds embrace a degree of technology, House Hawkshroud sees anything over and above what they need for continued operation as an unnecessary extravagance. Thus much of their world remains, in the eyes of observers, primitive. Peasants and Nobles alike live very much as they did ten thousand years ago, or earlier. Now, Krastellan is ravaged by war following the Ork invasion of Waaagh! Zagsmasha. The house has sent out many calls for aid, desperately needing reinforcements. Though many have not responded, the Knights of House Griffith, Astra Militarum regiments of Valhalla and Space Marines of the Valiant Blades are coming. Whether or not Krastellan can stand up to the xenos hordes remains to be seen, but regardless, they will make the Orks suffer.

THE OATHSWORN

Such is the unusually tight association between the Knights of House Hawkshroud and their allies that it is not uncommon for a Knight to remain on campaign far beyond the length of service that was initially offered or requested of them. In doing so, these Knights are, in theory, walking the path of the Freeblade Knight. Unlike many Freeblades, however, these lone Hawkshroud Knights, or Oathsworn, as they are often called, still display their house's heraldry and livery. Unless they are slain in battle, these Knights will one day seek to return to Krastellan, where they will be welcomed back with honour. One Oathsworn is Lady Oriyai, the only survivor of a lance that raced to the Yasan Sector to aid the White Scars against the Red Corsairs. To this day she fights beside the sons of Chogoris.

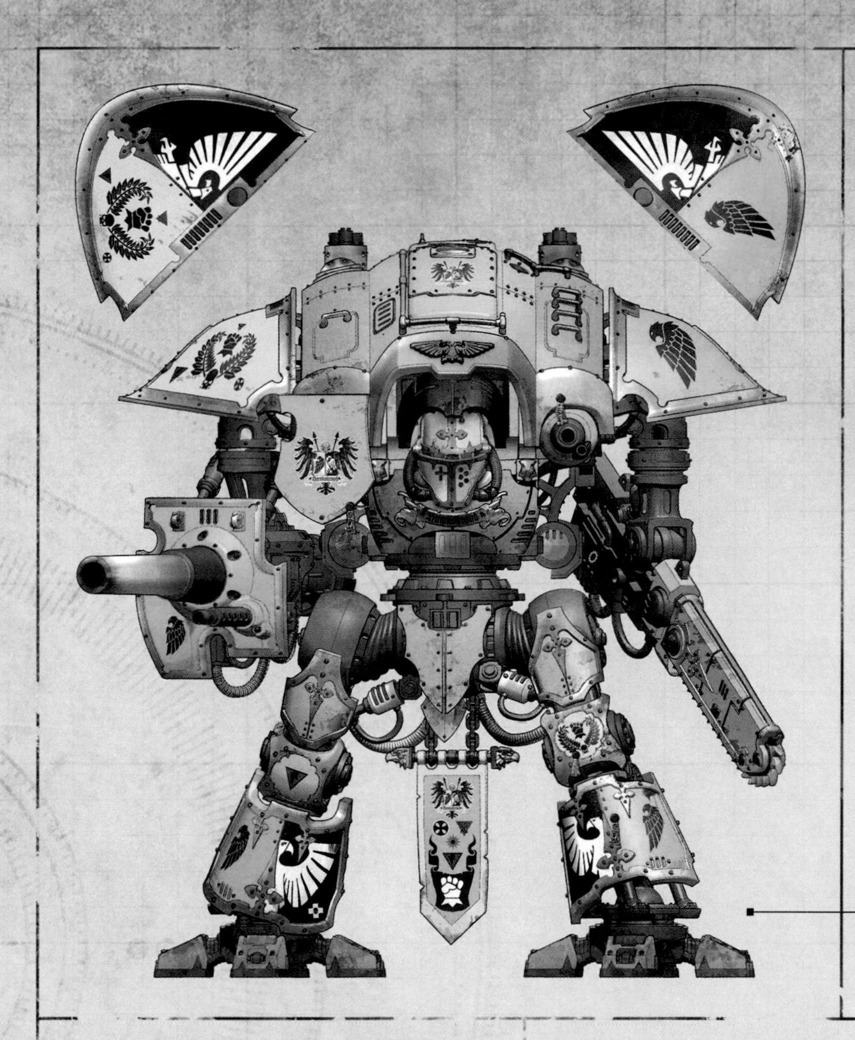

001
Crippled in body, Tormund's spirit bond with the Throne Mechanicum of his Knight Paladin is exceptionally strong. He fights now in memory of his wife, Ludgera, killed in battle by the same Tyranid bio-titan that injured him so badly. His hatred for Hive Fleet Leviathan burns as strongly as the acid which took his life-bond as well as his physical ability.

002
Piloted by the sure-sighted Sir Morlian, Oathkeeper has slain dozens of enemy aircraft to date. Often he fights beside his twin sisters, Morlia and Tegaria, who also pilot Armiger Helverins. Together, the three fill the skies over the battlefield with torrents of fire, denying airspace to all but the most foolhardy of enemy pilots.

003
The shamed Duke Ritter, pilot of Headsman vents his anger and resentment by beheading the war engines and monsters of the enemy in his Knight.

Tormund (001)

Morlian (002)

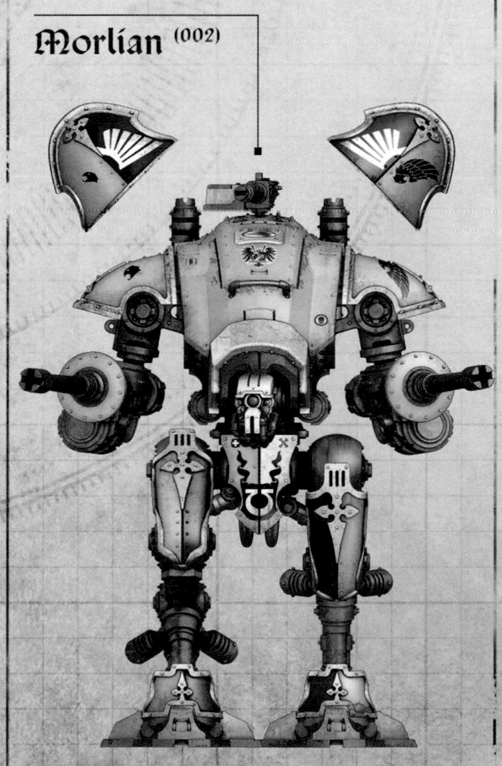

Ritter (003)

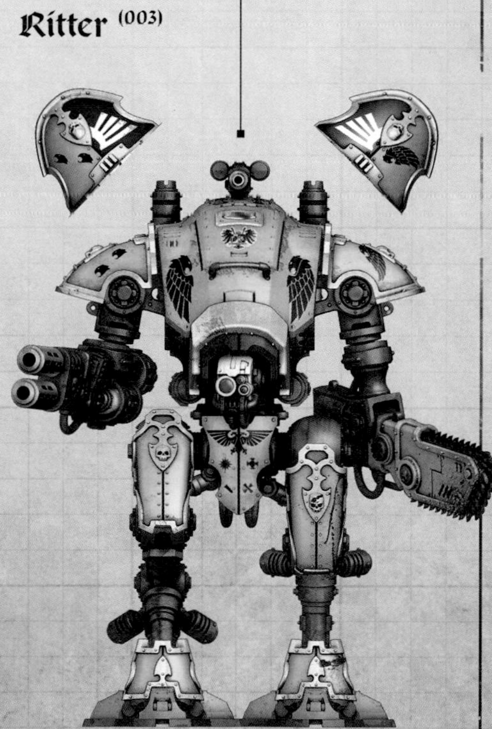

Honour thy word and honour thy debt, and you shall bring honour back to House Hawkshroud.

001

Ludwig has achieved a remarkable tally of a dozen Titan-class kills, denoted by the banding on his reaper chainsword. Despite his many years of service, he has lost none of the impulsiveness of youth, and no matter the carnage and bloodshed he has witnessed he is as eager as ever to get to grips with the foe. If anything, the more deaths of his fellows he has seen the more eager he has become to avenge them. It is fitting then, that he pilots the Knight Gallant War Strider, a particularly bellicose suit that went unpiloted for centuries. No scion of House Mortan had the mental fortitude to conquer its spirit in a Ritual of Becoming until Ludwig. The two have forged an especially strong bond in the thick of dozens of conflicts.

Such is Ludwig's reputation for daring he has unintentionally gathered about him Knights eager to win acclaim on the battlefield by defeating particularly powerful enemies. These include Wilhemina of the Knight Gallant Longsword and Sabine of the Knight Errant Beast Breaker. Though many of his following have met bloody ends in battle, this has dissuaded few. The rewards of killing a brute as powerful as a Titan are seen by many of House Mortan's youth as more than worth the risk.

002

Sir Dirkwald recently completed his thousandth watch-patrol on Kimdaria, allowing the Noble to serve off-planet, a tribute to his fighting prowess. Many have high hopes for him. On only his eighty-seventh watch-patrol he slew a fendrake single-handedly. A handful of actions later he hunted down the notorious Beast of Eckhaal, which had eluded trackers for years. His tally of kills on his watch-patrols is the highest of any of the House's scions for generations, and few doubt that one day he will reach the heights of the house's Exalted Court. Provided he survives the galaxy's wars, of course.

HOUSE MORTAN

'IN WAR, SHOW NO MERCY'

The Knights of House Mortan hail from Kimdaria, known also as the Black Planet. Until M35, a mysterious nebula known as the Black Pall hid the planet from the rest of the galaxy. It was only when this phenomenon partially dissipated that the Imperium finally re-established contact.

In the years before its reunification with the Imperium, the Nobles of House Mortan knew only Kimdaria. A world of eternal darkness and ink-black landscapes, it was inhabited by fell creatures who were well accustomed to the conditions. The Nobles had the singular task of holding back the endless variety of predatory monsters who stalked the desolate mountains, forbidding coastlines, twisted forests and boggy moors. So central did this duty become to their identity, a stylised depiction of a tusk-boar, one of Kimdaria's monstrous beasts, is included in the house crest to this day.

House Mortan's entire way of being has grown around surviving amongst its world's formidable environment. The Nobles and peasants alike of Kimdaria are stern, hard and rugged. They cling to traditions, rituals and orders that have seen them through unimaginable trials and horrors. They know their lessons have been hard-won, and never gained without great loss of life. Thus, they put little trust in experimentation or new ideas – on such a dangerous world, the house can ill afford the losses that testing innovative tactics would create.

The Nobles of House Mortan put much stock in towering walls and heavy gates to hold the nocturnal monsters of their world back. The surface of Kimdaria is dotted with bastions of varying size, which serve both as immense fortifications armed to break direct orbital assault from off-world invaders, as well as relatively smaller patrol bases that serve as rallying points and places of refuge for peasants and Knightly patrols alike. Kimdaria's principal fortress is Blackcrag, and it is here that the High Monarch of House Mortan has their seat of power. Other powerful fortifications include the Bleakmoat, which watches over the Dominus Rex archipelago. The Dimwall holds back the tides of migratory sand sharks of the Wildewind Desert. The Peak of Darkness stands atop one of Kimdaria's highest mountains, a statement from the house that no part of their planet is beyond their control. Umbral Keep and the Black Bastion lie at the heart of the Irchtwyst Forest, their Knights making more watch-patrols than any others. The Nightspire lies on an island in the Rauhart Sea, its enormous beacon helping prevent shipping moving through the most hazardous waters to avoid both coastal rocks and sea monsters.

The Nobles of House Mortan are as grim and as taciturn as any would expect of the warriors expected to fight the horrors of Kimdaria on a daily basis. Over the centuries they have learned to be as accustomed to darkness as the fell creatures that they hunt, and just as fierce. That their traditional monstrous foes kill with claw, fang, tooth and talon, they too have embraced fighting in close quarters. Few Nobles of other households can match them with thunderstrike gauntlets or reaper chainswords.

HIGH KING GERROLT

Perhaps due to his lofty station, Sir Gerrolt is dour, even by the standards of his house. Many, however, claim the reason for this is the Throne Mechanicum Gerrolt bonded with centuries ago – that of the Knight Warden Pride of Blackcrag. Tragedy haunts this ancient artefact the way fell beasts lurk within the dark forests of Kimdaria. Whatever dark whispers might fill Sir Gerrolt's mind, they do not seem to hamper his ability to rule over Kimdaria's people and lead House Mortan's Knights in battle, nor diminish the vehemence with which he destroys the enemy. Blasting rockets into the distance, blazing away with his avenger gatling cannon and smiting foes with his thunderstrike gauntlet, Gerrolt steers the Pride of Blackcrag into the thick of the fighting, slaughtering all that fall under its shadow.

Fear not the dark. Though many horrors lie within, know this: When we strike out, their terror at the sound of our iron tread is so much greater than any fear we might have.

HOUSE TERRYN

'GLORY IN HONOUR'

Hailing from the tropical world of Voltoris, the Knights of House Terryn can trace the existence of their line back fifteen thousand years in a history replete with tales of valour, strength and glory. Over the ages they have earned countless battle honours, and it is widely believed that no one Knight house exemplifies proud martial tradition greater than they.

House Terryn derives its name from Maximillian Terryn, the first ruler of Voltoris, which legends say was colonised early in the Age of Strife. The practises and culture that he instituted are still honoured today by his successors, and over time each generation has added to them as they have achieved their own battlefield triumphs worthy of remembrance. It is believed that the reason why House Terryn's heraldic colour is a cobalt blue is because Voltoris' oceans were once that hue, though today they are green due to the reaction of algae to the system's twin suns; Voltoris lies on the Eastern Fringe. Its vast green oceans surround tropical islands the size of continents. Bat-winged monstrosities hunt beneath the jungle eaves, and the giant amphibious predators that are similarly commonplace offer the Knights ample opportunity to perfect their hunting skills.

Over time House Terryn has amassed so many rituals and traditions that they have become as renowned for their laborious ceremonies as much as their magnificent battle skills. The daily intonation known as the Thousand Canticles of War Long Awaited is said to take three hours. It is joked by some of the house's observers that the tedium that these events cause in the Nobles is a primary reason why they are so eager to leave Furion Peak, their primary fortress, to go to war. Whatever the truth, when House Terryn forged their alliance with the Imperium, they ensured that Voltoris' law was changed so that any Knight under arms in the service of the Emperor was exempt from ceremonial obligations. After that, the Knights of House Terryn sought out conflict across the galaxy, pursuing foes with an aggression born of years of unrequited yearning for war. Now, once a Terryn Noble has completed the Ritual of Becoming, they will join one of the Imperium's military campaigns as soon as possible, returning only rarely to their home world in order to show fealty and ensure the continuation of their line.

Honour thy ancestors. Honour thy House.

Just as their rituals and ceremonies have evolved and grown over time, so has House Terryn's crest. The emblem is that of a white stallion's head emblazoned upon a field of blue. As members of an Questor Imperialis house, Terryn's Knights bear an demi-aquila as part of their crest, emblazoned upon red, representing the blood they have given in honour of the Emperor. At the time of the house's founding, however, the crest was merely a blue tilting shield with a stallion's head. It is believed that this symbol was chosen by Maximillian Terryn after he had mysterious visions of a white stallion. Millennia later, Lord Brutus Terryn led a victorious campaign against a monster the annals record as the Great Kroktar at the Battle of the Six Swords. After this, the crest was expanded to include six blades pointing inwards towards the tilting shield. It was Brutus' descendant, Seuitonius Thucidies Terryn, who made the crest what it is today after he swore allegiance to the Emperor.

House Terryn Knights utilise all manner of different iconography and symbols on the armour of their Knight suits. Many frequently repeat the icon of the white stallion's head. Battle honours, campaign badges and kill markings are a common sight. Family lineage is indicated using patterns and crests, in particular on their pauldrons and poleyns. There are also more bespoke symbols. To earn the right to display blue and red stripes on weapon arms requires the Noble to single-handedly slay a Titan-class foe. The Golden Arrow is the highest honour awarded to House Terryn Knights for fighting prowess. A Noble with this award displays it proudly on their armour and is regarded as a hero by their fellows.

In recent centuries the Knights of House Terryn have been forced to fight ever closer to home, despite a desire to fight further afield as they have done throughout the ages. The dual threats posed by Hive Fleet Leviathan and the rapidly expanding T'au Empire has ensured that Terryn's Knights remain on a constant war footing, lest Voltoris itself be threatened. This has proven to be of enormous benefit to the house. Since the emergence of the Great Rift, silvered automatons of the Necrons have risen from within Voltoris' once-tranquil lakes. As a result, Patriarch Tybalt, High King of House Terryn, has recalled numerous lances back to the home world to eliminate the Necron legions that threaten it. A veteran of many wars, Tybalt has defeated not only a T'au invasion of Voltoris in the past but one from the Aeldari of Craftworld Alaitoc; he is committed to vanquishing the Necrons, just as he has broken other xenos before. He will fight to the death to protect his home.

Hortensio (001)

001

Before the Great Crusade, the Knight Undeniable was so battle damaged that only desperation kept it in commission. After contact was re-established with Mankind, many needed repairs were undertaken. Once its new weapons were in place, Undeniable's livery was changed to reflect that bond – the gun shields of the new weapons bore the same blazing red background upon which the Aquila appeared. After a great many pilots, Sir Hortensio has now bonded with Undeniable, taking that venerable suit once more into battle.

002

The stern Sir Mercutane is as unyielding as the gates of an armoured fortress. His faith is unshakeable, and he would gladly give his life in defence of the Imperium. This would be no simple task for any enemy, especially while he sits within the indomitable Knight Valiant known as Adamant Wrath. This Dominus-class war engine is infamously stubborn, its machine spirit refusing to yield no matter how much damage it suffers.

003

As Master of Justice, Baron Darius – pilot of Intolerant – is the High King's chief military advisor and the appointed executioner of House Terryn's foes. He leads his own Knightly vassals upon missions at Tybalt's command, bringing judgement in his lord's stead. These include Ladies Rozalin and Aaliz, pilots of the Knights Gallant Azure Fury and Raging Stallion. They seek out the foe's leaders, taking their heads for the honour of the house.

Darius (003)

Mercutane (002)

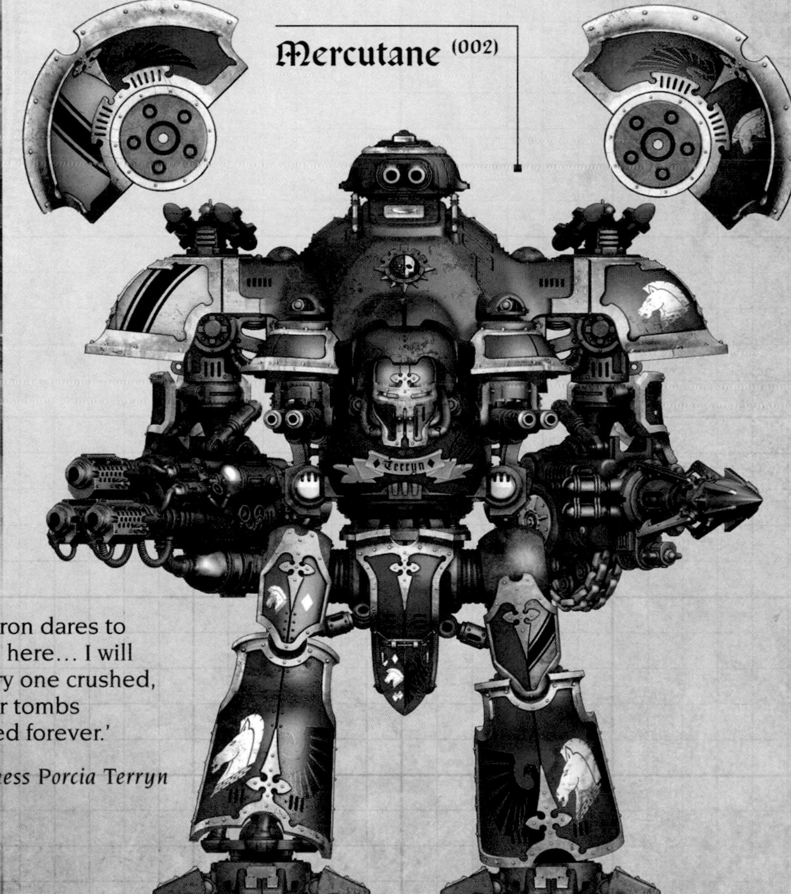

'The Necron dares to assail us here... I will see every one crushed, and their tombs destroyed forever.'

– Baroness Porcia Terryn

Gerantius, the Green Knight (001)

Manifest Vengeance (002)

001

Gerantius resides at the centre of Sacred Mountain on Alaric Prime's largest island. It is rumoured he stands guard over a vast hoard of archeotech and lost lore, and has done so since time immemorial. None know who the Green Knight is, only that in times of need he arises to defend Alaric Prime.

002

Once this dogged Freeblade sets his mind to the hunt, few forces in the galaxy can stop him. Manifest Vengeance has tracked foes across entire sectors in order to land a killing blow with his chain-cleaver.

003

It is believed that Retribution Incarnate was the last of a Knightly house destroyed in the Macharian Crusade. The truth has never come to light.

Retribution Incarnate (003)

FREEBLADES

LONE KNIGHTS

Some Nobles forsake their lineage to quest alone amongst the stars, are cast out as exiles or are the lone survivors of their house. Such warriors are known as Freeblades, and must carve out their own path to glory. Many quickly meet their end upon a battlefield far from home and kin, their past deeds buried with them – yet some prove themselves worthy of legend.

There is no one reason a Knight might become a Freeblade. Nobles who dishonour themselves may be banished from their household, or else decide themselves that they cannot remain. Some Freeblades are forged by force of circumstance; perhaps they were left stranded far from home, and have fought for so long across the stars that solitude is all they now know. In other cases, entire Knightly houses are destroyed, leaving a surviving Noble to fight on for vengeance alone.

So do lone Knights set off into the vast void of space. Some quest for a worthy cause to uphold, others search out a great wrong that they might set right. Rarely Freeblades will become reclusive, willing to fight only to protect their hermitage, while others may even be driven mad by their isolation or the circumstances of their exile, becoming murderous destroyers or silent avengers more akin to supernatural beings than the proud warriors they once were. Whatever the case, Freeblade Nobles become ever more bonded to their Knight suit, Human and machine living as one. Eventually, many become known only by the name of their Knight suit, as though the warrior inside is no longer a separate entity.

Freeblade Knights tend to travel alone, or with only a small group of retainers. Often those bondsmen who fought loyally beside a Noble while they were still part of a household will continue to do so after their master becomes a Freeblade, their Armigers supporting the larger Knight as they did in the past. It is also not uncommon for Freeblades to band together – perhaps having been drawn to the same war zones during campaigns – forming lances that fight in much the same manner as a household detachment. After achieving victory, such Freeblade groups typically disperse once more, although a few have been known to remain in each other's company for extended periods of time.

Regardless of their past tragedies or present company, and irrespective of the idiosyncrasies they develop after so long away from hearth and home, Freeblades still place great significance on acts of honour and duty, perhaps even more so than in their previous lives. Thus, wherever their travels may take them, a Freeblade Knight will fight to protect the people of the Imperium and punish the foes of Mankind.

My house is destroyed. I am all that remains. No matter. My Imperium and Emperor need me. And I need my vengeance.

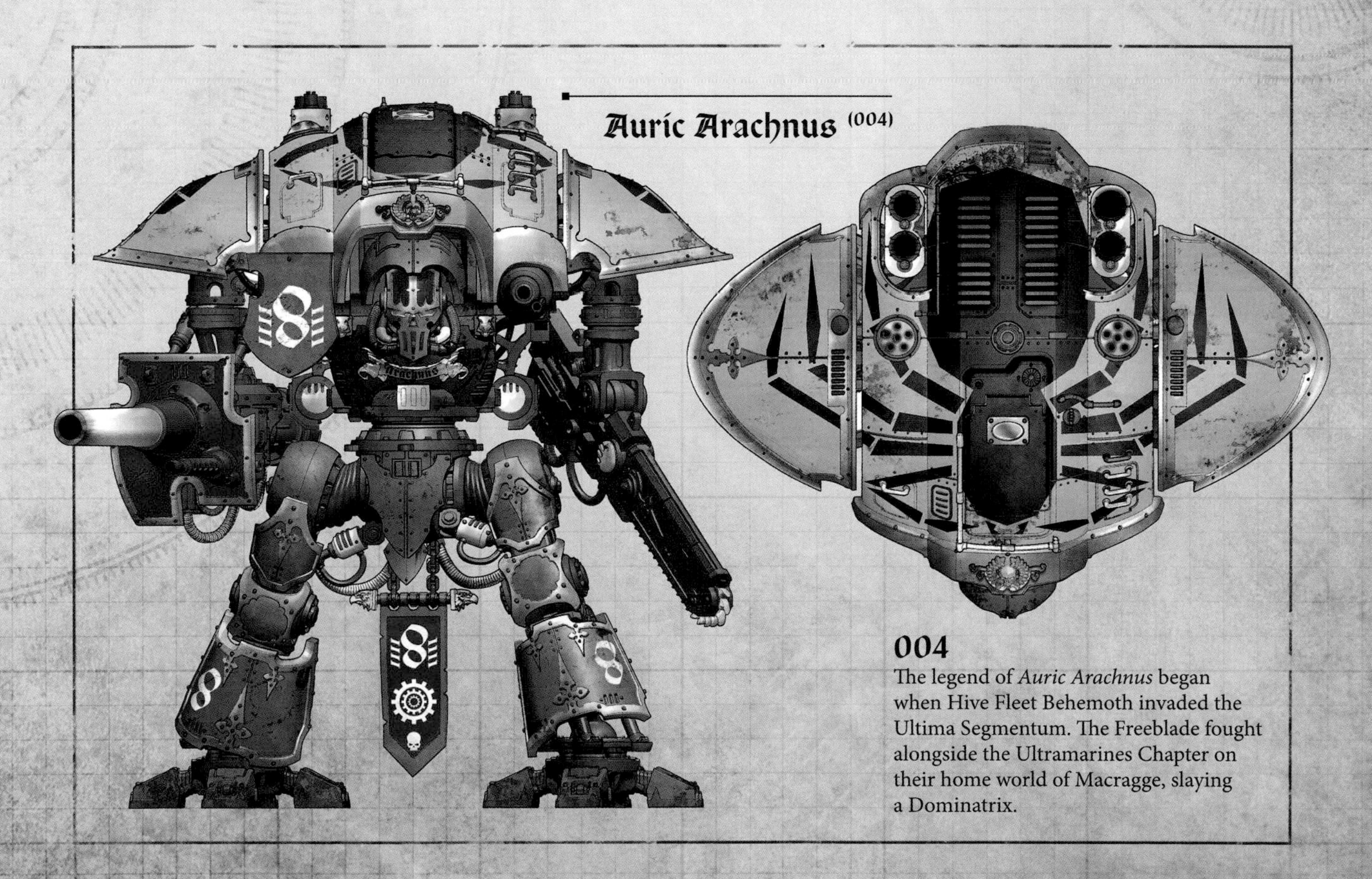

004

The legend of *Auric Arachnus* began when Hive Fleet Behemoth invaded the Ultima Segmentum. The Freeblade fought alongside the Ultramarines Chapter on their home world of Macragge, slaying a Dominatrix.

Dyros Kamata, the Scorched Knight (001)

Kalena Maxus, the Storm Walker (002)

No one knows how many Freeblades exist. It is impossible to count and track them as some are destroyed and more rise to the fore. The number, however, must be in the tens of thousands.

001

Dyros Kamata cast off his family obligations after learning that his older brother was murdered by their father. He rejected the caste system of Alaric Prime and scorched off the symbols of House Kamata from his Knight suit in the Damatoi volcano range. When the Red Waaagh! invaded his world he fought against the Orks alone, refusing to fight alongside other Nobles. It was in the final battle for the Sacred Mountain that finally he took his revenge, slaying his father.

002

Only a single Noble survived the fall of the Knight World of Kamador to the grotesque warriors of the Emperor's Children – Lady Kalena Maxus. Now she haunts the fringes of the Great Rift, fighting furiously against the forces of Chaos wherever she has found them and turning the tide of many battles in the Imperium's favour.

CANIS REX

THE CHAINBREAKER

Sir Hekhtur, Freeblade and pilot of the Knight suit Canis Rex, is a gruff old Noble. Wise, courageous and dutiful, he is a warrior of formidable mental strength as well of immense battlefield skill. He is the saviour of countless souls bound to slavery, and the death of countless followers of Chaos.

The Iron Warriors' siege of the Knight world of Randoryn Alpha was long and brutal. The ruling House Cerberan fought fiercely against the traitors, yet for all their efforts they were defeated and the survivors taken into captivity. In his enslavement, Sir Hekhtur prayed to the Emperor each day, and tried desperately to maintain the morale of his comrades as they were tortured. Despite his efforts, soon he was the only Noble yet to be broken by the Iron Warriors. There is no known true explanation for what happened next. Some argue the Emperor sent Sir Hekhtur a miracle. Others say the bond between him and his Knight was incredibly strong. Either way, Canis Rex broke free of its own chains and came to its pilot's rescue. From then on Sir Hekhtur, now a Freeblade as the last of his House, led the Randoryn resistance. He freed several of his household's living servants, helping them to escape – earning him the epithet of Chainbreaker. Despite his successes he knew his world was lost. Capturing a vessel, he and his remaining loyal followers escaped. Ever since, he has fought to slay followers of Chaos wherever he has found them, and liberate those they have enslaved.

Too many are bound in chains by our foes. Too many toil in slavery for xenos and heretical overlords. I shall be the salvation of the chained, the doom of the oppressor.

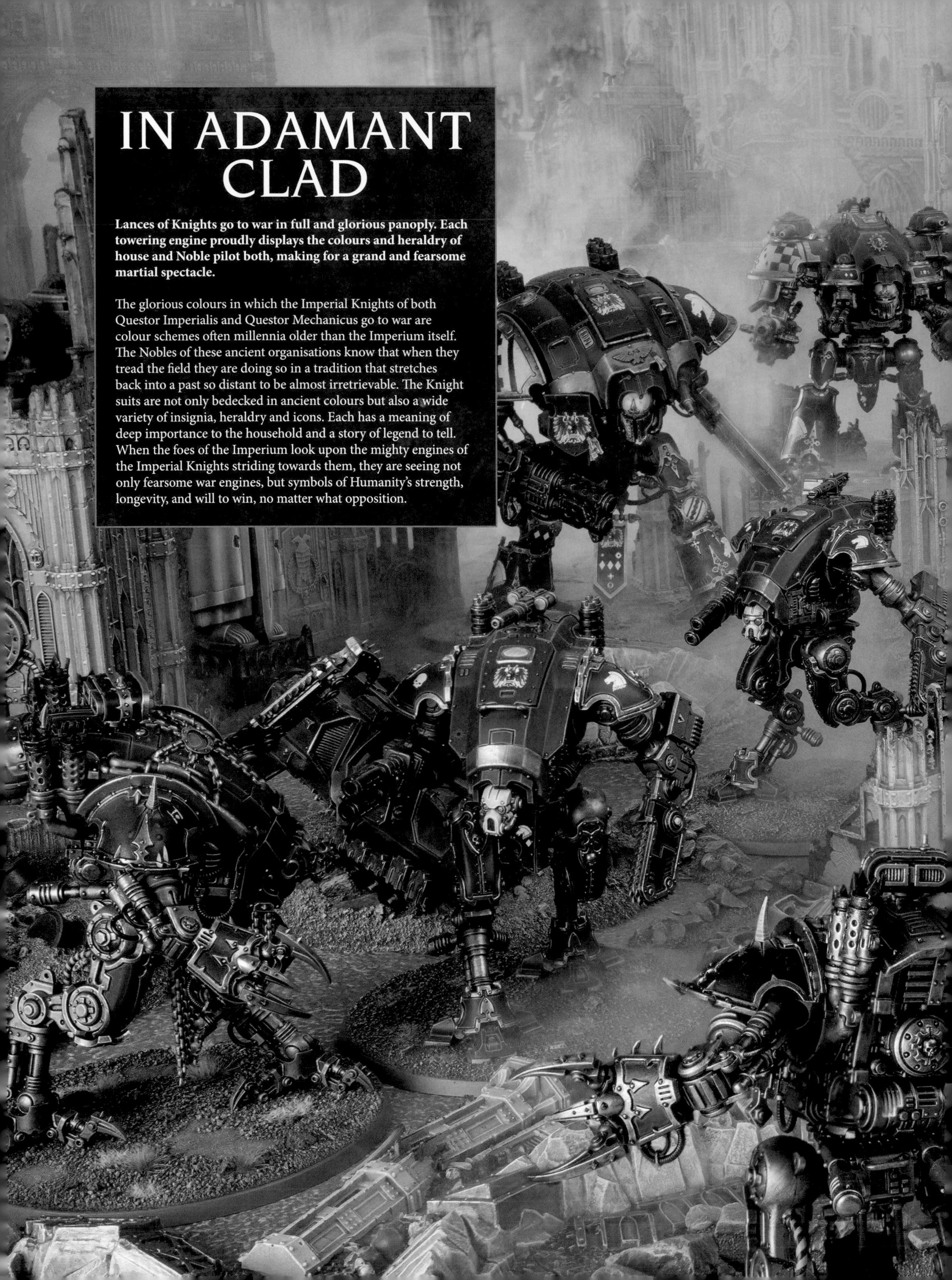

IN ADAMANT CLAD

Lances of Knights go to war in full and glorious panoply. Each towering engine proudly displays the colours and heraldry of house and Noble pilot both, making for a grand and fearsome martial spectacle.

The glorious colours in which the Imperial Knights of both Questor Imperialis and Questor Mechanicus go to war are colour schemes often millennia older than the Imperium itself. The Nobles of these ancient organisations know that when they tread the field they are doing so in a tradition that stretches back into a past so distant to be almost irretrievable. The Knight suits are not only bedecked in ancient colours but also a wide variety of insignia, heraldry and icons. Each has a meaning of deep importance to the household and a story of legend to tell. When the foes of the Imperium look upon the mighty engines of the Imperial Knights striding towards them, they are seeing not only fearsome war engines, but symbols of Humanity's strength, longevity, and will to win, no matter what opposition.

Terryn

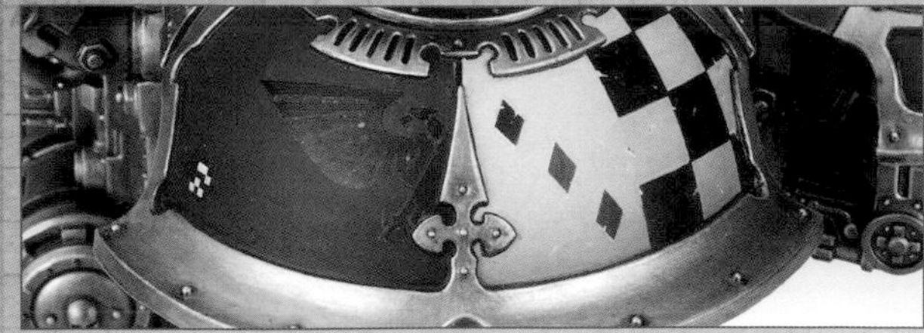

Volcano lance

Knight Castellan of House Terryn

The Knights of House Terryn are staunch warriors, loyal to Emperor and Imperium. In fighting for the Nachmund Gauntlet, they went toe to toe with the Black Legion Heretic Astartes.

Avenger gatling cannon

Knight Crusader of House Taranis

Reaper chainsword

Rapid-fire battle cannon

Knight Paladin of House Raven

Armiger Warglaive of House Raven with thermal spear, reaper chain-cleaver and heavy stubber

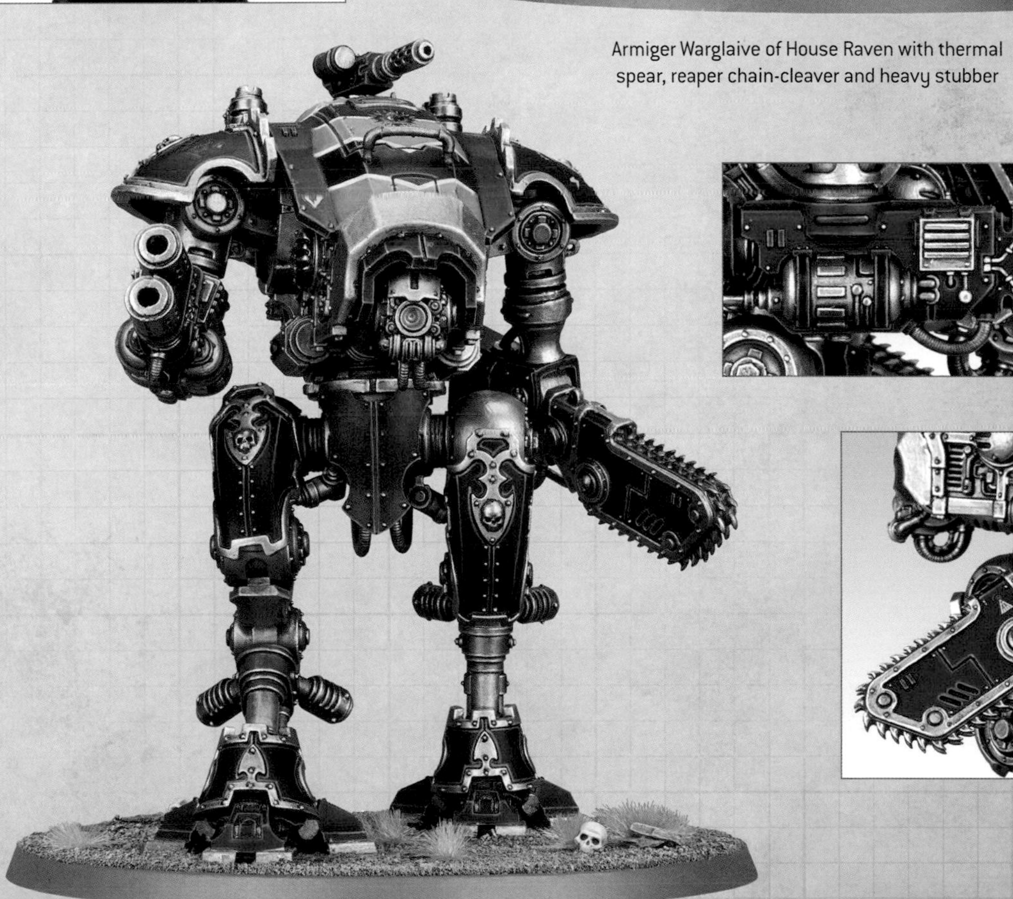

Armiger Warglaive of House Raven with thermal spear, reaper chain-cleaver and meltagun

Sir Hekhtur, dismounted and clad in his half-armoured bodyglove

Canis Rex, the Chainbreaker

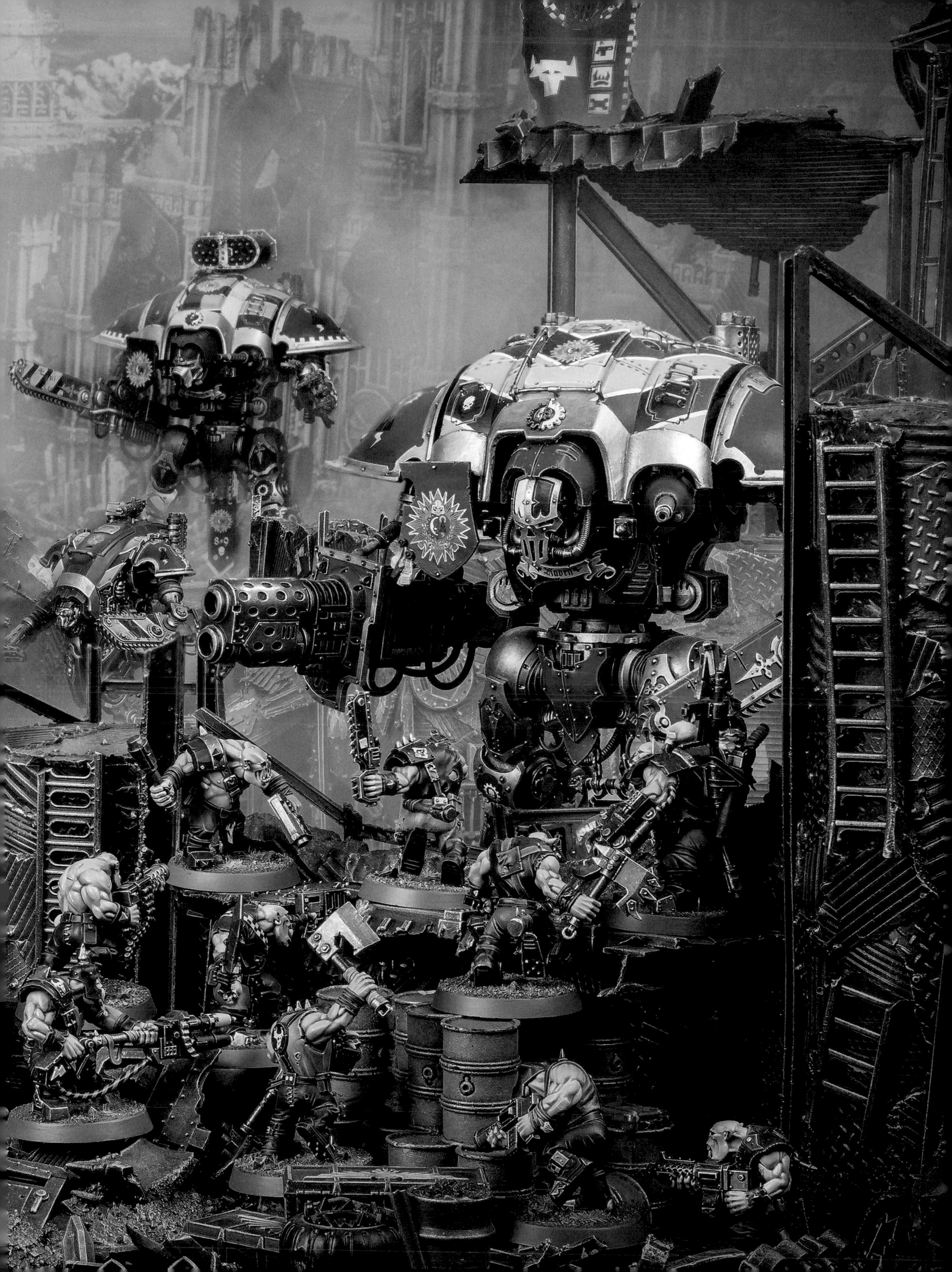

THE RULES

Welcome to the rules section of *Codex: Imperial Knights*. On the following pages you will find all the rules content you need to bring every aspect of the Imperial Knights to life on your tabletop battlefields. Maybe you're inspired to dive straight into some open play games, maybe you want to forge your own tales of horror and destruction with narrative play, perhaps you can't wait to pit yourself against your opponents in nail-biting matched play contests; whichever appeals to you – even if it's a bit of all three – this section of your Codex provides a modular toolbox that allows you to get the most out of your collection.

Of course, there's no need to take it all in at once! Some of the content on the following pages, things like your army's datasheets and the rules for its weapons, will be useful no matter what kind of game you're playing. Others – such as your army's Stratagems, Warlord Traits and Relics – will become relevant once you start playing games with Battle-forged armies. Then there's content such as the Knightly Teachings, which you will unlock by including particular models in your tabletop army. In each case, you can include these new elements at your own pace; whether you're a brand new hobbyist playing your first few games or a veteran general ready to vanquish your foes, there's plenty here to provide countless hours of fresh and exciting gameplay.

On top of this, the Imperial Knights are a unique faction in Warhammer 40,000 in that their battlefield prowess rises and falls as it gains or loses honour. There are a myriad of rules within this section – such as the knight households and Exalted Court – that provide you with an opportunity to further upgrade and customise your army into a lance of noble heroes prepared to hold back the tide of darkness enveloping the Imperium. In addition to unique Agendas, Battle Traits and Crusade Relics that reflect the Imperial Knights' bespoke backgrounds and methods of war, you will find unique content for your Imperial Knights Crusade force, including exciting Requisitions that enable your young Armiger pilots to be promoted to wield a larger Knight suit to war, or rules that can be used to exile a Knight from their household in order to forge a new and noble path as a Freeblade. Finally, your Imperial Knights can undertake mighty heroic quests, gaining Glory points from battle to battle until they accomplish their Knightly Deed, or else failing and earning Shame points and a stain upon their honour. In either case, such a model will gain new abilities in the forms of Qualities and Burdens, forming part of each Knight's unique history and character.

We have been Humanity's sword and shield since the first colony ships left ancient Terra. We failed not then, we will fail not now.

BATTLE-FORGED RULES

DETACHMENT ABILITIES (PG 64-65)

Units in **IMPERIAL KNIGHTS** Detachments gain additional abilities to better reflect how Imperial Knights armies operate together and wage war on the battlefield. You can find out more about Detachment abilities in the Battle-forged Armies section of the Warhammer 40,000 Core Book.

THE NOBLE HOUSEHOLDS (PG 66-79)

IMPERIAL KNIGHTS Detachments in your army can be from a noble household, or they can be a Freeblade. In either case, units in those Detachments will have access to unique rules that reflect the way those noble households fight on the battlefields of the 41st Millennium, and you will be able to create a fighting style that best suits the individualistic nature of **FREEBLADE** units.

STRATAGEMS (PG 80-83)

Imperial Knight armies have access to unique battlefield strategies and tactics that they can utilise to best their foes in any theatre of war; these are represented by the Stratagems in this section, which you can spend Command points to use in your games. You can find out more about Stratagems and Command points in the Warhammer 40,000 Core Book.

EXALTED COURT (PG 84-86)

Imperial Knights can be upgraded to their household's Exalted Court. In doing so, these noble warriors will gain several new abilities, including some that are specific to Crusade armies.

ARMY OF RENOWN: FREEBLADE LANCE (PG 88-89)

You can use the rules found in this section to forge an Army of Renown – a highly specialised army in which every model in your army must be a Freeblade. If you field such an army you will have the varied and eclectic battle experience of several mighty heroes to command.

Designer's Note: *The rules for the Freeblade Lance Army of Renown were originally published in* War Zone Charadon 1: The Book of Rust. *With the updates found in this book, it is necessary to update the Army of Renown rules previously published, and so the rules found in this section replace those previously published.*

ARMY RULES

RELICS (PG 90-93)

IMPERIAL KNIGHTS characters can take powerful artefacts and called Heirloom Relics into battle; these Relics and the rules they bestow are described in this section.

WARLORD TRAITS (PG 94)

The **WARLORD** of an Imperial Knights army can have one of the traits presented in this section. These help to personalise the leader of your force and better reflect their individual combat preferences and command style on the battlefield.

KNIGHTLY TEACHINGS (PG 95)

Some Imperial Knights can act as mentors to the young nobles that pilot Armiger-class suits, and instruct them in the knightly virtues and martial traditions to become a fully fledged Knight. The list of Knightly Teachings that each Mentor in your army can choose from can be found in this section.

MATCHED PLAY RULES

CHAPTER APPROVED RULES (PG 96-97)

If you are playing a battle that instructs you to select secondary objectives, then you can choose from the Imperial Knights ones printed here. These represent goals unique to the Imperial Knights. You can find out more about secondary objectives in many matched play mission packs, including the Eternal War mission pack in the Warhammer 40,000 Core Book.

CRUSADE RULES

CRUSADE (PG 98-115)

Imperial Knights have access to a host of additional rules that enhance your Crusade experience. These include bespoke Agendas, Requisitions, Battle Traits, Battle Scars and Crusade Relics that reflect the honourable background of the Imperial Knights. Amongst these rules are the Sworn to a Quest rules, where an Imperial Knight can embark upon mighty quests, earning glory with their victories, and shame with their failures, and in doing so receive new bonuses in the form of Qualities, and afflictions in the form of Burdens.

DATASHEETS

DATASHEETS (PG 116-130)

This section is essential to all Imperial Knights players, regardless of play style, containing as it does the datasheets for **IMPERIAL KNIGHTS** units. Each datasheet describes, among other things, the profiles of its models, the wargear they can be equipped with and the abilities they have. You can find out more about datasheets in the Warhammer 40,000 Core Book.

POINTS & WARGEAR

WEAPON PROFILES (PG 132-133)

This section provides wargear lists referenced in the wargear options of certain Imperial Knights datasheets, as well as profiles for all of the weapons **IMPERIAL KNIGHTS** units can be equipped with.

POINTS VALUES (PG 133)

If you are playing a game that uses points values, you can use the alphabetical lists in this section to determine the cost of each unit from your army. These will be reviewed annually.

RULES REFERENCE

GLOSSARY (PG 134-135)

In this section you will find a glossary of rules terms used in this Codex that is designed to aid in resolving any complex rules interactions that may arise.

REFERENCE (PG 136)

Here you will find a handy bullet-pointed rules reference that summarises some common Imperial Knights rules.

COMBAT PATROL

Combat Patrol is the smallest size game, and this Imperial Knights force is a great way to start – regardless of whether you want to play an open play game, forge a narrative with a Crusade army, or compete in a matched play mission.

Created from the contents of two Armiger Warglaive boxed sets, this force can be used in a Battle-forged army, and in itself comprises a Super-heavy Auxiliary Detachment, as described in the Warhammer 40,000 Core Book.

On the battlefield, every Imperial Knights model – even the Armiger-class Knights such as these – is a towering engine of destruction. Each one is as powerful as two or more units form most other armies, and is equipped with powerful weaponry and tough armour. As part of a Battle-forged army, these units will also gain the Objective Secured ability (see the Warhammer 40,000 Core Book) enabling them to hold on to objectives even when outnumbered by the foe.

The models here are equipped with deadly heavy weapons in the form of thermal spears, meltaguns and heavy stubbers. The thermal spears and meltaguns are particularly deadly to armoured targets, such as tanks and monsters, but they are short-ranged and unlikely to make a dent against any enemy hordes you encounter. A heavy stubber provides a modicum more anti-infantry firepower, and makes such a Knight a better choice for defensive duties in your deployment zone, where an objective marker may need securing, without putting all of its weapons out of range. A Warglaive's melee attacks are perhaps the most versatile of its weapons, able to eliminate both numerous foes with its sweep profile, or elite foes with its strike profile. As these models are likely to be at the fore of your army, marching forth to get their ranged weapons into range and secure objectives, close combat is a very likely prospect. Thankfully, there are few foes that can best an Imperial Knight in the cut and thrust of melee.

The models in this Combat Patrol force must be aggressive and work together to secure victory. Whilst each is mighty, you only have 3 models, and they will doubtless be outnumbered by your foes and at risk of being overrun. To minimise the risk of this, try and ensure your models can team up and are close enough to one another to provide support when needed. You may struggle to do this while simultaneously holding onto more than one objective, so if different objectives yield you better rewards, concentrate on those; do not squander your forces guarding areas of the battlefield that will not yield you victory.

DETACHMENT ABILITIES

An **IMPERIAL KNIGHTS** Detachment is one that only includes models with the **IMPERIAL KNIGHTS** keyword (excluding models with the **AGENT OF THE IMPERIUM** or **UNALIGNED** keyword).

- **IMPERIAL KNIGHTS** Detachments gain the Knight Lances and Wandering Hero abilities.
- **IMPERIAL KNIGHTS** units in **IMPERIAL KNIGHTS** Detachments gain the Unyielding Knight, Household Traditions and Questor Allegiance Oaths abilities.
- **ARMIGER-CLASS** units in **IMPERIAL KNIGHTS** Detachments gain the Objective Secured ability (this ability is described in the Warhammer 40,000 Core Book).

Note that **IMPERIAL KNIGHTS** Super-heavy Auxiliary Detachments still get these Detachment abilities, even though Super-heavy Auxiliary Detachments do not normally gain any Detachment abilities.

KNIGHT LANCES

On the battlefield, Knights gather in formations called lances, earth-shaking spearheads of towering war engines led by the highest ranking amongst them.

- If this Detachment is a Super-heavy Detachment, or if you are playing a Combat Patrol battle and this Detachment is a Super-heavy Auxiliary Detachment, select one **ARMIGER-CLASS**, **QUESTORIS-CLASS** or **DOMINUS-CLASS** model in this Detachment. That model gains the **CHARACTER** keyword.
- If this Detachment contains between 1 and 2 **QUESTORIS-CLASS** models, or if it contains between 3-5 **ARMIGER-CLASS** models, this Detachment's Command Benefits are changed to: '+3 Command points if your **WARLORD** is part of this Detachment.'
- If this Detachment contains 3 or more **QUESTORIS-CLASS** models, or if it contains 6 or more **ARMIGER-CLASS** models and 1 or more **TITANIC** units, this Detachment's Command Benefits are changed to: '+6 Command points if your **WARLORD** is part of this Detachment.'

WANDERING HERO

Freeblades often wander the galaxy, aiding the armies of the Imperium as they can against the enemies that surround the Emperor's realm.

If this Detachment is a Super-heavy Auxiliary Detachment that contains one **FREEBLADE** unit, until the end of the battle, that unit gains the **AGENT OF THE IMPERIUM** keyword. Only one **FREEBLADE** unit in your army can have this keyword.

UNYIELDING KNIGHT

Every Knight is an army unto themselves, capable of engaging entire enemy forces and holding their ground against them.

This model counts as 5 models for the purposes of determining control of an objective marker (if this model is **TITANIC**, it instead counts as 10 models when determining control of an objective marker).

The only way to show a foe respect is to annihilate them utterly.

HOUSEHOLD TRADITIONS

Noble houses are ancient institutions with martial traditions that stretch back for millennia. Each fights in its own distinctive way.

All **IMPERIAL KNIGHTS** units with this ability, and all the models in them, gain a Household Tradition so long as their Detachment contains at least 3 models (excluding **FREEBLADES**) when you muster your army, and every **IMPERIAL KNIGHTS** unit from your army (excluding **FREEBLADES**) is from the same noble household. The Household Tradition gained depends upon which noble household they are from, as shown on the following pages.

Example: *A* **HOUSE KRAST** *unit with the Household Traditions ability gains the Cold Fury Household Tradition.*

If your noble household does not have an associated Household Tradition, you must instead select a Martial Tradition for them, as described on pages 76-78; this allows you to customise the rules for your noble household.

If a Detachment includes any **FREEBLADES**, you must instead select a Martial Tradition for each of them, as described on pages 76-79. Each **FREEBLADE** must have a unique Martial Tradition and so you cannot select a Martial Tradition for a **FREEBLADE** if any other model in your army has the same Martial Tradition. If your army includes **CANIS REX** (pg 130), then you must select the Mythic Hero Martial Tradition for him. Note that **FREEBLADES** always receive a Martial Tradition, regardless of how many models are in their Detachment.

Write down all of your models' Household Traditions and Martial Traditions on your army roster.

FREEBLADES IN CRUSADE

When you add a **FREEBLADE** unit to your Order of Battle, you must select its Martial Tradition and make a note of this on its Crusade card(s). You cannot select a Martial Tradition for this unit if any other unit in your Crusade army already has that tradition, and its tradition cannot be changed. Note that if this unit contains more than one model, each of those models will have the same tradition even though each will have a separate Crusade card. If you add Canis Rex to your Order of Battle, he will have the Mythic Hero Martial Tradition even if another model in your Crusade army has this tradition.

QUESTOR ALLEGIANCE OATHS

When the Knight worlds were rediscovered after the isolation and terror of the Age of Strife, there was a race for their allegiance between the Imperial Administratum and the Cult Mechanicus. Fealty and integrity are so intrinsic to the Knightly households that these oaths remain a linchpin of their existence millennia later.

All **IMPERIAL KNIGHTS** units with this ability (excluding **FREEBLADES**), and all the models in them, gain a Questor Allegiance Oath so long as every unit in their Detachment has the same Questor Allegiance i.e. every model in their Detachment has the **QUESTOR MECHANICUS** keyword or every model in their Detachment has the **QUESTOR IMPERIALIS** keyword. The Questor Allegiance Oath gained depends upon which allegiance they have, as shown on the following pages, and you must write down all of your Detachments' Questor Allegiance Oaths on your army roster.

Example: *A* **HOUSE KRAST** *unit with the Questor Allegiance ability gains the Sacristan Pledge Questor Allegiance Oath.*

QUESTOR MECHANICUS: SACRISTAN PLEDGE

Those noble households that swear allegiance to the Adeptus Mechanicus preserve the mutual pledge that saw their Knight worlds raised out of technological oblivion. Their failing Knight suits were restored and the arcane knowledge granted to the formative Sacristan orders raised them to a holy perfection of function.

- Add 1 to the Wounds characteristic of a model with this Questor Allegiance Oath (if this model is **TITANIC**, add 2 to its Wounds characteristic instead).
- At the start of each of your Command phases, a model with this Questor Allegiance Oath regains 1 lost wound.

QUESTOR IMPERIALIS: VOW OF HONOUR

These noble households pledged their undying allegiance to the Emperor, and swore to defend the Imperium with neither question nor hesitation. In the millennia since, their Knights have endured hardships and fought monstrous foes in fulfilment of those ancient oaths.

- Add 1 to Advance and charge rolls made for a model with this Questor Allegiance Oath.
- Each time an Advance or charge roll is made for a model with this Questor Allegiance Oath, you can ignore any or all modifiers to that roll.
- Each time this model makes a pile-in move or consolidation move, it can move an additional 1".

THE NOBLE HOUSEHOLDS

If your army is Battle-forged, **<NOBLE HOUSEHOLD>** units (excluding **FREEBLADES**) in **IMPERIAL KNIGHTS** Detachments gain access to the following noble household rules, provided that Detachment contains at least 3 models (excluding **FREEBLADES**) and every **IMPERIAL KNIGHTS** unit in your army (excluding **FREEBLADES**) is from the same noble household. If every **<NOBLE HOUSEHOLD>** unit (excluding **FREEBLADES**) in an **IMPERIAL KNIGHTS** Detachment is from the same noble household, that Detachment is referred to as a Noble Household Detachment.

QUESTOR ALLEGIANCE OATH

The noble households owe their allegiance to either the Imperium or the Adeptus Mechanicus, and so can gain a Questor Allegiance Oath (pg 65). A reminder of what associated Questor Allegiance Oaths can be gained is found here.

HOUSEHOLD TRADITIONS

All **<NOBLE HOUSEHOLD>** units (excluding **FREEBLADES**) in a Noble Household Detachment will gain a Household Tradition, as described on pages 67-75. On these pages you will find the Household Traditions associated with each noble household, as well as the list of Martial Traditions (pg 76-79) that you must use if your noble household does not have an associated Household Tradition or if your Detachment includes any **FREEBLADES**.

WARLORD TRAITS

Each noble household has an associated Noble Household Warlord Trait. If an **IMPERIAL KNIGHTS <NOBLE HOUSEHOLD> CHARACTER** model gains a Warlord Trait, they can have the relevant Noble Household Warlord Trait instead of a Warlord Trait from page 94. **FREEBLADES** can never be given a Noble Household Warlord Trait.

STRATAGEMS

Each noble household has an associated Noble Household Stratagem. If your army includes a Noble Household Detachment, then you will gain access to the relevant Noble Household Stratagem, and can spend CP to use them.

HOUSEHOLD RELICS

Each noble household has an associated Noble Household Heirloom Relic. If your army is led by an **IMPERIAL KNIGHTS <NOBLE HOUSEHOLD> WARLORD** (excluding a **FREEBLADE**), you can give the relevant Noble Household Heirloom Relic to an **IMPERIAL KNIGHTS <NOBLE HOUSEHOLD> CHARACTER** model from your army instead of giving them a Heirloom Relic from pages 90-93. **FREEBLADES** can never be given a Noble Household Heirloom Relic.

Note that some Relics replace one of the model's existing items of wargear. Where this is the case, you must, if you are using points values, still pay the cost of the wargear that is being replaced. Write down any Noble Household Heirloom Relics your models have on your army roster.

Example: *A Battle-forged army includes an* **IMPERIAL KNIGHTS** *Detachment containing 6* **HOUSE TERRYN** *models. All* **HOUSE TERRYN** *units in that Detachment gain the Gallant Warriors Household Tradition and the Vow of Honour Questor Allegiance Oath. A* **HOUSE TERRYN CHARACTER** *model in that Detachment that is given a Warlord Trait can instead be given the Champion of the Household trait and you have access to the Glory in Honour Stratagem and can spend CPs to use it. If the army's* **WARLORD** *is selected from this Detachment and is from* **HOUSE TERRYN**, *then a* **HOUSE TERRYN CHARACTER** *model from your army that could be given a Relic can instead be given the Thunder of Voltoris.*

THE NOBLE HOUSEHOLDS

HOUSE TERRYN

The Knights of House Terryn have earned countless battle honours over the ages. Their house's storied history is replete with tales of valour, strength and glory in battles fought from one side of the galaxy to the other. Some say the tedium of their daily life at Furion Peak only encourages them to campaign away from their home planet. There is a kernel of truth behind this – after all, House Terryn is famed almost as much for their laborious ceremonies as they are for the magnificent skills their Knights display in battle.

'The Ivory Horse and the Ebon Eagle. Such are the great symbols of our House. The former is the acknowledgement of our heritage, without which we would not be the mighty force we are today. The latter is the acknowledgement of our allegiance, proclaiming to all who oppose us that we stand for the Emperor, and all Mankind.'

- Lady Ellania Terryn

QUESTOR ALLEGIANCE OATH: VOW OF HONOUR

House Terryn models in this Detachment gain the Vow of Honour Questor Allegiance Oath (pg 65) if every model in their Detachment has the **Questor Imperialis** keyword.

HOUSEHOLD TRADITION: GALLANT WARRIORS

The Nobles of House Terryn are ever hungry for combat, driving their towering steeds hard across the field. The Knights are as eager as their pilots to take the fight to the foe, striding fleet and sure into the white heat of battle with ferocious determination.

Each time an Advance roll or a charge roll is made for a model with this tradition, roll one additional D6 and discard one of the dice results.

GLORY IN HONOUR 1CP

House Terryn – Epic Deed Stratagem

Drawing upon the heroism that is their birthright and inspired by the spirits of the Noble ancients within their Throne Mechanicum, the pilot unleashes their full fury upon the foe.

Use this Stratagem in the fight phase when a **House Terryn** model from your army is selected to fight. Until the end of the phase:

- Add 1 to that model's Attacks characteristic.
- Each time that model makes a melee attack, re-roll a hit roll of 1.

WARLORD TRAIT: CHAMPION OF THE HOUSEHOLD

Terryn's rulers can always be found at the forefront of their house's armies.

You can re-roll Advance and charge rolls made for this **Warlord**.

RELIC: THUNDER OF VOLTORIS

Originally, Thunder of Voltoris was a defensive cannon mounted upon the battlements of House Terryn's mountainous stronghold. During the Khybus Schism, the traitors of the Sevenskull Cult attempted to assassinate the house's ruler as he walked beyond the safety of his fortress walls. Thunder of Voltoris is said to have fired of its own volition, a miraculous discharge that slew the traitors in a ball of flame and saved High King Nathanial. To honour the weapon's machine spirit, Nathanial had the artillery piece removed and fashioned into a battle cannon that could be borne to glory by his scions until the end of days.

House Terryn model with rapid-fire battle cannon only. This Relic replaces a rapid-fire battle cannon and has the following profile:

WEAPON	RANGE	TYPE	S	AP	D
Thunder of Voltoris	72"	Heavy D6+6	9	-2	3

Abilities: Blast.

THE NOBLE HOUSEHOLDS

HOUSE GRIFFITH

The Knights of House Griffith are a fierce and proud warrior caste who value courage and skill at arms above all else. Duels of honour are commonplace amongst Griffith's hot-headed Knights. A regular jousting tourney, the Field of Adamantine, dictates the standings of each family in society; a Knight can be pre-eminent one day, but overshadowed the next, should one of their rivals emerge triumphant.

'Our ancestors, slayers of great drakes all, could not have imagined the beasts which plague the wider galaxy. Tyranid horrors, Orkoid brutes, mutant terrors. Despite this, thanks to their legacy, we have slain them all.'

- Baroness Eyelda Griffith

QUESTOR ALLEGIANCE OATH: VOW OF HONOUR

House Griffith models in this Detachment gain the Vow of Honour Questor Allegiance Oath (pg 65) if every model in their Detachment has the **Questor Imperialis** keyword.

HOUSEHOLD TRADITION: GLORY OF THE CHARGE

Seeking supreme martial glory, the Nobles of House Griffith slam into the enemy formation like an avalanche. Their momentum and pitiless wrath are such that the foe are scattered before them like leaves upon a gale, their battle lines sundered by the apocalyptic charge of ironclad giants.

Each time a model with this tradition fights, if it made a charge move, was charged or performed a Heroic Intervention this turn, then until that fight is resolved, add 1 to the Attacks characteristic of this model.

Praise thy lance. Love thy sword. Revere thy shield. Honour thy steed. Glorify thy Emperor.

DRAGONSLAYER — 2CP

House Griffith – Epic Deed Stratagem

The Nobles of House Griffith have a long and proud history of ruthlessly hunting down and expertly slaying the most monstrous of foes.

Use this Stratagem in your Shooting phase, when a **House Griffith** model from your army is selected to shoot, or in the Fight phase, when a **House Griffith** model from your army is selected to fight. Until the end of the phase, each time that model makes an attack, if the target of that attack contains any **Vehicle** or **Monster** models, add 1 to that attack's wound roll.

WARLORD TRAIT: MASTER OF THE JOUST

The lords of Griffith are experts at striking pinpoint blows while at full stride.

This **Warlord** is eligible to declare a charge in a turn in which it Advanced.

RELIC: MARK OF THE LANCE

A Noble who has won victory in the fabled Field of Adamantine tourney earns the right to bear this unique mark of honour into battle. Micro-circuitry woven into the honour pennant sends jolts of electrical force surging through the Knight's melee weaponry, enhancing the pilot's already proven skill in one-to-one combat.

House Griffith Questoris-class model only. Each time the bearer finishes a Charge move, select one enemy unit within Engagement Range of it and roll one D6; on a 2-3, that enemy unit suffer D3 mortal wounds; on a 4-5, that enemy unit suffers 3 mortal wounds; on a 6, that enemy unit suffer D3+3 mortal wounds.

HOUSE CADMUS

For thousands of years, the Knights of House Cadmus have gathered every midsummer's eve to prepare for an annual hunt to keep the mutant numbers of their forested world in check. This much-celebrated event is known as the Cull. Bio-reading cogitators are attached to their Knight suits before every event, enabling each to track their kills. The Knight who claims the greatest number is the winner, and will rule the affairs of the house for the next year.

'We are Cadmus! Slaughterers of mutants, aliens and traitors! Let it be known that no horde of abominable horrors can stop us.'

- Lord Harolde Cadmus

QUESTOR ALLEGIANCE OATH: VOW OF HONOUR

HOUSE CADMUS models in this Detachment gain the Vow of Honour Questor Allegiance Oath (pg 65) if every model in their Detachment has the **QUESTOR IMPERIALIS** keyword.

HOUSEHOLD TRADITION: HUNTERS OF THE FOE

House Cadmus' Knights are accomplished at wading through hordes of lesser enemies, culling them like vermin.

Each time a model with this tradition makes a melee attack:

- Unless the target of that attack contains any **VEHICLE** or **MONSTER** models, re-roll a wound roll of 1
- If the target of that attack contained 6 or models when this model was selected to fight, you can re-roll the wound roll.

BIO-SCRYER COGITATOR ARRAY 1CP/2CP

House Cadmus – Wargear Stratagem

Some Knights of Cadmus use cogitator arrays within their cockpits, salvaged from Gryphonne IV, that allows them to track their prey.

Use this Stratagem at the end of the Reinforcements step of your opponent's Movement phase. Select one **HOUSE CADMUS** model from your army that is not within Engagement Range of any enemy units. That unit can shoot as if it were your Shooting phase, but its models can only target a single eligible enemy unit that was set up as Reinforcements this turn and that is within 12" of them when doing so. If that model is an **ARMIGER-CLASS** model, this Stratagem costs 1CP; otherwise, it costs 2CP.

WARLORD TRAIT: VETERAN OF GRYPHONNE IV

Those Knights of Cadmus who survived the destruction of Gryphonne IV by Hive Fleet Leviathan proved their endurance time and again.

Each time a melee attack is allocated to this **WARLORD**, subtract 1 from the Damage characteristic of that attack (to a minimum of 1). This is not cumulative with any other rules that reduce the Damage characteristic of an attack.

RELIC: THE HUNTER'S EYE

This remarkable data-manifold was recovered by the Nobles of House Cadmus almost eight millennia ago, during a crusade amidst the blighted tech-graves of Kossok's World. It surrounds a Noble's Throne with a remarkable holo-projected bio-scan and engine-signature read-out whose gaze penetrates the densest terrain as though it were not there. Thus, the pilot is able to direct their fury against even those enemies who believe themselves wholly safe and undetected.

HOUSE CADMUS ARMIGER-CLASS or **HOUSE CADMUS QUESTORIS-CLASS** model only. Each time the bearer makes a ranged attack, the target does not receive the benefits of cover against that attack.

THE NOBLE HOUSEHOLDS

HOUSE HAWKSHROUD

To the Knights of Hawkshroud, honour is the single most important virtue of all. So essential to their way of life is the esteem and reputation of their house that Hawkshroud's Knights will honour almost any call to arms from those that have earned their loyalty or respect. It is for this reason that, at any given time, almost all of House Hawkshroud's Knights are away on campaigns to uphold past alliances.

'Failing to uphold a vow? Painful death is preferable.'

- Sir Ottwald Hawkshroud

QUESTOR ALLEGIANCE OATH: VOW OF HONOUR

HOUSE HAWKSHROUD models in this Detachment gain the Vow of Honour Questor Allegiance Oath (pg 65) if every model in their Detachment has the **QUESTOR IMPERIALIS** keyword.

HOUSEHOLD TRADITION: OATHKEEPERS

The Nobles of Hawkshroud uphold the honour of their house above all, and refuse to yield whilst an oath remains unfulfilled.

- Models with this tradition whose characteristics can change as they suffer damage are considered to have double the number of wounds remaining for the purposes of determining what those characteristics are.
- When you are determining which Chivalric abilities are active for **IMPERIAL KNIGHTS** models in your army, provided your army is not Dishonoured (pg 99), models with this tradition count the number of Honour points your army currently has as being 1 higher than it actually is. This may mean that different Chivalric abilities are active for models with this tradition than are active for other **IMPERIAL KNIGHTS** models in your army.

STAUNCH ALLIES 2CP

House Hawkshroud – Epic Deed Stratagem

So ingrained is House Hawkshroud's reputation for loyalty that they won't hesitate to come to an ally's aid, storming in to join the fray.

Use this Stratagem in the Heroic Interventions step of your opponent's Charge phase, before making any other Heroic Interventions (if any). Select one **HOUSE HAWKSHROUD** model from your army and one enemy unit that is within 12" horizontally and 5" vertically of it that made a charge move during this phase. Your model is eligible to perform a Heroic Intervention and when this model makes a Heroic Intervention move this phase, so long as it ends that move within Engagement Range of the enemy unit you selected, it can move up to 6+D6". All other rules for Heroic Interventions still apply. If your model successfully performs a Heroic Intervention, then in the subsequent Fight phase, it can fight first that phase.

WARLORD TRAIT: DUTY OF THE FORSWORN

The champions of Hawkshroud often take to the field having sworn a binding oath to slay a particular foe.

At the start of your first Command phase, select one unit in your opponent's army. Each time this **WARLORD** makes an attack against that unit, add 1 to that attack's hit roll.

RELIC: ANGEL'S GRACE

This gilded halo fits into the data-couplings atop a Throne Mechanicum. It was crafted by the artificers of the Blood Angels Chapter to honour a debt to one of House Hawkshroud's devoted Knights who fought alongside them on Theska II. Unnatural manifestations of empyric power, the malefic conjurations of damned sorcerers, and all other forms of foul witchery are warded away by the Angel's Grace, lending credence to the claim that whoever sits their Throne beneath the ornate device enjoys the personal protection of the Primarch Sanguinius himself.

HOUSE HAWKSHROUD ARMIGER-CLASS or **HOUSE HAWKSHROUD QUESTORIS-CLASS** model only.

- Each time the bearer would lose a wound as the result of a mortal wound, roll one D6: on a 5+, that wound is not lost.
- The bearer has the following ability:

Angel's Grace (Aura): While a friendly **HOUSE HAWKSHROUD ARMIGER-CLASS** model is within 6" of the bearer, each time that **ARMIGER-CLASS** model would lose a wound as the result of a mortal wound, roll one D6: on a 5+, that wound is not lost.

HOUSE MORTAN

House Mortan was not reunited with the Imperium until M35. For as long as twenty millennia, its Knights stood firm against the countless horrors and brutes that dwelled in the forests of its world of Kimdaria alone. It was a mysterious phenomenon known as the Black Pall which isolated Kimdaria from the rest of the galaxy for so long, and House Mortan has ever been grateful for it, believing that in their isolation they were forced to become strong.

'Our ancestors settled a world no other would take. Alone they took a foothold, and alone they held it for millennia. Only with blades and mettle did they succeed. No foe of ours can match either.'

- Lady Sieglinde Mortan

QUESTOR ALLEGIANCE OATH: VOW OF HONOUR

House Mortan models in this Detachment gain the Vow of Honour Questor Allegiance Oath (pg 65) if every model in their Detachment has the **Questor Imperialis** keyword.

HOUSEHOLD TRADITION: CLOSE-QUARTERS KILLERS

The Nobles of House Mortan are hardened and merciless, preferring to finish their foes with fist and blade.

Each time a model with this tradition makes a melee attack, re-roll a hit roll of 1.

SLAYERS OF SHADOWS 1CP

House Mortan – Battle Tactics Stratagem

Used to fighting in the dark, House Mortan Nobles close their eyes and let their ancestors' whispers guide their aim.

Use this Stratagem in your Shooting phase, when a **House Mortan** model from your army is selected to shoot, or in the Fight phase, when a **House Mortan** model from your army is selected to fight. Until the end of the phase, each time that model makes an attack, you can ignore any or all hit roll, Ballistic Skill and Weapon Skill modifiers.

WARLORD TRAIT: LEGACY OF THE BLACK PALL

The gloom of their home world of Kimdaria seems to cling to the Knights of House Mortan.

Each time a ranged attack is made against this **Warlord**, if the attacker is more than 18" away, subtract 1 from that attack's hit roll.

RELIC: HONOUR'S BITE

Honour's Bite was fashioned by a conclave of tech-magi from the forge world of Ionus X. It was created as payment for the heroic sacrifice of High King Garthalomew Mortan, who stood alone in his Knight Paladin Lord of the Hunt *against three enraged Squiggoths during the Dastorvol Evacuation. Garthalomew held off the trio of savage greenskin beasts, slaying the third even as it laid him low. In the process, he protected the entire tech-magi conclave of Dastorvol, allowing them to successfully escape their overrun planet without a single casualty. Garthalomew's descendants have wielded Honour's Bite in his name ever since.*

House Mortan model with reaper chainsword only. This Relic replaces a reaper chainsword and has the following profile:

WEAPON	RANGE	TYPE	S	AP	D
Honour's Bite					
Each time an attack is made with this weapon, select one of the profiles below to make that attack with.					
- Strike	Melee	Melee	+6	-5	6
Abilities: Each time an attack is made with this weapon profile, on an unmodified wound roll of 6, the target suffers 3 mortal wounds in addition to the normal damage.					
- Sweep	Melee	Melee	User	-4	2
Abilities: Each time an attack is made with this weapon profile, make 3 hit rolls instead of 1. Each time an attack is made with this weapon profile, on an unmodified wound roll of 6, the target suffers 1 mortal wound in addition to the normal damage.					

THE NOBLE HOUSEHOLDS

HOUSE RAVEN

House Raven is a household without a home, for its world of Kolossi was taken, ripped from realspace during the Charadon Campaign whilst the bulk of its enormous numbers were fighting off-world. Still a powerful force indeed, the Knights of House Raven march across the stars, purging heretics and traitors wherever they go in their quest to find out what happened to their home world, and slay whomever is responsible for its loss.

'We shall seek not know rest of any kind until Kolossi is avenged. We shall not stop our march across the stars until the ones responsible for its loss are put to the sword or crushed beneath our iron tread. I vow this today, before all of us who remain, and before the Omnissiah.'

- Princeps Grevan Raven

QUESTOR ALLEGIANCE OATH: SACRISTAN PLEDGE

House Raven models in this Detachment gain the Sacristan Pledge Questor Allegiance Oath (pg 65) if every model in their Detachment has the **Questor Mechanicus** keyword.

HOUSEHOLD TRADITION: RELENTLESS ADVANCE

The Knights of House Raven grind inexorably forwards, hammering their enemies with fire all the while.

Each time a model with this tradition makes a Normal Move or Advances in your Movement phase, until the end of your Shooting phase, it can ignore any or all modifiers to its Move characteristic and Advance rolls, and each time it is selected to shoot it counts as having Remained Stationary.

ORDER OF COMPANIONS 1CP

House Raven – Requisition Stratagem

The Order of Companions use little in the way of visible markings to denote their elite status, but instead maintain constant noospheric communication to aid each other in battle. The first warning most enemies receive that such warriors are coordinating their demise is when a volley of fire tears through their ranks.

Use this Stratagem before the battle, when you are mustering your army, if your **Warlord** has the **House Raven** keyword. Select one **House Raven Questoris-class** model from your army. That model gains the following ability:

Order of Companions: Each time this model is selected to shoot or fight, you can re-roll one hit roll, one wound roll or one damage roll when resolving that model's attacks.

You can only use this Stratagem once, unless you are playing a Strike Force battle (in which case, you can use this Stratagem twice) or an Onslaught battle (in which case, you can use this Stratagem three times).

WARLORD TRAIT: MASTER OF THE TRIAL

Those elite Nobles who emerge triumphant from House Raven's Trial of the Companions are forever hardened by the experience.

Each time an attack is allocated to this **Warlord**, if that Attack has an Armour Penetration characteristic of -1 or -2, the Armour Penetration characteristic of that attack is reduced by 1.

RELIC: THE BANNER INVIOLATE

Taken with reverence from the walls of the Keep Inviolate, this magnificent banner inspires all Knights of House Raven to greater glories. The youth of House Raven who fight within sight of the banner feel the eyes of their ancestors upon them, and hear their whispered encouragements from the depths of their Thrones.

House Raven Questoris-class model only. The bearer gains the following ability:

Banner Inviolate (Aura): While a friendly **House Raven Armiger-class** model is within 6" of this model, each time that **Armiger-class** model makes an attack, re-roll a hit roll of 1.

HOUSE TARANIS

The first of the noble houses to be established was that of House Taranis. This truly ancient house predates any other by many hundreds of years, for it was first founded on Mars during the Age of Terra. As the industries of the Red Planet developed into a vast metropolis of technological mastery, so too did it evolve to become the first and foremost of the forge worlds, and the Knights of House Taranis were its guardians.

'It was our ancestors who paved the way for all who followed. Our blood cakes the earliest worlds claimed by Mankind during the Great Crusade. There is no foe of Humanity we have not faced, no foe we have not conquered. We are the blade of the Omnissiah, and are ever sharp.'

- Lady Xentir Taranis

QUESTOR ALLEGIANCE OATH: SACRISTAN PLEDGE

HOUSE TARANIS models in this Detachment gain the Sacristan Pledge Questor Allegiance Oath (pg 65) if every model in their Detachment has the **QUESTOR MECHANICUS** keyword.

HOUSEHOLD TRADITION: OMNISSIAH'S GRACE

No Noble house is higher in the Omnissiah's favour than Taranis. They enjoy his singular blessings.

Each time a model with this tradition loses a wound, unless that wound was lost as the result of a mortal wound, roll one D6: on a 6, that wound is not lost.

OUR DARKEST HOUR — 1CP/2CP

House Taranis – Epic Deed Stratagem

Almost annihilated once before, the same tenacity that saved them then still runs in the Nobles' blood and the veins of their Knights.

Use this Stratagem in any phase, when a **HOUSE TARANIS CHARACTER** model from your army is destroyed, but does not explode. Place a marker on the battlefield in the centre of where the destroyed model's base was. You can choose to roll one D6 at the end of the phase instead of using any rules (other than Explodes, which must be rolled for first) that are triggered when that model is destroyed. If you do, then on a 4+, set that model back up on the battlefield as close as possible to the marker you placed and within 6" of that marker, and not within Engagement Range of any enemy models, with 3 wounds remaining. If it is not possible to set up the model, it is destroyed. This Stratagem can only be used once per battle. If that model is an **ARMIGER-CLASS** model, this Stratagem costs 1CP; otherwise, it costs 2CP.

WARLORD TRAIT: KNIGHT OF MARS

The data-manifolds of House Taranis' lords are thrice-blessed by the priests of the Red Planet.

- Once per battle, after rolling a D6 or a D3 when making an Advance roll, hit roll, wound roll, damage roll, charge roll or saving throw for this **WARLORD**, after any re-rolls (if any) have been made, you can change the result of one of those dice to be a 6 (or, in the case of a D3, a 3).
  Example: *After rolling 2D6 to see what the charge distance is when making a charge roll, you can turn one of the dice into a 6. If you rolled a 4 and a 1, you could change the 1 into a 6 to change its charge distance into 10".*
- While your army is Virtuous (pg 99), this **WARLORD** can use the above rule once per turn, instead of once per battle.

RELIC: FURY OF MARS

The remarkable machine spirit of this weapon channels the fires of the Red Planet's hottest forges, eradicating its victims even at extreme range. It is said that to face the Fury of Mars is to be subjected to the killing ire of the Omnissiah himself, and to be struck down without mercy.

HOUSE TARANIS model only. Select one meltagun, twin meltagun, thermal spear or thermal cannon that model is equipped with.

- That weapon is now a Relic for all rules purposes.
- Add 1 to that weapon's Strength characteristic.
- Delete that weapon's abilities.
- Add 2 to that weapon's Damage characteristic.

We are the First. You need not know anything else about us.

THE NOBLE HOUSEHOLDS

HOUSE KRAST

The Knight world of Chrysis, home to House Krast, was the first of its kind to be rediscovered during the Great Crusade. All of the noble houses of the planet were re-armed and re-supplied by Mars, and the Nobles of House Krast swiftly joined Imperial crusade fleets. In their absence, Chrysis was stormed by the forces of the Arch-enemy, the Warmaster Horus. The planet was devastated, and all the other houses wiped out. Ever since, House Krast has fought the forces of Chaos with extreme prejudice.

'The heretic, the mutant, the traitor, the witch. All are our hated foes. They are worse than a blight upon the realms of Mankind. They are worse than parasites sucking the blood of a larger animal, worse than biting insects or scurrying vermin. They are worse than plague. There is only one thing for them - total annihilation.'

- Lady Taraga Krast

QUESTOR ALLEGIANCE OATH: SACRISTAN PLEDGE

House Krast models in this Detachment gain the Sacristan Pledge Questor Allegiance Oath (pg 65) if every model in their Detachment has the **Questor Mechanicus** keyword.

HOUSEHOLD TRADITION: COLD FURY

The Knights of House Krast are fuelled by their rage, which burns hottest when faced by the most dreaded of foes.

Each time a model with this tradition makes a melee attack, an unmodified hit roll of 6 automatically wounds the target (if the target of that attack is **Titanic**, then an unmodified hit roll of 5+ automatically wounds the target instead).

CONTROLLED AGGRESSION — 1CP

House Krast – Battle Tactics Stratagem

When the Knights of House Krast enter close-quarters combat, they do so certain in the knowledge that their attack speed and aggression protocols are optimal.

Use this Stratagem at the start of the Fight phase. Select up to 2 **House Krast Armiger-class** models from your army, or one other **House Krast** unit from your army. Until the end of the phase:

- Add 1 to the Attacks characteristic of the selected models.
- Each time the selected models make a melee attack, improve the Armour penetration characteristic of that attack by 1.

WARLORD TRAIT: FIRST KNIGHT

As exemplars of the first rediscovered Noble house, the leaders of Krast constantly strive to uphold a long and glorious history.

- Improve this **Warlord's** Weapon Skill characteristic by 1 (to a maximum of 2+).
- At the end of each of your Command phases, if your army is Honoured (pg 99), you can select one Virtuous Chivalric ability from one of your selected Oaths. Until the end of your next Command phase, that Virtuous ability is active for this **Warlord**. This may mean that different Chivalric abilities are active for this **Warlord** than are active for other **Imperial Knights** models in your army.

RELIC: THE HEADSMAN'S MARK

The Nobles of House Krast have a particular hatred for the traitorous Legio Mortis, and hunt down Chaos Titans wherever they get the chance. Those amongst their ranks who have struck the killing blow against such an enemy earn the right to bear the Headsman's Mark. More than just a badge of respect, this amulet feeds the pilot with targeting data that bolsters their giant-slaying skills still further.

House Krast model only.

- Each time an attack made by the bearer is allocated to a **Monster** or **Vehicle** model, the Damage characteristic of that attack is increased by 1.
- Each time the bearer makes an attack against a **Titanic** unit, add 1 to that attack's wound roll.

HOUSE VULKER

The Knights of House Vulker are reclusive and mysterious. They hail from Aurous IV, a mineral-rich world surrounded by asteroid belts and other planets, all similarly possessing vast quantities of natural resources. The forge world of Bellus Prime was established to exploit all of these, and its tech-magi share a close bond with the Knights of House Vulker. When at war, the Knights place a premium on well-coordinated plans, engaging the enemy at optimum distance based on carefully calculating ranges and trajectories.

'The Canticle of the Auric Debt; the Rites of Bellus; the Orders of the Crimson Cog; the Threnody of the Emerald Laurel, the Seventeen - none outside our hallowed ranks shall know what these are or what they mean. Why? Because they are ours, meant for us. They are no business of the outsiders.'

- Forge Mistress Narassa

QUESTOR ALLEGIANCE OATH: SACRISTAN PLEDGE

HOUSE VULKER models in this Detachment gain the Sacristan Pledge Questor Allegiance Oath (pg 65) if every model in their Detachment has the **QUESTOR MECHANICUS** keyword.

HOUSEHOLD TRADITION: FIRESTORM PROTOCOLS

House Vulker fights from afar with coldly methodical logic, targeting and eliminating their enemies with steely efficiency before they can ever reach friendly lines.

Each time a model with this tradition makes a ranged attack, if the target of that attack is the closest enemy unit to this model, re-roll a hit roll of 1.

SATURATION BOMBARDMENT 1CP/2CP

House Vulker – Battle Tactics Stratagem

The saturation bombardments of House Vulker are infamous, their Nobles elevating their guns and letting fly on pre-cogitated trajectories. The enemy are caught in a firestorm as the Omnissiah's wrath rains down upon them.

Use this Stratagem in your Shooting phase, when a **HOUSE VULKER** model from your army is selected to shoot. Until the end of the phase, each time that model makes a ranged attack, on an unmodified hit roll of 6, one additional hit is scored. If that unit is an **ARMIGER-CLASS** model, this Stratagem costs 1CP; otherwise, this Stratagem costs 2CP.

WARLORD TRAIT: ADAMANTINE KNIGHT

The most accomplished of House Vulker's Knights are fitted with a sub-layer of adamantine weave.

Each time an attack is made against this **WARLORD**, an unmodified wound roll of 1-3 for that attack fails, irrespective of any abilities that the weapon or the model making the attack may have.

RELIC: THE AURIC MASK

A massive upscaling of the eerie masks worn by the Nobles of House Vulker, this faceplate radiates terrifying contra-empathetic waves that spread panic and terror throughout the foe's ranks. Few can bear to even hold the gaze of the Knight suit that bears this mask, let alone stand defiant in battle against it.

HOUSE VULKER model only. The bearer has the following ability:

Auric Mask (Aura): While an enemy unit is within 12" of the bearer, subtract 1 from the Leadership characteristic of models in that unit. While an enemy unit is within 6" of the bearer, subtract an additional 1 from the Leadership characteristic of models in that unit (for a total modifier of -2 Leadership) and each time a Combat Attrition test is taken for that unit, subtract 1 from that Combat Attrition test.

THE NOBLE HOUSEHOLDS

MARTIAL TRADITIONS

If your chosen noble household does not have an associated Household Tradition on pages 67-75, you must instead select a Martial Tradition for it from the lists here. In addition, **FREEBLADE** units from your army must also have a Martial Tradition from the lists here. If your army includes **CANIS REX**, he must have the Mythic Hero Martial Tradition. Remember that each **FREEBLADE** unit must have a unique Martial Tradition and so you cannot select a Martial Tradition for a **FREEBLADE** if any other model in your army has the same Martial Tradition.

Unless otherwise stated, **QUESTOR IMPERIALIS** units have one Martial Tradition from the Questor Imperialis Martial Traditions list, and **QUESTOR MECHANICUS** units have one Martial Tradition from the Questor Mechanicus Martial Traditions list. **FREEBLADE** units can have one Martial Tradition from the **FREEBLADE** Martial Traditions list instead of the other lists, if you so choose. You cannot select the Glorified History or Fealty to the Cog Martial Traditions for a **FREEBLADE** unit.

'Each of us has our pride. Each of us has our honour. And rightly so, for we are the pilots of Knights. To become such few have the will. But remember also, we belong to a house, and the Imperium, and the Emperor. These keep us humble in our pride. They are our armour against hubris.'

- Baron Enelcia Cadmus

ON ADAMANT THRONES

Even the smallest noble household has a seat of power, whether it be a fortified tower upon an outlying moon, a slab-sided bastion looming over the house's fiefdom, mountaintop fastness, vacuum-resistant hab-dome or armoured cave-system. The foundations of the largest and oldest of these sit upon the archeotech remains of the Long March ships themselves. Within the throne room or audience chamber of each noble house, its rulers hold court. Ranging from a single Baron and their direct courtiers, to vast assemblages of Nobles, bondsmen, courtiers and more, these gatherings observe the endless rituals of their world, deal with matters of rulership for the common folk, and politick constantly amongst themselves. The figures involved in such intrigues are many and varied, including sages, advisors, Imperial preachers, tech-magi, Sacristans, house militia officers and countless others. While marriage and the continuation of the Noble bloodlines is often regulated by formal arranged pacts, many Knights join themselves romantically and politically to a consort. These individuals may be the daughters or sons of other Noble families, high-placed members of court, or even – in unusual cases – other Knights of a different or lesser rank. What matters more than their origin is their incisive minds, their skill at courtly politics and their dedication to being a societal power behind their Noble's martial throne.

QUESTOR IMPERIALIS MARTIAL TRADITIONS

FRONT-LINE FIGHTERS

The Knights of this household unleash the full power of their fury only when in the very heart of the enemy, honour demanding no less of their Nobles.

Each time a model with this Martial Tradition makes a ranged attack, if the target of that attack is within 18" of this model, add 1 to the Strength characteristic of that attack.

GLORIFIED HISTORY

This household strives to maintain its hard-won prestige, earned through countless centuries of honourable service to the Imperium.

Select one of the following noble households: **HOUSE TERRYN**, **HOUSE GRIFFITH**, **HOUSE CADMUS**, **HOUSE MORTAN** or **HOUSE HAWKSHROUD**.

- Use the Household Tradition of the noble household you selected, as listed on pages 67-75.
- If a **CHARACTER** model with this Martial Tradition gains a Warlord Trait, they can have a Noble Household Warlord Trait associated with the noble household you selected, instead of a Warlord Trait from page 94. If a **CHARACTER** has such a Warlord Trait, replace all instances of the **<NOBLE HOUSEHOLD>** keyword on that Warlord Trait (e.g. **HOUSE TERRYN**), if any, with the name of the noble household that this **CHARACTER** is from.
- You will gain access to the Noble Household Stratagems associated with the noble household you selected. When using such a Stratagem, replace all instances of the **<NOBLE HOUSEHOLD>** keyword on that Stratagem (e.g. **HOUSE TERRYN**) with the **<NOBLE HOUSEHOLD>** keyword that the units with this Martial Tradition have.

HUNTERS OF BEASTS

A millennia-old culture of hunting the great beasts of their home world has accustomed the Knights of this household to the movements of such hulking brutes.

- Each time a model with this Martial Tradition makes an attack against a **MONSTER** or **VEHICLE** unit, add 1 to that attack's hit roll.
- Each time an attack made by a model with this martial Tradition is allocated to a **TITANIC** model, add 1 to that attack's Damage characteristic.
- If you have sworn the Lay Low the Tyrants Oath (pg 119), and one or models with this Martial Tradition destroy a **MONSTER** or **VEHICLE** model during a battle round, then at the end of that battle round, you gain 2 Honour points from that Oath's Pledge, instead of 1.

NOBLE COMBATANTS

Drilled in the honourable art of duelling, every blade thrust, parry and swipe is a breathtaking study in finesse.

Each time a model with this Martial Tradition fights, if all of its attacks target one enemy unit and none of those attacks are made using the Sweep or Strike profiles of a melee weapon, after resolving all of those attacks, it can make a number of additional attacks against that enemy unit equal to the number of attacks that did not reach the Inflict Damage step of the attack sequence during that fight (these additional attacks cannot be made using the 'Sweep or Smash profiles of a melee weapon).

PARAGONS OF HONOUR

This noble household upholds the tenets of the Code Chivalric with zealous passion, exemplifying teachings regardless of the wider tactical situation.

If every unit from your army has the **IMPERIAL KNIGHTS** keyword (excluding units with the **AGENTS OF THE IMPERIUM** or **UNALIGNED** keywords), then after you have sworn 2 Oaths for your army (pg 118), you must, if any models in your army have this Martial Tradition, swear one additional Oath. This Oath applies to all models in your army with this Martial Tradition (i.e. that Oath's Pledge, Troth and Chivalric abilities only apply to models in your army that have this Martial Tradition).

STRIKE AND SHIELD

Mastery of both attack and defence in close quarters is something all Nobles aspire to attain. Those as capable in both will swiftly dispatch their enemies, and live to fight on many battlefields to come.

- Each time a melee attack is made against a model with this Martial Tradition, an unmodified hit roll of 1-3 always fails, irrespective of any abilities that the weapon or the model making the attack may have.
- Each time a melee attack with an Armour Penetration characteristic of -1 is allocated to a model with this Martial Tradition, that attack has an Armour penetration characteristic of 0 instead.

'To sit within the Throne Mechanicum feels like ascending to godhood. Piloting your Knight into battle, it is easy to believe you are invincible. Make no mistake, you are not. Your enemies will try to destroy you with massed firepower from afar. They will surround you, and hope to overrun you with sheer numbers. Your very might makes them desperate, and in their terror they will resort to any means, no matter how underhanded, to lay you low. Be wise. Be vigilant. Fight with your mind, as well as your weapons, and they will never defeat you.'

- Precept Artur Dol Nassatar

BATTLE-FORGED RULES

THE NOBLE HOUSEHOLDS

QUESTOR MECHANICUS MARTIAL TRADITIONS

BLESSED ARMS

This household reverently maintains the masterwork weapons of former ages, their power undimmed.

- Add 6" to the Range characteristic of ranged weapons models with this Martial Tradition are equipped with.
- If a model has this Martial Tradition, the Type of every cognis heavy stubber it is equipped with is changed to Assault 6.
- If a model has this Martial Tradition, the Armour Penetration characteristic of every cognis heavy stubber it is equipped with is improved by 1.

FEALTY TO THE COG

This noble household has such close ties to one of the greater households that over the centuries they have grown more alike, seeking to emulate their examples at every opportunity and in doing so, bring honour to the Omnissiah.

Select one of the following noble households: **HOUSE RAVEN**, **HOUSE KRAST**, **HOUSE TARANIS** or **HOUSE VULKER**.

- Use the Household Tradition of the noble household you selected, as listed on pages 67-75.
- If a **CHARACTER** model with this Martial Tradition gains a Warlord Trait, they can have a Noble Household Warlord Trait associated with the noble household you selected, instead of a Warlord Trait from page 94. If a **CHARACTER** has such a Warlord Trait, replace all instances of the **<NOBLE HOUSEHOLD>** keyword on that Warlord Trait (e.g. **HOUSE RAVEN**), if any, with the name noble household that this **CHARACTER** is from.
- You will gain access to the Noble Household Stratagems associated with the noble household you selected. When using such a Stratagem, replace all instances of the **<NOBLE HOUSEHOLD>** keyword on that Stratagem (e.g. **HOUSE RAVEN**) with the **<NOBLE HOUSEHOLD>** keyword that the units with this Martial Tradition have.

HONOURED SACRISTANS

The Sacristans of this household are amongst the greatest of their calling, maintaining the iron-hard skin of their masters' Knights with esoteric techniques

Each time an attack with a Damage characteristic of 1 is allocated to a model with this Martial Tradition, add 1 to any armour saving throws taken against that attack.

MACHINE FOCUS

The Nobles of this household are minutely attuned to the fabric and soul of their Knight suits, in a seamless fusion of man and machine that refines their sensorium and ensures that when foes go down, they stay down.

Each time a model with this Martial Tradition is selected to Shoot, you can re-roll either one wound roll or one Damage roll.

STEEL-SINEWED AIM

When standing their ground and engaging the enemy at point-blank range, the Knights of this household direct even indiscriminate weapons with a rare calm and preternatural stability.

Each time a ranged attack is made by a model with this Martial Tradition against an enemy unit that is within Engagement Range of their unit, add 1 to that attack's hit roll

UNREMITTING

Never ceasing in their prosecution of fell enemies, this household's Knights each unleash devastating barrages of firepower.

Each time a model with this Martial Tradition is selected to Shoot, for the purposes of determining how many attacks are made by weapons with the Blast ability, double the number of models in the target unit. For example, if a model with this Martial Tradition targets an enemy unit that contains 6 models, then for the purposes of the Blast ability, this is doubled to 12, meaning that weapon makes the maximum number of attacks against that target.

FREEBLADE MARTIAL TRADITIONS

LAST OF THEIR LINE

With no kin left to stand beside but many to avenge, this Freeblade fights outnumbered but never outgunned.

- Each time a model with this Martial Tradition makes an attack that targets a unit containing 11 or more models, you can re-roll the hit roll.
- Each time an **ARMIGER-CLASS** model with this Martial Tradition makes an attack that targets a unit containing 6 or more models, you can re-roll the hit roll.

MYSTERIOUS GUARDIAN

This Freeblade manifests as though from nowhere, an elemental force of vengeance against Mankind's foes.

If a model with this Martial Tradition is placed into Strategic Reserves, it can arrive from Strategic Reserves in the Reinforcements step of any of your Movement phases as if the battle round was one higher than it currently is, regardless of any mission rules.

PEERLESS WARRIOR

Through endless battle and practice, this Freeblade seeks to become the greatest of all.

Once per battle, when you use an Imperial Knights Epic Deed Stratagem, if you select a model with this Martial Tradition to use that Stratagem, it costs 0 Command points.

MYTHIC HERO

Tales of this Freeblade's exploits and their deeds of honour have spread far and wide, and they are not exaggerations. This Knight is a mythic figure that embodies the Code Chivalric.

When you are determining which Chivalric abilities are active for **IMPERIAL KNIGHTS** models in your army, models with this Martial Tradition count the number of Honour Points your army currently has as being 2 higher than it actually is. This may mean that different Chivalric abilities are active for models with this tradition than are active for other **IMPERIAL KNIGHTS** models in your army.

'We march out now, an army of adamantine giants stepping from the shadows, a hunting party of apex predators. What possible answer can our enemies have in the face of such fearsome strength?'

- Sir Percivus of House Mortan

STRATAGEMS

If your army includes any **IMPERIAL KNIGHTS** Detachments, you have access to these Stratagems, and can spend CPs to use them. When one of these Stratagems instructs you to select a unit from your army, replace all instances of **<NOBLE HOUSEHOLD>** on that Stratagem (if any) with the name of the noble household that your selected unit is drawn from (if the selected unit is a **FREEBLADE**, replace all instances of **<NOBLE HOUSEHOLD>** on that Stratagem (if any) with **FREEBLADE** instead).

CALCULATED TARGETING 2-4CP

Imperial Knights – Battle Tactics Stratagem

With an icy and calculating menace, this knightly lord establishes the end of the Omnissiah's foes in violent displays of unremitting firepower.

Use this Stratagem in your Shooting phase, when a **QUESTOR MECHANICUS** model from your army is selected to shoot. Until the end of the phase, each time that model makes a ranged attack, on an unmodified wound roll of 6, that attack inflicts a number of mortal wounds on the target equal to the Damage characteristic of that attack, and the attack sequence ends. If that model is an **ARMIGER-CLASS** model, this Stratagem costs 2CP; if that model is a **QUESTORIS-CLASS** model, this Stratagem costs 3CP; otherwise, it costs 4CP.

FULL TILT 1CP

Imperial Knights – Battle Tactic Stratagem

With the enemy before them, their Knight's machine spirit snarling, and the rush of battle coursing through their veins, the Noble pilot pours power into their motive actuators and thunder forwards.

Use this Stratagem in your Movement phase, when an **IMPERIAL KNIGHTS VEHICLE** model from your army Advances. Do not make an Advance roll. Instead, until the end of the phase, add 6" to the Move characteristic of this model (if this model is an **ARMIGER-CLASS** model, add 9" instead).

THUNDERSTOMP 1CP

Imperial Knights – Battle Tactic Stratagem

The Knight brings its foot crashing down with the force of an industrial piledriver. Few can survive such a blow.

Use this Stratagem in the Fight phase when an **IMPERIAL KNIGHTS TITANIC** model from your army is selected to fight. Until the end of the phase, each time that model makes a melee attack with its titanic feet:

- Subtract 1 from that attack's hit roll.
- If that attack successfully hits the target, unless the target of that attack is a **VEHICLE**, **MONSTER** or a **CHARACTER** unit, the target suffers 2 mortal wounds and the attack sequence ends.

IMPETUOUS GLORY 1CP

Imperial Knights – Battle Tactic Stratagem

Some aspiring youths are so keen to prove their worth that they recklessly plunge into the fray, putting their every ounce of skill and valour into the fight at hand in the name of honour.

Use this Stratagem when an **ARMIGER-CLASS** model from your army is selected to fight in the Fight phase. Until the end of the phase, each time that model makes a melee attack, on an unmodified hit roll of 6, one additional hit is scored.

LINEBREAKER 1CP

Imperial Knights – Battle Tactic Stratagem

Aggressively pushing through the swirl of melee with piles of dead in its wake, nothing can stop the Knight's bloody advance.

Use the Stratagem in your Fight phase, when a **QUESTOR IMPERIALIS VEHICLE** model from your army makes a consolidation move. Until the end of the phase, when making that consolidation move, that model:

- Can move up to 6" instead of up to 3" (this is cumulative with the Vow of Honour Questor Allegiance Oath (pg 65), meaning that such a model would move up to 7" when it consolidates this phase).
- Can move in any direction, provided it ends that consolidation move either within Engagement Range of an enemy model, or it ends that move at least 3" closer to your opponent's battlefield edge.

MARTIAL PROWESS 1CP/2CP

Imperial Knights – Battle Tactics Stratagem

The households place great emphasis on a Knight's skill in combat, and they spend countless hours learning how to angle their Knight's armour to deflect all but the most powerful blows.

Use this Stratagem in the fight phase when an **IMPERIAL KNIGHTS VEHICLE** unit from your army is selected as the target of an attack. Until the end of the phase, each time an attack is allocated to that model, add 1 to any armour saving throw taken against that attack. If that model is an **ARMIGER-CLASS** model, this Stratagem costs 1CP; otherwise, it costs 2CP.

PACK TACTICS 1CP

Imperial Knights – Battle Tactic Stratagem

Hunting in teams, the Nobles who pilot Armigers attack as one, rending apart and smashing aside their prey.

Use this Stratagem at the start of the Fight phase. Select one enemy unit that is within Engagement Range of 2 or more **ARMIGER-CLASS** models from your army. Until the end of the phase, add 1 to the Attacks characteristic of each **ARMIGER-CLASS** model from your army that started the phase in Engagement Range with that enemy unit.

PAINS OF OLD NIGHT 1CP

Imperial Knights – Battle Tactics Stratagem

Deep were the wounds suffered by this household when they fought the terrors of Old Night, and the fires lit in that time continue to burn within their hearts.

Use this Stratagem in the Fight phase, when an **IMPERIAL KNIGHTS** model from your army is selected to fight. Until the end of the phase, each time that model makes an attack against a **CHAOS** model, re-roll a wound roll of 1.

SKYFIRE PROTOCOLS 1CP

Imperial Knights – Battle Tactics Stratagem

The Armiger's pilot intones prayers to the machine spirits of their weapons, beseeching them to guide their aim against fast-moving airborne targets.

Use this Stratagem in your Shooting phase when an **ARMIGER-CLASS** model from your army is selected to shoot. Until the end of the phase, each time that model makes an attack against an **AIRCRAFT** unit, add 1 to that attack's hit roll.

THIN THEIR RANKS 1CP

Imperial Knights – Battle Tactic Stratagem

Not even the largest hordes or mightiest foes can long survive the fusillade of bondsworn young Nobles.

Use this Stratagem at the start of the Shooting phase. Select up to 3 **ARMIGER-CLASS** models from your army. Until the end of the phase, each time a selected model makes a ranged attack, an unmodified hit roll of 6 automatically wounds the target.

TROPHY CLAIM 1CP

Imperial Knights – Epic Deed Stratagem

The worthiest of foes is the mightiest! Only against such enemies can you test your true mettle, and once such a foe is laid low the Knight's emitters blare its triumph, announcing the glory and the honour brought to its House.

Use this Stratagem in the Fight phase when an **IMPERIAL KNIGHTS** model from your army destroys an enemy **TITANIC** unit with a melee attack.

- Until the end of the battle, add 1 to this model's Attacks characteristic.
- If every unit from your army has the **IMPERIAL KNIGHTS** keyword (excluding units with the **AGENTS OF THE IMPERIUM** or **UNALIGNED** keywords), you gain 1 Honour point (pg 118).
- Until the end of the battle, when you are determining which Chivalric abilities (pg 118-119) are active for **IMPERIAL KNIGHTS** models in your army, this model always counts as if your army was Virtuous (pg 99). This may mean that different Chivalric abilities are active for different models in your army.

BENEVOLENCE OF THE MACHINE GOD 1CP

Imperial Knights – Epic Deed Stratagem

As the forces of the enemy rain destruction down upon the Knight, its Noble pilot offers up a binharic prayer to the Omnissiah for protection.

Use this Stratagem in any phase, when a **QUESTOR MECHANICUS** model from your army would lose a wound as the result of a mortal wound. Until the end of the phase, each time that model would lose a wound as the result of a mortal wound, roll one D6: on a 5+, that wound is not lost.

CRUSHED 1CP

Imperial Knights – Epic Deed Stratagem

The servo-articulated digits of the Knight's fist close around the victim with piston pressure and begin to squeeze…

Use this Stratagem in the Fight phase when an attack made with Freedom's Hand or a thunderstrike gauntlet (or a Relic that replaces such a weapon) by an **IMPERIAL KNIGHTS** model from your army is allocated to an enemy model. Before any saving throw is taken against that attack, both players roll off (if the Strength characteristic of this **IMPERIAL KNIGHTS** is greater than that of the model the attack has been allocated to, add 1 to your result). If you win the roll off, invulnerable saving throws cannot be taken against that attack; otherwise the Damage characteristic of that attack is 0.

MACHINE SPIRIT RESURGENT 1CP/2CP

Imperial Knights – Epic Deed Stratagem

Through the broadcasting of auto-sequenced data-hymnals, the pilot reinvigorates their Knight's machine spirit, stoking its predatory ire and directing it at the foe.

Use this Stratagem in your Command phase. Select one **QUESTOR MECHANICUS** model from your army. Until the start of your next Command phase, that model is considered to have its full wounds remaining for the purposes of determining what characteristics on its profile to use. If that model is an **ARMIGER-CLASS** model, this Stratagem costs 1CP; otherwise, it costs 2CP.

VALIANT LAST STAND 1CP/2CP

Imperial Knights – Epic Deed Stratagem

Badly wounded, their Knight's generator on the verge of overload, still the Noble fights on, drawing upon their reserves of chivalric heroism to sell their life as dearly as they can.

Use this Stratagem in the Fight phase, when a **QUESTOR IMPERIALIS** model from your army that has not already been selected to fight this phase is destroyed (but did not explode). Do not remove that model from play – it can fight after the attacking model's unit has finished making attacks. When resolving these attacks, assume the model has 1 wound remaining when determining which characteristics to use. After resolving the destroyed model's attacks, it is then removed. If that model is an **ARMIGER-CLASS** model, this Stratagem costs 1CP; otherwise, it costs 2CP.

NOBLE SACRIFICE 1-3CP

Imperial Knights – Epic Deed Stratagem

Sensing their end drawing close, the pilot overloads their Knight's plasma core to take the enemy with them.

Use this Stratagem when an **IMPERIAL KNIGHTS VEHICLE** model from your army is destroyed. Do not roll to see if that model explodes: it does so automatically (if that model is a **DOMINUS-CLASS** model, roll one D6: on a 4+, the range of the explosion is 3D6"). If that model is an **ARMIGER-CLASS** model, this Stratagem costs 1CP; if that model is a **QUESTORIS-CLASS** model, this Stratagem costs 2CP; otherwise, it costs 3CP. You can only use this Stratagem once.

RECOUNT THE VIRTUES 1CP

Imperial Knights – Epic Deed Stratagem

A mentor's role is not only to teach the aspiring youth in the practice fields, but also to remind them of their duties in the heart of battle itself.

Use this Stratagem at the start of any of your phases other than your Command phase. Select one **MENTOR** unit from your army that has not recounted a teaching this turn. That model can recount one teaching that has not already been recounted by a friendly model this turn. That teaching is automatically inspiring (do not roll) and takes effect until the start of your next Command phase.

SURVIVORS OF STRIFE 1CP

Imperial Knights – Epic Deed Stratagem

The home world of this household fared better than some during the Age of Strife, thus its Knight suits remain girded with ancient protective technologies long thought lost.

Use this Stratagem in any phase, when an **ARMIGER-CLASS** model from your army is selected as the target of an attack. Until the end of the phase, each time an attack is made against that model, an unmodified wound roll of 1-3 for that attack fails, irrespective of any abilities that the weapon or the model making the attack may have.

HEIRLOOMS OF THE HOUSEHOLD 1CP

Imperial Knights – Requisition Stratagem

The catacombs beneath many knightly strongholds delve deep, and are replete with ancient technological wonders.

Use this Stratagem before the battle, when you are mustering your army, if your **WARLORD** has the **IMPERIAL KNIGHTS** keyword. Select one **IMPERIAL KNIGHTS** model from your army. That model can have one Heirloom Relic, even if they are not a **CHARACTER** model (this must be a Relic they could have). Each Relic in your army must be unique, and you cannot use this Stratagem to give a model two Relics. You can only use this Stratagem once, unless you are playing a Strike Force battle (in which case, you can use this Stratagem twice) or an Onslaught battle (in which case, you can use this Stratagem three times).

Read the Code Chivalric. Heed its lessons. Absorb its wisdom. No matter how difficult its demands may be – it will bring you victory.

KNIGHT BARON 1CP

Imperial Knights – Requisition Stratagem

It is a truly glorious day for the Imperium when the Barons of the noble households take to the battlefield, for these storied heroes bring wisdom and strength in equal measure

Use this Stratagem before the battle, when you are mustering your army, if your **WARLORD** has the **IMPERIAL KNIGHTS** keyword. Select one **IMPERIAL KNIGHTS** model from your army (excluding named characters). That model gains the **CHARACTER** keyword and you must determine one Warlord Trait for it (this must be a Warlord Trait it can have); that model is only regarded as your **WARLORD** for the purposes of that Warlord Trait. Each Warlord Trait in your army must be unique (if randomly generated, re-roll duplicate results), and you cannot use this Stratagem to give a model two Warlord Traits. You can only use this Stratagem once, unless you are playing a Strike Force battle (in which case, you can use this Stratagem twice) or an Onslaught battle (in which case, you can use this Stratagem three times).

REVERED PARAGON 1CP

Imperial Knights – Requisition Stratagem

Either through countless martial triumphs or by one truly heroic act, this Knight champion has distinguished themselves above and beyond their peers and is a true paragon of their house.

Use this Stratagem after nominating an **IMPERIAL KNIGHTS CHARACTER** model to be your **WARLORD**. You can generate one additional Warlord Trait for them. Each Warlord Trait in your army must be unique (if randomly generated, re-roll duplicate results). You can only use this Stratagem once and you cannot use this Stratagem if your **WARLORD** is a named character.

EXACTING CHARGE 1CP/2CP

Imperial Knights – Strategic Ploy Stratagem

During every thunderous step of their charge, the Nobles of this household are utterly focused. When their strike hits home, it is with piercing precision.

Use this Stratagem in your Charge phase, when an **IMPERIAL KNIGHTS VEHICLE** model from your army finishes a charge move. Select one enemy unit within Engagement Range of your model and roll four D6s (if this model is **TITANIC**, roll six D6s instead). For each dice result that equals or exceeds that enemy unit's Toughness characteristic, it suffers 1 mortal wound; for each unmodified roll of a 6, that enemy unit instead suffers 2 mortal wounds. If this model is an **ARMIGER-CLASS** model, this Stratagem costs 1CP; otherwise, it costs 2CP.

A SQUIRE'S DUTY 2CP

Imperial Knights – Strategic Ploy Stratagem

Under the scrutiny and judgment of their Noble betters, an Armiger pilot will redouble their efforts and plunge into the fray once more.

Use this Stratagem in your Movement phase when an **ARMIGER-CLASS** model from your army Falls Back. That model is still eligible to shoot and charge this turn even though it Fell Back.

FLANKING MANOEUVRES 1CP

Imperial Knights – Strategic Ploy Stratagem

Eager to earn glory, Knight Armigers focus on swiftly redeploying mid-battle to flank the foe.

Use this Stratagem at the start of your Movement phase. Select up to two **ARMIGER-CLASS** models from your army that are more than 6" from any enemy models and within 6" of any battlefield edge. If the mission you are playing is using the Strategic Reserves rule, place that unit into Strategic Reserves – that model cannot arrive from Strategic Reserves in the same turn it is placed into Strategic Reserves.

STORMSTRIDERS 1CP

Imperial Knights – Strategic Ploy Stratagem

Nothing can halt the ever moving Knights of this household, their path punctuated with wrathful strikes.

Use this Stratagem in your Movement phase, when you select one **QUESTOR IMPERIALIS TITANIC** model from your army to make a Normal Move or Advance. After this model has moved, select one enemy unit it moved across (excluding **AIRCRAFT** units) and roll one D6. Add 1 to the result if that enemy unit contains between 6-10 models, and add 2 to the result if that enemy unit contains 11 or more models: on a 3-6, that enemy unit suffers D3 mortal wounds; on a 7+, that unit suffers D6 mortal wounds.

DEFIANT FURY 2CP

Imperial Knights – Strategic Ploy Stratagem

Incensed by those who dare harm their Noble lords, the squires of this house let their righteous wrath invigorate them.

Use this Stratagem in any phase, when an **IMPERIAL KNIGHTS <NOBLE HOUSEHOLD> CHARACTER** unit from your army is destroyed by an enemy unit. Select one friendly **<NOBLE HOUSEHOLD> ARMIGER-CLASS** model from your army.

- At the end of the phase, that **ARMIGER-CLASS** model can shoot as if it were your Shooting phase, but it can only target that enemy unit (and only if that enemy unit is an eligible target for that attack).
- Until the end of the battle, each time that **ARMIGER-CLASS** model makes an attack that targets that enemy unit, you can re-roll the hit roll.

POINT BLANK BARRAGE 1CP

Imperial Knights – Strategic Ploy Stratagem

Imperial Knights know too well that, despite the dangers, a point blank barrage can mean the difference between victory and defeat.

Use this Stratagem in your Shooting phase, when an **IMPERIAL KNIGHTS** model from your army is selected to shoot. Until the end of the phase:

- That model can make attacks with Blast weapons against units within Engagement Range of it.
- Each time this model makes an attack with a Blast weapon against a unit within Engagement Range of it, on an unmodified hit roll of 1, this model suffers 1 mortal wound after all of its attacks have been resolved.

CHAINSWEEP 1CP

Imperial Knights – Wargear Stratagem

With a snarl, the Noble swings their Knight's chainsword in a howling arc that rips through the enemy ranks and sends sundered foes tumbling through the blood-misted air.

Use this Stratagem in the Fight phase when an **IMPERIAL KNIGHTS** model from your army that is equipped with a reaper chainsword or reaper chain-cleaver (or a Relic that replaces such a weapon) is selected to fight. Until the end of the phase, each time that model makes an attack, you can never re-roll that attack's hit roll, but if that attack is made using the Sweep profile of a reaper chainsword or reaper chain-cleaver (or a Relic that replaces such a weapon), make 1 additional hit roll.

ROTATE ION SHIELDS 1CP/2CP

Imperial Knights – Wargear Stratagem

Veteran Knight pilots can swiftly angle their ion shields to better defect incoming fire.

Use this Stratagem in your opponent's Shooting phase, when an **IMPERIAL KNIGHTS VEHICLE** model from your army is selected as the target of a ranged attack. Until the end of the phase, that model has a 4+ invulnerable save against ranged attacks. If that model is an **ARMIGER-CLASS** model, this Stratagem costs 1CP; otherwise, it costs 2CP.

ION AEGIS 2CP

Imperial Knights – Wargear Stratagem

Redirecting power from its secondary plasma core, the Dominus-class Knight projects its ion shield over squires.

Use this Stratagem in your opponent's Command phase. Select one **DOMINUS-CLASS** model from your army. Until the end of the turn, that model has the following ability:

Ion Aegis (Aura): While a friendly **<NOBLE HOUSEHOLD> ARMIGER-CLASS** model is within 6" of this model, that **ARMIGER-CLASS** model has a 4+ invulnerable save against ranged weapons.

HURLED WRECKAGE 1CP

Imperial Knights – Wargear Stratagem

Spying another brutish silhouette, the Noble unerringly hurls the remains of their Knight's victim towards it.

Use this Stratagem at the end of the Fight phase. Select one **IMPERIAL KNIGHTS** model from your army equipped with Freedom's Hand or a thunderstrike gauntlet (or a Relic that replaces such a weapon). If a **VEHICLE** or **MONSTER** model was destroyed within Engagement Range of the selected **IMPERIAL KNIGHTS** model during that phase, you can now select one enemy unit within 9" of and visible to that **IMPERIAL KNIGHTS** model that is not within engagement range of any friendly units. Roll one D6, subtracting 1 from the result if the enemy unit you selected is a **CHARACTER** with a Wounds characteristic of 9 or less: on a 3-5, that enemy unit suffers D3 mortal wounds; on a 6, that enemy unit suffers 3 mortal wounds.

EXALTED COURT

If your army is Battle-forged and includes any **IMPERIAL KNIGHTS** Detachments, then when you muster your army, with the exception of **FREEBLADES**, you can upgrade any **QUESTORIS-CLASS CHARACTER** or **DOMINUS-CLASS CHARACTER** model in your army to be a member of the Exalted Court. Note that the Knight Lances Detachment ability (pg 64) can grant **IMPERIAL KNIGHTS** models the **CHARACTER** keyword, as can the Knight Baron Stratagem (pg 82).

Each time you upgrade a model, its Power Rating is increased by the amount shown for that upgrade, as shown in the table to the right. If you are playing a matched play game, or a game that uses a points limit, then the points value of that model is also increased by the amount shown in the same table. Make a note on your army roster each time you upgrade a model using these rules. These models are still considered to be the same datasheet for the purposes of any mission rules that limit the number of times any particular datasheet can be included in your army.

Each time you upgrade a model to become a member of the Exalted Court, it gains the **EXALTED COURT** keyword, the Exalted Court ability (see below) and other additional abilities, as shown in the appropriate section over the following pages. Each upgrade also includes a Noble Exemplar ability and a Crusade Duty (see below). An upgraded model can only use its Noble Exemplar ability while your army is Honoured or Virtuous (pg 99). If your army is Dishonoured, or if the upgraded model has no Bondsman abilities (pg 117), its Noble Exemplar ability cannot be used.

Exalted Court: If the bearer has a Bondsman ability (pg 117), it can use that Bondsman ability one additional time in each of your Command phases.

An army (or a Crusade force) cannot include the same upgrade more than once (i.e. you can only have one Monarchsward, one Herald etc.). A Crusade force cannot start with any upgraded **CHARACTER** models – to include one in a Crusade force, you must use the Exalted Court Requisition (pg 108).

An upgraded model also gains a Crusade Duty. This is a new type of Battle Honour that only applies when such a model is part of your Crusade force. Having a Crusade Duty does not count towards the maximum number of Battle Honours a model can have, and it does not increase the models' Crusade points total.

EXALTED COURT

MODEL	POWER	POINTS
High Monarch	+2	+45
Master of Justice	+2	+30
Monarchsward	+2	+35
Herald	+1	+20
Gatekeeper	+2	+35
Princeps	+2	+35
Master Tactician	+2	+30
Master of Lore	+2	+35
Master of Vox	+1	+20
Forge Master	+2	+30

MASTER OF JUSTICE

The Master of Justice is the executor of the High Monarch's military might, and their superior skill on the battlefield is unquestionable. In addition to their role as chief military advisor, they are typically styled the Executioner of the Household, an unmerciful station that punishes wrongdoing both in the courtrooms and on the battlefield, and ensures that the household's entire efforts remain focused on winning the war.

- **QUESTOR IMPERIALIS CHARACTER** only.
- When you select this upgrade, select one Questor Imperialis Martial Tradition (pg 77) that no model in your army has (you cannot select Glorified History) – this model gains that Martial Tradition in addition to any others it has.
- **Noble Exemplar ability:** Once per battle, when you use an Imperial Knights Strategic Ploy Stratagem, if the model you select to use that Strategic Ploy is under the effects of this model's Bondsman ability, then that Stratagem costs 0 Command points.
- **Crusade Duty:** If this model is in your Crusade force, at the end of the battle, if you won, roll one D6: on a 4+, you gain 1 additional Requisition point.

HIGH MONARCH

The High Monarch is the Noble who exemplifies the honour of their house and uphold the Code Chivalric. They're in charge, they're expert warriors, and they inspire great loyalty in their aspiring Nobles.

- **QUESTOR IMPERIALIS CHARACTER** only.
- If this model is included in your army, it must be your **WARLORD**. If more than one model in your army has a rule to this effect, then one of those models must be your army's **WARLORD**.
- Each time your army gains an Honour point, roll one D6: on a 5+, you gain 1 additional Honour point.
- **Noble Exemplar ability:** Each time this model uses its Bondsman ability, it also applies to every friendly **<NOBLE HOUSEHOLD> ARMIGER-CLASS** model within 6" of this model.
- **Crusade Duty:** While this model is in your Crusade Force, each time you use the Exalted Court Requisition, it costs 1 fewer Requisition points to use.

MONARCHSWARD

To be Monarchsward is a great honour and burden, given not just to a superlative warrior, but to one whose loyalty is more firm than adamantine. In battle, the Monarchsward matches their charge stride for stride, always angling their Knights, and their ion shields, to best protect their charge. And, as they protect their liege, so too does a Monarchsward's bondsmen act to protect them. At battle's end, it is their duty to stand sentinel over those comrades who fell in battle, protecting their wounded forms while a rescue and recovery can be mounted.

- **QUESTOR IMPERIALIS CHARACTER** only.
- While another friendly **<NOBLE HOUSEHOLD> CHARACTER** model is within 3" of this unit, enemy models cannot target that **CHARACTER** model with ranged attacks unless it is the closest eligible target to the attacking model.
- **Noble Exemplar ability:** While an **ARMIGER-CLASS** model is under the effects of this model's Bondsman ability, at the start of the Fight phase, if that **ARMIGER-CLASS** model is within Engagement Range of any enemy units, it can fight first that phase.
- **Crusade Duty:** If this model is part of your Crusade force, and if it was not destroyed during the battle, then at the end of the battle you can ignore one failed Out of Action test taken for one **<NOBLE HOUSEHOLD>** model from your Crusade force – that test is treated as having been passed instead.

GATEKEEPER

The Gatekeeper is tasked with the solemn duty of protection. To them falls the sacred honour of defending the strongholds of the household, a tradition that stretches back to the Long Night.

- **QUESTOR IMPERIALIS CHARACTER** only.
- While this model is wholly within your deployment zone, each time an attack is made against this model, an unmodified wound roll of 1-3 for that attack fails, irrespective of any abilities that the weapon or the model making the attack may have.
- **Noble Exemplar ability:** While an **ARMIGER-CLASS** model is under the effects of this model's Bondsman ability, while that **ARMIGER-CLASS** model is in range of an objective marker, add 1 to that model's Toughness characteristic.
- **Crusade Duty:** If this unit is part of your Crusade force and you are the Defender, then you start the battle with 1 additional Command point.

HERALD

A Herald's duties are plentiful, but mercifully streamlined upon the battlefield. The Herald ensures the fanfare – trumpet-blasts blared through his vox-grilles – as befits each Knight who enters the battlefield. It is the Herald's role to issue first warning of enemy attacks, and the ion shields of the entire household pivot upon his alerts. Finally, from a central position, they also relay vox orders and lays down supporting firepower.

- **QUESTOR IMPERIALIS CHARACTER** only.
- Each time a friendly **<NOBLE HOUSEHOLD>** model uses a Bondsman ability, if they are within 9" of this Herald, they can select one **<NOBLE HOUSEHOLD> ARMIGER-CLASS** model that is within 9" of this Herald for that Bondsman ability to apply to.
- **Noble Exemplar ability:** While an **ARMIGER-CLASS** model is under the effects of this model's Bondsman ability, that **ARMIGER-CLASS** model has a 4+ invulnerable save.
- **Crusade Duty:** While this model is in your Crusade Force, each time you use the Specialist Reinforcement or the Warlord Trait Requisition, it costs 1 fewer Requisition points to use.

PRINCEPS

The Princeps is in charge of the entire household, juggling the needs of both logic and honour. Even the most stubborn and prideful Knight will submit to the will of the Princeps.

- **QUESTOR MECHANICUS CHARACTER** model only.
- If this model is included in your army, it must be your **WARLORD**. If more than one model in your army has a rule to this effect, then one of those models must be your army's **WARLORD**.
- Each time your army would lose an Honour point, roll one D6: on a 5+, that Honour point is not lost.
- **Noble Exemplar ability:** Once per Command phase, when this model uses its Bondsman ability, it can select a **<NOBLE HOUSEHOLD> QUESTORIS-CLASS** model (excluding itself) for that ability to apply to instead of an **ARMIGER-CLASS** model.
- **Crusade Duty:** While this model is in your Crusade force, each time you use the Exalted Court Requisition, it costs 1 fewer Requisition points to use.

FORGE MASTER

To the Forge Master falls the defence of the household's home. Amongst their duties are the protection of the keep's heirlooms and the entire armies of Sacristans. They command utmost authority in mustering the household to protect their strongholds. Their Knights are expected to endure some of the worst punishment, and is accordingly the one most ministered to by the Sacristans.

- **QUESTOR MECHANICUS CHARACTER** model only.
- While this model is wholly within your deployment zone, each time a wound is allocated to it, reduce the Damage characteristic of that attack by 1 (to a minimum of 1). This is not cumulative with any other rules that reduce the Damage characteristic of an attack.
- **Noble Exemplar ability:** While an **ARMIGER-CLASS** model is under the effects of this model's Bondsman ability, each time that **ARMIGER-CLASS** model makes an attack against a unit that is within your deployment zone, add 1 to that attack's hit roll and add 1 to that attack's wound roll.
- **Crusade Duty:** While this model is in your Crusade force, each time you use the Relic or the Repair and Recuperate Requisition, it costs 1 fewer Requisition points to use.

Listen always to your betters! Many years have they fought and bled! By their leadership have countless battles been won.

MASTER TACTICIAN

Master Tacticians are one of the very best fighters of their household. They can be trusted to cogitate numerous potential battlefield strategies at once, lead armies of Knights in the Princeps' absence and provide sage wisdom on any course of action decided by a superior.

- **QUESTOR MECHANICUS CHARACTER** model only.
- When you select this upgrade, select one Questor Mechanicus Martial Tradition (pg 78) that no model in your army has (you cannot select Fealty to the Cog) - this model gains that Martial Tradition in addition to any others it has.
- **Noble Exemplar ability:** Once per battle, when you use an Imperial Knights Battle Tactic Stratagem, if the model you select to use that Battle Tactic Stratagem is under the effects of a Bondsman ability, then that Stratagem costs 0 Command points.
- **Crusade Duty:** If this unit is part of your Crusade force and you are the Attacker, then you start the battle with 1 additional Command point.

MASTER OF LORE

The Master of Lore, the keeper of sacred data, the Cogitator Prime. They are the lord of their household's traditions, the guardian of its valued principles as well as the adjudicator and judge whenever transgressions against the house or the Code Chivalric occur.

- **QUESTOR MECHANICUS CHARACTER** model only.
- If this model is a **KNIGHT PRECEPTOR**, in your Command phase, it can recount one additional teaching it knows that has not already been recounted by a friendly model that turn.
- If this model is not a **KNIGHT PRECEPTOR**, it gains the **MENTOR** keyword and it knows one teaching from the Knightly Teachings (pg 95) and, in your Command phase, if this model is on the battlefield, it can recount one teaching it knows that has not already been recounted by a friendly model this turn. Roll one D6: on a 3+, the recounted teaching is inspiring and takes effect until the start of your next Command phase.
- **Noble Exemplar ability:** Each time this model uses its Bondsman ability on a model that is already under the effects of a Bondsman ability, the new ability applies to it in addition to the existing one, instead of replacing it.
- **Crusade Duty:** While this model is in your Crusade Force, each time you use the Arts of War Duty Requisition, it costs 0 Requisition points to use.

MASTER OF VOX

The Master of Vox, sometimes known as a Broadhailer, bears the internal comms equipment that can network together all the fighting detachments of the household's Knights as well as broadcast vox hails to distant allies.

- **QUESTOR MECHANICUS CHARACTER** model only.
- While this model is on the battlefield, each time you spend a Command point to use a Stratagem you can roll one D6: on a 5+, that Command point is refunded.
- **Noble Exemplar ability:** Each time this model uses its Bondsman ability, it can select any **<NOBLE HOUSEHOLD> ARMIGER-CLASS** model on the battlefield for that ability.
- **Crusade Duty:** If this unit is part of your Crusade force and you are using the Strategic Reserves rule, you can halve the Command point cost required to place units into Strategic Reserves (rounding fractions down). You can find out more about the Strategic Reserves rule in the Warhammer 40,000 Core Book.

FREEBLADE LANCE

Freeblades are exiles – Nobles either cast out from their houses and undertaking some self-imposed quest of penance, or striding to war as the last avenging scions of their sundered lines. They live solitary and often tragic lives, bearing terrible burdens even as they fight on in the Emperor's name. Yet they need not always fight alone. For every Freeblade who becomes an almost supernatural figure that comes and goes from Imperial battle lines without a word, there are others not so lost. Such wandering Nobles seek comradeship with other exiles like themselves, and sometimes form entire lances.

Fighting with a Freeblade Lance has many advantages. It simulates the structure of a noble household – often the hardest thing for long-indoctrinated and hidebound Nobles to lose. It also allows its members to form a sort of martial alloy, each covering for one another's quirks or aiding with their struggles even as they fight side by side as a force that is greater than the sum of its parts.

Some Freeblade Lances – such as the Forgotten Company, the Voidstriders and the Unfettered – have fought together so long and so successfully that they have gained notoriety to equal a noble house in their own right. New exiles travel far to soldier beneath the banner of such a famed company, for in joining their ranks there is the chance to earn again the redemption and glory that all such Freeblades crave.

A Freeblade Lance is an Army of Renown.

RESTRICTIONS

- All units in your army must be **FREEBLADES**.

BENEFITS

- All units in your army gain the **FREEBLADE LANCE** keyword.
- You have access to the Freeblade Lance Warlord Trait, Relic and Stratagems.
- **FREEBLADE LANCE** models in your army gain the Indomitable Heroes Martial Tradition (see below), in addition to any others they have (note that this is an exception to the rule that says that every Martial Tradition a **FREEBLADE** model has must be unique).
- **FREEBLADE LANCE CHARACTER** models in your army gain the Legendary Knight ability (see opposite).

INDOMITABLE HEROES

The warriors of a Freeblade lance are remarkable for their sheer resilience and bloody-minded determination.

- At the start of each of your Command phases, a model with this Martial Tradition regains 1 lost wound.
- Each time an Advance or charge roll is made for a model with this Martial Tradition, you can ignore any or all modifiers to that Advance or charge roll.

ARMY OF RENOWN

An Army of Renown is a specialised force that has earned fame or infamy across the 41st Millennium, the experience of which has given its warriors unique skills to use on the battlefield.

An Army of Renown is a variant army list for a particular Faction in Warhammer 40,000 that is themed around a particular disposition of forces. Each imposes certain restrictions on what units can be included, but it also grants access to a wider range of rules such as Stratagems, Relics etc. to reflect that Army of Renown's unique methods of waging war in the 41st Millennium.

If you wish for your army to become an Army of Renown, it must first adhere to all the restrictions laid out for that Army of Renown, it must be Battle-forged and it must not include any Specialist Detachments. You can then make a note in the Army Faction section of your Army Roster of which Army of Renown your army is. Some, or all the units in an Army of Renown then gain the benefits listed, such as new keyword, abilities, Stratagems etc. Note that your army does not automatically become an Army of Renown just because it happens to abide by the restrictions – you must choose for it to be an Army of Renown.

CRUSADE ARMY OF RENOWN

You can use any of the rules listed in an Army of Renown to make a Crusade Army of Renown when you start a Crusade force. In this case, the Restrictions and Benefits apply to your entire Crusade force – replace all instances of 'army' listed in the Restrictions and Benefits sections to instead say 'Crusade force', and make a note in the Crusade Faction section of your Order of Battle of which Army of Renown your Crusade force is. Note that means that certain units can never be added to your Order of Battle; but it will result in a particularly focussed and themed collection. Whenever you select a Crusade army from such an Order of Battle, it must be Battle-forged and cannot include any Specialist Detachments.

LEGENDARY KNIGHT

Freeblade lances are made up of Imperial Knights who once were of esteemed rank and who have continued to win mighty victories across the galaxy, forging a new path of valour and dread.

- A **Freeblade Lance Character** can be upgraded to have one of the Exalted Court upgrades (pg 84-86), even though they are a **Freeblade**. If a **Freeblade Lance** model is so upgraded, replace all instances of the **<Noble Household>** keyword on that upgrade's abilities (if any) with **Freeblade Lance.**

WARLORD TRAIT

If a **Freeblade Lance Character** model is your **Warlord**, they can have the Warlord Trait below instead of one from another source.

ECHOES FROM THE PAST

Though this Noble is in exile, they still cling to the vestiges of honour from their former household.

This **Warlord** gains and the Glorified History Martial Tradition (if it has the **Questor Imperialis** keyword) or the Fealty to the Cog Martial Tradition (if it has the **Questor Mechanicus** keyword), as described on pages 77 and 78 respectively, even though they are a **Freeblade**. This **Warlord** will only gain the Martial Tradition of the selected house, however – it will not gain access to the selected Noble Household Relic, Noble Household Warlord Trait or Noble Household Stratagem. Write down your selected tradition on your army roster or Crusade card when this Warlord Trait is selected.

RELIC

If your army is led by a **Freeblade Lance Warlord**, you can, when mustering your army, give the following Heirloom Relic to a **Freeblade Lance Character** model from your army, instead of one from another source. Named characters cannot be given the following Relic. Note that this Relic replaces one of the model's existing items of wargear. You must, if you are using points values, still pay the cost of the wargear that is being replaced. Write down any Heirlooms Relics your models have on your army roster.

BRINGER OF JUSTICE

It is said that whenever this famed weapon is brought roaring to life, it shall not fall silent until it has slaked its thirst for justice.

Freeblade Lance model with a reaper chainsword only. Bringer of Justice replaces the bearer's reaper chainsword and has the following profile:

MELEE WEAPON	RANGE	TYPE	S	AP	D
Bringer of Justice					
Each time the bearer fights, it makes one additional attack with this weapon. Each time an attack is made with this weapon, select one of the profiles below to make that attack with.					
- Strike	Melee	Melee	+8	-4	6
- Sweep	Melee	Melee	+2	-3	2
Abilities (Sweep): Each time an attack is made with this weapon profile, make 3 hit rolls instead of 1.					

STRATAGEMS

If your army is a Freeblade Lance, you have access to these Stratagems, and can spend CPs to use them.

BROTHERS AND SISTERS IN BURDEN — 1CP

Freeblade Lance – Epic Deed Stratagem

Only another who also walks the path of a Freeblade can have any hope of understanding the burdens that such warriors must bear.

Use this Stratagem in your Command phase if your army is Dishonoured. Select one **Freeblade Lance Character** model from your army. Until the start of your next Command phase, that model has the following ability:

Brothers and Sisters in Burden (Aura): While a friendly **Freeblade Lance** model is within 12" of this character, the Honoured Chivalric ability from your selected Oaths are still active for this **Warlord**. This may mean that different Chivalric abilities are active for these models than are active for other **Imperial Knights** models from your army.

STRENGTH FROM EXILE — 1CP

Freeblade Lance – Epic Deed Stratagem

Freeblades spend years fighting without support, and when they fight alongside others, such hard-won knowledge is not lost.

Use this Stratagem in your Shooting phase, when a **Freeblade Lance** model from your army is selected to shoot, or in the Fight phase, when a **Freeblade Lance** model from your army is selected to fight. Until the end of the phase, while that model is more than 12" away from any friendly models, each time it makes an attack, re-roll a hit roll of 1 and re-roll a wound roll of 1.

DEEDS OF LEGEND — 1CP

Freeblade Lance – Epic Deed Stratagem

Freeblades seek out the mightiest of foes to vanquish in battle.

Use this Stratagem in any phase, when a **Freeblade Lance** model from your army destroys an enemy **Vehicle**, **Monster** or **Character** unit. Select one Chivalric ability (pg 118-119). Until the end of the battle, this model has that Chivalric ability, and it is active for that model, regardless of your army's current level of Honour. If you selected the Martial Legacy ability, you can only re-roll rolls made for this model. You can only use this Stratagem once.

FAVOURED KNIGHT — 2CP

Freeblade Lance – Requisition Stratagem

Some revered Freeblades wield several weapons of legend.

Use this Stratagem before the battle, when you are mustering your army. Select one **Freeblade Lance Character** model (excluding named characters) from your army that has one Heirloom Relic. That model can have a second Heirloom Relic (this must be a Relic they could have). Each Relic in your army must be unique. You can only use this Stratagem once.

RELICS

If your army is led by a **IMPERIAL KNIGHTS WARLORD**, you can, when mustering your army, give one of the following Heirloom Relics to a **IMPERIAL KNIGHTS CHARACTER** model from your army. Recall that **IMPERIAL KNIGHTS** Detachments gain the Knight Lancés ability (pg 64) that will enable you to select one model in that Detachment to be a **CHARACTER**. Named characters cannot be given any of the following Relics.

Note that some Relics replace one of the model's existing items of wargear. Where this is the case, you must, if you are using points values, still pay the cost of the wargear that is being replaced. Write down any Heirloom Relics your models have on your army roster.

SANCTUARY

Despite whispers of xenos taint in its origins, the potent ion shield generator known as Sanctuary is a venerated war relic. Through the projection of rapidly modulating and overlapping energy fields, coupled with a steady emission of warding incense and a cycling barrage of data-hymnals, this device wards away the furious fire of the enemy. It does not even require tilting and angling like a typical ion shield, for its effects wreathe the Knight suit in an all-encompassing fog of protective energies and holy wards. The resultant field clings to the Knight like an energised second skin, flexing and shifting with its movement and protecting it from close-quarters attacks.

QUESTORIS-CLASS or **ARMIGER-CLASS** model only. The bearer has a 4+ invulnerable save against melee attacks.

RAVAGER

This scarred chainsword has claimed millions of lives during its service to the noble houses. Its razor-sharp teeth were harvested from the canines of a long-extinct species of bio-horror called a Balethrox. What makes this fact so startling is that dozens of the fell creatures must have been hunted down and slain by brave Knights in order to secure enough fangs to line Ravager's blade. However, witnessing the wrath of this chainblade's touch in battle more than justifies the dedication of those long-dead Knights, and its bearer fights all the harder to honour their sacrifice.

Model with a reaper chainsword only. Ravager replaces the bearer's reaper chainsword and has the following profile:

MELEE WEAPON	RANGE	TYPE	S	AP	D
Ravager					
Each time an attack is made with this weapon, select one of the profiles below to make that attack with. Each time an attack is made with this weapon profile, on an unmodified hit roll of 6, one additional hit is scored.					
- Strike	Melee	Melee	+7	-4	6
- Sweep	Melee	Melee	+1	-3	2
Abilities (Sweep): Each time an attack is made with this weapon profile, make 3 hit rolls instead of 1.					

'Sound the horns! Sound the horns! The Blade of Antiaz is brought forth to war!'

- Herald Rardos ven Restorilg, House Arakon

HELM OF THE NAMELESS WARRIOR

Though many great heroes through the ages have mounted this faceplate upon their Knight suits, the names of both the suit and the valiant pilot who first bore this helm have been lost to history. Regardless of its origins, the Helm of the Nameless Warrior has become synonymous with murderous ferocity in battle.

QUESTOR IMPERIALIS QUESTORIS-CLASS or **QUESTOR IMPERIALIS ARMIGER-CLASS** models only. Each time the bearer makes a melee attack, on an unmodified wound roll of 6, that attack inflicts a number of mortal wounds equal to the Damage characteristic of that attack and the attack sequence ends.

THE HELM DOMINATUS

This noospheric interface boosts the bearer's ability to communicate with their bondsmen and enables them to emit a temporary cerebral override that beckons bonded Armigers to aid the bearer to defeat the foe.

QUESTORIS-CLASS model with a Bondsman ability (pg 117) only. At the end of each of your Command phases, you can select one **ARMIGER-CLASS** model that is being affected by the bearer's Bondsman ability. While the bearer is on the battlefield, that ability will affect that **ARMIGER-CLASS** model until the end of the battle (instead of until the start of your next Command phase), or until that **ARMIGER-CLASS** model is affected by another Bondsman ability – whichever happens first.

ENDLESS FURY

This remarkable avenger gatling cannon is fitted with ballistic micro-fabricators that churn out fresh ammunition as fast as it can be fired. Rumours persist of the weapon's wielders being driven slowly mad with bloodlust, but even if there is truth to these claims, it is seen as a small price to pay for the power unleashed.

Model with an avenger gatling cannon only. Endless Fury replaces the bearer's avenger gatling cannon and has the following profile:

WEAPON	RANGE	TYPE	S	AP	D
Endless Fury	36"	Assault D6+12	6	-3	2

THE BASTARD'S HELM

This Helm Mechanicum was said to have been crafted for the beloved illegitimate son of a fabled Noble Lord. Though technically lowborn, the son was raised as any other highborn Knight, and proved to be a skilled warrior and a natural leader, becoming an inspirational hero amongst the squires of the household and a lord in all but name. Generations later, and the essence of that first low-born hero still commands the loyalty and inspiration of squires.

ARMIGER-CLASS model only.

- Each time the bearer makes an attack, add 1 to that attack's wound roll.
- The bearer cannot be affected by any Bondsman abilities or any Knightly Teachings.
- The bearer gains the following ability:

The Bastard's Helm (Bondsman): In your Command phase, you can select one other friendly **<NOBLE HOUSEHOLD> ARMIGER-CLASS** model within 12" of this model. Until the start of your next Command phase, each time that **ARMIGER-CLASS** model makes an attack, add 1 to that attack's wound roll.

ARMOUR OF THE SAINTED ION

This carapace body glove is worn by the Noble pilot. It is studded with electro-sockets that couple with the machineries of the Throne Mechanicum. Once bonded, the micro-generators within the armour thrum to life. They project streams of ionic energy, not only wreathing the pilot and their Throne in a protective shield, but reinforcing and protecting the Knight's internal systems. Thus, even shots and blows that penetrate the outer shell of the Knight's armour may fail to cause any harm.

QUESTORIS-CLASS or **ARMIGER-CLASS** model only. The bearer has a Save characteristic of 2+.

MARK OF THE OMNISSIAH

Forged in the shape of the cog of Mars, the Mark of the Omnissiah is an incredibly potent self-repair device. If the Knight suit upon which it is affixed takes battle damage, reconstruction protocols automatically engage to repair rents and restore lost power.

QUESTOR MECHANICUS QUESTORIS-CLASS or **QUESTOR MECHANICUS ARMIGER-CLASS** model only. At the start of each of your Command phases, this model is repaired and regains up to D3 lost wounds. Each model can only be repaired once per turn. Note that if this model has the Sacristan Pledge Questor Allegiance Oath, it means at the start of each of your Command phases it will regain D3+1 wounds.

BANNER OF MACHARIUS TRIUMPHANT

A gift from Lord Solar Macharius himself to honour the noble houses that accompanied his crusade, this banner was borne to battle by a Knight Seneschal in every engagement in which the Knights fought alongside the Warmaster. Legend has it that the Banner of Macharius Triumphant has never seen defeat: every time a Knight has carried it to war, a great victory has been won. To see its form fluttering in the wind instils the Emperor's warriors with a sense of honour, for to fight in its shadow is to all but assure victory.

QUESTORIS IMPERIALIS QUESTORIS-CLASS model only.

- The bearer has the Objective Secured ability (see the Warhammer 40,000 Core Book).
- If every unit from your army has the **IMPERIAL KNIGHTS** keyword (excluding units with the **AGENTS OF THE IMPERIUM** or **UNALIGNED** keywords), then you start the battle with 1 additional Honour point, but if the bearer is destroyed, you lose 1 Honour point.

MENTOR'S SEAL

These purity seals list the deeds of every founder of the household who epitomised the teachings and virtues of the Code Chivalric, inked in the blood of the master Knight who instructed them. They are a link to the household's inception, and a reminder that following the Code Chivalric is one of the most important duties.

KNIGHT PRECEPTOR only.

- The bearer knows one additional teaching from the Knightly Teachings (pg 95).
- Each time the bearer recounts a teaching, add 1 to the roll to see if that teaching is inspiring.

'Bathe it in the sacred unguents as it has bathed in the unholy blood of our blasphemous foes. Plunge it within its scabbard, so it is as embedded within its resting place as deeply as it was buried into the armour of our heretic enemies. Bless its name and sing its praises, for it has done the Emperor's work today. Thanks to He on the Throne.'

- Sacristan maxim for the proper care-taking and cleaning of weapons after battle has been fought against traitors

---

'Such artefacts as the Diadem of Aramos, the Auric Seal, the Shroud of Erinn, Cenkis' Fist and all nine volumes of the Code Rapturis lie within our vaults. Each has millennia of history, stories which each speak to a part of our glorious traditions. I would gladly die than see them fall into enemy hands. As should we all.'

- Herald Iniaska Aramos, House Aramos

ARMY RULES

THE HEART OF ION

This fabled plasma reactor is thought to have been one of the original STC construct templates created in the Dark Age of Technology. It is capable of channelling the primal wrath of plasma fire, imbuing the Knight with immense, if temporary, bursts of power. Such surges of the Omnissiah's holy lifeblood invariably damage the Knight, but it is only through sacrifice that great deeds can be achieved.

QUESTOR MECHANICUS QUESTORIS-CLASS or **QUESTOR MECHANICUS ARMIGER-CLASS** model only. Once per turn, at the end of your Command phase, the bearer can use this Relic. When it does, the bearer suffers 1 mortal wound, you must select one weapon that the bearer is equipped with, and until the start of your next Command phase:

- Add 1" to the bearer's Move characteristic.
- Add 1 to Advance and charge rolls made for the bearer.
- Each time the bearer makes an attack with the selected weapon, add 1 to that attack's wound roll.

THE PARAGON GAUNTLET

It is believed that this masterwork weapon was the prototype for the thunderstrike gauntlet – the first, perfect copy fabricated by a long lost STC that was developed on Mars during the Age of Technology. It was that same STC that was integral to the founding of the Knight worlds themselves, by equipping Mankind's first colonisation fleets with the knowledge to build the mighty armoured suits. If true, it would certainly explain the incredible level of artifice that went into the gauntlet's creation.

Model with a thunderstrike gauntlet only. The Paragon Gauntlet replaces the bearer's thunderstrike gauntlet and has the following profile:

MELEE WEAPON	RANGE	TYPE	S	AP	D
The Paragon Gauntlet					
Each time an attack is made with this weapon, select one of the profiles below to make that attack with.					
- Strike	Melee	Melee	x2	-4	9
Abilities: Each time an attack is made with this weapon profile, on an unmodified wound roll of 6, invulnerable saving throws cannot be taken against that attack.					
- Sweep	Melee	Melee	+2	-2	4
Abilities: Each time an attack is made with this weapon profile, make 2 hit rolls instead of 1 and, on an unmodified wound roll of 6, invulnerable saving throws cannot be taken against that attack.					

TRAITOR'S PYRE

This ornate conflagration cannon was borne upon a three-hundred and-fifty year pilgrimage to the cardinal world of Basphoria, so that it might be blessed by Saint Gauschwyn the Wrathful. The saint's spiritual influence fortified the weapon's machine spirit and greatly enhanced its ferocity, imparting a portion of Gauschwyn's infamous wrath upon it.

QUESTOR IMPERIALIS KNIGHT VALIANT model only. Traitor's Pyre replaces the bearer's conflagration cannon and has the following profile:

WEAPON	RANGE	TYPE	S	AP	D
Traitor's Pyre	18"	Heavy 3D6	8	-2	2
Abilities: Each time an attack is made with this weapon, that attack automatically hits the target and, on an unmodified wound roll of 6, invulnerable saves cannot be taken against that attack.					

CAWL'S WRATH

During his centuries-long efforts to reduce the size and increase the portability of advanced plasma weaponry, Archmagos Cawl created this singular plasma decimator. Its enhanced containment fields and machine spirit data-shackles allow it to generate even more lethal volumes of energy than a typical example of such a weapon.

QUESTOR MECHANICUS KNIGHT CASTELLAN only. Cawl's Wrath replaces the bearer's plasma decimator and has the following profile:

WEAPON	RANGE	TYPE	S	AP	D
Cawl's Wrath	48"	Heavy 2D6	8	-4	3
Abilities: Blast					

JUDGEMENT

This unique rocket pod fires self-propelled adamantine-tipped warheads fitted with servitor brains and running venatoris auto-targeting protocols. Once launched, these projectiles mercilessly hunt their prey across the battlefield.

Model with a stormspear rocket pod only. Judgement replaces the bearer's stormspear rocket pod and has the following profile:

WEAPON	RANGE	TYPE	S	AP	D
Judgement	48"	Heavy 3	8	-2	D3+3
Abilities: This weapon can target units that are not visible to the bearer.					

WARLORD TRAITS

If an **IMPERIAL KNIGHTS TITANIC CHARACTER** model is your **WARLORD**, you can use the Imperial Knights Warlord Traits table below to determine what Warlord Trait they have. You can either roll one D6 to randomly generate one, or you can select one. If an **IMPERIAL KNIGHTS ARMIGER-CLASS CHARACTER** model is your **WARLORD**, they can only have the Cunning Commander, Blessed by the Sacristans or Ion Bulwark traits. Alternatively, you can roll one D3 to randomly generate one from the table below.

1. CUNNING COMMANDER

A master tactician, this warlord instinctively knows how best to use the battlefield.

At the start of your Command phase, if this **WARLORD** is on the battlefield, roll one D6: on a 5+, you gain 1 Command point.

2. BLESSED BY THE SACRISTANS

This warlord bears a token of favour from Sacristans in the form of an artificer weapon of unrivalled quality.

Each time this **WARLORD** makes a ranged attack, on an unmodified wound roll of 6 that attack inflicts 1 mortal wound on the target in addition to the normal damage (to a maximum of 6 mortal wounds per unit per phase).

3. ION BULWARK

A survivor of countless battles, this warlord has learnt to angle their Knight suit's ion shield with exceptional deftness.

This **WARLORD** has a 4+ invulnerable save against ranged attacks.

4. KNIGHT SENESCHAL

Veteran warriors who have proved themselves worthy time and again are awarded the rank of Knight Seneschal. To be named so is an honour.

- Add 1 to this **WARLORD**'s Attacks characteristic.
- Even if your army is Dishonoured (pg 99), the Honoured Chivalric ability from your selected Oaths are still active for this **WARLORD**. This may mean that different Chivalric abilities are active for this **WARLORD** than are active for other **IMPERIAL KNIGHTS** models from your army.

5. LANDSTRIDER

This warlord has fought across hundreds of battlefields, and is an expert at reading strat-map inloads and coordinating their forces' advance.

- Add 2" to this **WARLORD**'s Move characteristic.
- Each time an Advance roll is made for this **WARLORD**, treat a dice roll of 1-2 as 3 instead.
- Each time a charge roll is made for this **WARLORD**, treat each dice roll of 1-2 as 3 instead.

6. REVERED KNIGHT

Never hesitating before tyrannical invaders, the warlord is beheld as the very epitome of honour – a towering and monolithic incarnation of the Imperium made manifest.

- At the start of the Fight phase, if this **WARLORD** is within Engagement Range of any enemy units, it can fight first that phase.
- If every unit from your army has the **IMPERIAL KNIGHTS** keyword (excluding units with the **AGENTS OF THE IMPERIUM** or **UNALIGNED** keywords), and this **WARLORD** is part of your army, then you start the battle with 1 additional Honour point (pg 118) but, if this **WARLORD** is destroyed, you lose 1 Honour point.

NAMED CHARACTERS AND WARLORD TRAITS

If **CANIS REX** gains a Warlord Trait, it must be Revered Knight. Note that if **CANIS REX** is destroyed and **SIR HEKHTUR** is set up on the battlefield, **SIR HEKHTUR** will also have the Revered Knight Warlord Trait.

March, Knights of Araphos! Into the maws of war, the fires of battle! Show them that no thought of pain, misery or death put fear in you!

KNIGHTLY TEACHINGS

Before the battle, generate the teachings for **MENTOR** models from your army that know teachings from the Knightly Teachings using the table below. You can either roll one D6 to generate each teaching randomly (re-rolling duplicate results), or you can select which teachings the model knows. When a **MENTOR** model from your army recounts a teaching, replace all instances of the **<NOBLE HOUSEHOLD>** keyword on that teaching (if any) with the name of the noble household that your **MENTOR** is drawn from (if your model is a **FREEBLADE**, this is instead replaced with **FREEBLADE**, unless that **FREEBLADE** is **CANIS REX**, in which case this is instead replaced with **IMPERIAL KNIGHTS**).

1. THE VIRTUE OF COURAGE (AURA)

A Knight must have the courage to face the greatest horrors in the galaxy.

If this teaching is inspiring, while a **<NOBLE HOUSEHOLD> ARMIGER-CLASS** model is within 6" of this **MENTOR**, each time that model makes an attack, on an unmodified hit roll of 6, one additional hit is scored.

2. THE OATH OF JUSTICE (AURA)

A Knight's honour is their life, and they must hold themselves to the highest standard of the Chivalric Code.

If this teaching is inspiring, while a **<NOBLE HOUSEHOLD> ARMIGER-CLASS** model is within 6" of this **MENTOR**, if that model is being affected by any Chivalric abilities (pg 118-119), you count as having 2 more Honour points than you currently do when determining what those Chivalric abilities are. This may mean that different Chivalric abilities are active for different **IMPERIAL KNIGHTS** models from your army.

3. THE FOLLY OF MERCY

The Emperor's foes deserve no mercy, and you must never relent in exacting punishment upon them.

If this teaching is inspiring, select one **<NOBLE HOUSEHOLD> ARMIGER-CLASS** model within 12" of this **MENTOR**. That model can perform an action and make a normal move and shoot without that action failing.

'Through faith, acceptance. Through acceptance, obedience. Through obedience, honour. Through honour, chivalry. Through chivalry, glory eternal.'

- *The Bondsman's Motto*

4. THE KNIGHT'S FAITH (AURA)

A true Knight knows that honour and faith are mightier bulwarks than any armour.

If this teaching is inspiring, while a **<NOBLE HOUSEHOLD> ARMIGER-CLASS** model is within 6" of this **MENTOR**, each time that **ARMIGER-CLASS** model would lose a wound, roll one D6: on a 6, that wound is not lost. If that **ARMIGER-CLASS** model is under the effects of a Bondsman ability (pg 117), that wound is not lost on the roll of a 5+ instead.

5. THE WARRIOR'S HOPE

When you are outnumbered and beset on all sides, look to the Code Chivalric and you will find the inner strength to light the darkness and earn glory for your household.

If this teaching is inspiring, select one **<NOBLE HOUSEHOLD> ARMIGER-CLASS** model within 12" of this **MENTOR**. Select one Oath from the Code Chivalric (pg 118-119) that is not active for your army. That Oath is active for that **ARMIGER-CLASS** model and it gains all of the relevant Chivalric abilities for your army's level of honour (but it does not gain that Oath's Pledge or Troth). Note that this Oath is active, even if every unit from your army does not have the **IMPERIAL KNIGHTS** keyword.

6. THE WISDOM OF NOBILITY

Listen to the teachings of your lords, ladies and betters well, for they have been honed on the field of battle. Take these lessons and pass them onto your fellow aspirants so that they may learn from your own noble example.

If this teaching is inspiring, select one **<NOBLE HOUSEHOLD> ARMIGER-CLASS** model with 12" of this **MENTOR**. Each time that **ARMIGER-CLASS** model is selected for a Bondsman ability, you can select one other **<NOBLE HOUSEHOLD> ARMIGER-CLASS** model that is within 6" of that model. Both of these **ARMIGER-CLASS** models are affected by that Bondsman ability.

CHAPTER APPROVED RULES

If every model in your army has the **IMPERIAL KNIGHTS** keyword (excluding models with the **AGENT OF THE IMPERIUM** or **UNALIGNED** keyword), and your **WARLORD** has the **IMPERIAL KNIGHTS** keyword, you can, if you are playing a matched play battle that instructs you to select secondary objectives (e.g. a mission from the Eternal War mission pack in the Warhammer 40,000 Core Book), select one of them to be from the Imperial Knights secondary objectives listed below.

Like all other secondary objectives, each of the secondary objectives listed below has a category, and they follow all the normal rules for secondary objectives (for example, when you select secondary objectives, you cannot choose more than one from each category, you can score no more than 15 victory points from each secondary objective you select during the mission etc.).

PURGE THE ENEMY

DUEL OF HONOUR

End Game Objective

The foe is a dastardly coward, a cur that has preyed on the weak and the innocent for too long and whose mere existence is an affront to the Code Chivalric. Such a tyrant cannot be allowed to besmirch your honour much longer. Slay them with impunity in personal combat, as honour demands.

If you select this objective, then before the battle, after you have deployed armies, you must identify your opponent's **WARLORD**, and the two units from your opponent's army that have the highest points value (excluding your opponent's **WARLORD**), and make a note of them on your army roster (if two or more units are tied, your opponent can choose between them). If your opponent's army has three or fewer units, then you instead identify all the units in your opponent's army. A unit's points cost includes the points of all weapons and wargear it is equipped with.

At the end of the battle, for each identified enemy unit that is destroyed, you score a number of victory points if that unit was destroyed during the battle by an **IMPERIAL KNIGHTS** unit from your army. The number of victory points scored depends on how the enemy unit was destroyed, as shown in the Manner of Destruction table below.

MANNER OF DESTRUCTION	VICTORY POINTS
Honour to the King: The unit was destroyed by a melee attack made by your **WARLORD**.	5
Personal Combat: The unit was destroyed by a melee attack made by any other **IMPERIAL KNIGHTS** model from your army.	4
Cowardly Cur: The unit was destroyed because it was not on the battlefield at the end of the battle and so counted as destroyed (note, this does not apply if the enemy unit is embarked in a **TRANSPORT** that is itself on the battlefield at the end of the battle).	4
Inglorious Demise: The enemy unit was destroyed by any other means.	3

At the end of any battle round in which Honour to the King or Personal Combat was achieved, you gain 1 Honour point (pg 118).

At the end of the battle, if the enemy's **WARLORD** has been destroyed, you gain 1 additional victory point, but you must reduce the number of victory points you have earned from this secondary objective by 1 (to a minimum of 0) for each of the identified units that has not been destroyed.

For example, if the enemy **WARLORD** was destroyed by a melee attack made by your **WARLORD**, one of the other identified units was destroyed by a ranged attack made by a model in your army, and the third identified unit was still on the battlefield at the end of the battle, you would score 8 victory points from this secondary objective.

NO MERCY, NO RESPITE

HONOUR OF THE HOUSE

Progressive and End Game Objective

Duty. Honour. Fealty. Upholding the tenets of the Code Chivalric is more important than breath to a Knight.

If you select this objective, at the end of each battle round, if you have 6 Honour points or if you have more Honour Points than you did at the start of the battle round, gain 2 victory points.

At the end of the battle:

- If your army is Virtuous, gain 3 additional victory points.
- If your army is Honoured, gain 2 additional victory points.
- If your army is Dishonoured, reduce the number of victory points you have earned from this secondary objective by 3 (to a minimum of 0).

BATTLEFIELD SUPREMACY

YIELD NO GROUND

Progressive Objective

The time has come to plant your adamantine feet and make a stand against the enemy. Take not one step back!

If you select this objective, at the end of your turn, you score victory points as follows (for a maximum of 5 victory points):

- Score 2 victory points if you control half or more of the total number of objective markers on the battlefield, and one or more **IMPERIAL KNIGHTS** models from your army are within range of each of those objective markers.
- Score 2 victory points if no enemy units (excluding **AIRCRAFT** units) are wholly within your deployment zone.
- Score 1 victory point so long as no **IMPERIAL KNIGHTS** units from your army ended that turn closer to your battlefield edge than they started the turn, and no **IMPERIAL KNIGHTS** units from your army Fell Back during that turn.

This secondary objective cannot be scored in the first battle round.

SHADOW OPERATIONS

RENEW THE OATHS

Progressive Objective

In ages past, the household fought upon this very battlefield and only through a noble sacrifice was victory assured. As part of their trials, a Knight is expected to perform a pilgrimage to this hallowed site, and pay their respects by recounting their chivalric deeds and renewing their oaths of loyalty. Only then, can honour and tradition be satisfied.

If you select this objective, then **IMPERIAL KNIGHTS** units from your army can attempt the following action:

Renew the Oaths (Action): One **IMPERIAL KNIGHTS** model from your army can start to perform this action at the end of your Movement phase if it is within 6" of the centre of the battlefield. This action is completed at the end of your turn provided the unit attempting it is still within 6" of the centre of the battlefield.

Each time a unit from your army completes this action:

- You score 3 victory points if the action was completed by a non-**TITANIC** model.
- You score 4 victory points if the action was completed by a **TITANIC** model.
- You score 1 additional victory point if the action was completed by a **CHARACTER** model.
- You must roll one D6: on a 4+, you gain 1 Honour point (pg 118).

CRUSADE RULES

In this section you'll find additional rules for playing Crusade battles with Imperial Knights, such as Agendas, Battle Traits and Crusade Relics that are bespoke to IMPERIAL KNIGHTS units. You can find out more about Crusade armies in the Warhammer 40,000 Core Book.

This section contains the following additional rules:

SWORN TO A QUEST
On pages 99-105 you will find rules for your IMPERIAL KNIGHTS models to swear mighty oaths, the successful completion of which will bring them much glory and honour, and with it, new abilities in the form of Qualities. However, should a Knight fail in their appointed task, they will instead acquire the Burden of shame, and a permanent stain upon their honour.

AGENDAS
IMPERIAL KNIGHTS units can attempt to achieve unique Agendas in Crusade battles, which can be found on pages 106-107. These Agendas reflect the unique quests of Imperial Knights armies on the battlefield and help to reflect their particular fighting styles. You can find out more about Agendas in Crusade mission packs, such as that presented in the Warhammer 40,000 Core Book.

REQUISITIONS
Imperial Knights armies have access to a number of additional Requisitions, suited to their methods for waging war. You can find these on page 108.

CRUSADE RELICS
In addition to the Crusade Relics presented in the Warhammer 40,000 Core Book, IMPERIAL KNIGHTS CHARACTER models can quest to search for one of the Crusade Relics described on page 109; these Relics are unique to the noble households, and they are glorious artefacts.

BATTLE TRAITS
IMPERIAL KNIGHTS models can be given one of the Battle Traits presented on pages 110-111 as they gain experience and are promoted in your Crusade force. These help to better reflect the unique upgrades and Battle Honours that are bestowed to noble households.

BATTLE SCARS
If an IMPERIAL KNIGHTS model gains a Battle Scar, you can select one from those presented on pages 112-113. These Battle Scars represent the damage that an Imperial Knight suit can sustain and the afflictions that can affect its pilot, and help to add further character to your Crusade force.

SHOWCASE CRUSADE ARMY
On pages 114-115 you will find James Karch's excellent House Taranis Imperial Knights Crusade army, with a description of the force and its upgrades, and details of its exploits on the battlefield.

IMPERIAL KNIGHTS CHARACTERS IN CRUSADE
IMPERIAL KNIGHTS Detachments have a Detachment ability called Knight Lances. The part of this ability that enables a model to gain the CHARACTER keyword does not apply to Crusade armies. The only method by which an IMPERIAL KNIGHTS model can gain the CHARACTER keyword when it is added to your Order of Battle is by purchasing the Specialist Reinforcements Requisition (see the Warhammer 40,000 Core Book) in order to use the Knight Baron Stratagem* (pg 82).

Note, however, that using this Stratagem will only result in that model gaining the CHARACTER keyword – it will not grant them a Warlord Trait as described on the Stratagem (as per the Specialist Reinforcement Requisition's rules). To give such a model a Warlord Trait you would have to additionally purchase the Warlord Trait Requisition (see the Warhammer 40,000 Core Book).

It is also possible for an IMPERIAL KNIGHTS model to gain the CHARACTER keyword later, either by using the above Requisition and Stratagem, or by gaining the Knight Commander Battle Trait.

***Designer's Note:** *This rule also appears in the Crusade section of the Warhammer 40,000 Core Book, but there it mentions the 'Exalted Court' Stratagem. Since the Core Book was published, this Stratagem has been renamed 'Knight Baron' to help avoid confusion with the Exalted Court rules presented on pages 84-86.*

FREEBLADES IN CRUSADE
When you add a FREEBLADE unit to your Order of Battle, you must select its Martial Tradition and make a note of this on its Crusade card(s). You cannot select a Martial Tradition for this unit if any other unit in your Crusade army already has that tradition, and its tradition cannot be changed. Note that if this unit contains more than one model, each of those models will have the same tradition even though each will have a separate Crusade card. If you add Canis Rex to your Order of Battle, he will have the Mythic Hero Martial Tradition even if another model in your Crusade army has this tradition.

SWORN TO A QUEST

If, when you start a Crusade Force, there are any **Imperial Knights** models on your Order of Battle, you can select one of them. That model gains the **Questsworn** keyword and will start to earn Glory points and Shame points as you play, which you must keep track of on its Crusade card. You can give additional **Imperial Knights** the **Questsworn** keyword by using the Knightly Quest Requisition (pg 108). Note that there is no limit to the number of models that can be **Questsworn**, but once a model embarks upon a quest, it cannot be abandoned without incurring consequences. They will end in either glory or shame.

When you first select a model to be a **Questsworn**, select one of the Quests on page 100. That model is now said to be undertaking that Quest, and in addition to gaining a Knightly Deed to complete (these are detailed in the Quests themselves), that model will accrue Glory points and Shame points depending on its performance in battle. At the end of each battle, every **Questsworn** model in your Crusade army will gain a Glory point or a Shame point depending on your army's level of Honour at the end of the battle, and that model's current rank, as shown below. A model cannot have more than 3 Glory points.

ARMY'S HONOUR			
MODEL'S RANK	ARMY LEVEL OF HONOUR AT THE END OF THE BATTLE		
	Dishonoured	Honoured	Virtuous
Battle-ready	+1 Shame point	+1 Glory point	+2 Glory points
Blooded or Battle-hardened	+1 Shame point	Nothing	+1 Glory point
Heroic or Legendary	+2 Shame points	Nothing	+1 Glory point

There are additional rules found within this Crusade section, such as Battle Traits and Crusade Relics, that can adjust a model's current number of Glory points and Shame points.

Questsworn MODELS IN IMPERIUM CRUSADE ARMIES

If your Crusade army includes any **Questsworn** models, you must use the Code Chivalric ability (pg 118-119), even if every unit from your army doesn't have the **Imperial Knights** keyword. Note that in this case, the Code Chivalric ability is solely used to track your army's level of Honour for the purposes of determining whether or not **Questsworn** models in your army can use Honour Extremis abilities (pg 102) and whether they gain any Glory points or Shame points at the end of the battle. You swear Oaths and your army's level of honour is adjusted according to the Pledge and Troths of those Oaths, but **Imperial Knights** models in your army are not affected by those Oaths' Chivalric abilities.

Once a **Questsworn** model has earned 3 Glory points and it has completed the Knightly deed listed in the Quest it is undertaking, that model's quest ends in success, that model's Glory points total is reset to 0 and that model gains one Quality, which are abilities that make the model more powerful.

If a **Questsworn** model earns 3 Shame points before the Quest it is undertaking ends in success, that model's quest ends in failure, that model's Glory points and Shame points totals are both reset to 0 and that model gains one Burden, which are abilities that afflict the model.

At the end of any battle, a **Questsworn** model can abandon the Quest they are currently undertaking and you can select a new one for them. If you do so, their Quest ends, their Glory points are reset to 0 and the model immediately gains 1 Shame point.

Note that a model's number of Shame points is only reset to 0 when a Quest is failed. If a model successfully completes a Quest, they carry over any Shame points that they have acquired with them when they undertake their next Quest.

Once a model's quest has ended, you must then select a new Quest for them to undertake before your next battle and begin again.

- **Questsworn** models gain Glory points and Shame points.
- Glory points and Shame points are earned depending on your army's level of Honour at the end of the battle.
- If a model has 3 Glory points and it has completed its Quest's deed, that Quest ends in success; it gains 1 Quality and its Glory points are reset to 0.
- If a model has 3 Shame points, that Quest ends in failure; it gains 1 Burden and its Glory points and Shame points are reset to 0.
- Each time a model gains a Quality or Burden, it gains abilities and either gains or loses Crusade points.

QUESTS

The Quests that can be undertaken by **QUESTSWORN** models from your army, and their associated Knightly deeds, are shown below. The same model can undertake the same Quest more than once. A model cannot undertake a Quest that another model from your Order of Battle is currently undertaking unless each and every one of the 6 Quests listed below is currently being undertaken by other models from your Order of Battle. Make a note on a model's Crusade Card of what Quest it is currently undertaking (and which ones it has completed successfully).

RECOVER ANCIENT RELIC

This Knight swears an oath to recover a fabled ancient artefact.

Knightly Deed: While undertaking this Quest, this model must either gain one Crusade Relic or, if this model has the **QUESTOR MECHANICUS** keyword, gain 1 or more experience points from the Martian Pact Agenda (pg 107).

CALL TO ARMS

This Knight vows to hone their skills and answer any call to war.

Knightly Deed: While undertaking this Quest, this model must either gain one Battle Trait or, if this model has the **QUESTOR IMPERIALIS** keyword, gain 1 or more experience points from the Imperial Petition Agenda (pg 107).

SETTLE A GRUDGE

This Knight pledges to right a terrible wrong, enduring any hardship until the task is done.

Knightly Deed: While undertaking this Quest, this model must either gain 1 or more experience points from the Honour Must Be Satisfied Agenda (pg 106), or if this model has one or more Battle Scars, it must increase its Battles Survived tally (see the Warhammer 40,000 Core Book) by at least 2 whilst it has those Battle Scars.

TO SLAY A TYRANT

This Knights sets out on a quest to find one of the most dangerous foes in the galaxy, or the weapon needed to slay it.

Knightly Deed: While undertaking this Quest, this model must either gain 1 or more experience points from the Slayer of Beasts Agenda (pg 107), or it must gain one Weapon Enhancement.

ASSAIL THE FOE

This Knight never relents while their enemies still stand.

Knightly Deed: While undertaking this Quest, this model must gain 1 or more experience points from the Sally Forth Agenda (pg 107), or it must gain 3 or more experience points from Dealers of Death (see the Warhammer 40,000 Core Book).

HOLD BACK THE DARK

This Knight undertakes to uphold the highest principles of the Code Chivalric and use its tenets to drive back the enemy through great acts of nobility.

Knightly Deed: While undertaking this Quest, this model must earn 1 or more experience points from the Paragons of Honour Agenda (pg 106) and it must be Marked for Greatness in the same battle.

Few foes arouse such ire in Imperial Knights of any house as the Chaos Knights. Such monstrosities must be destroyed for their betrayal of the Omnissiah for turning their gifts against their creators.

QUALITIES

Whether they be heroes of their household or exiled Freeblades travelling a lone adventurer's path, all Knights develop and hone a unique set of traits and skills. A Knight must always adhere to the tenets of the Code Chivalric as their legend grows, and never give into wanton, dishonourable destruction, for victory without honour is meaningless.

Each time a model gains a Quality, you can use one of the tables to determine what Quality the model has gained. To do so, first roll one D6 to determine which of the Quality tables you should select from – Sword, Shield or Lance – and then roll another D6 on the appropriate table. Alternatively, just select a Quality from a table that tells the best narrative for your model.

A model can have more than one Quality, but it can only have 1 Quality of the Sword, 1 Quality of the Shield and 1 Quality of the Lance – if a **QUESTSWORN** model already has a particular type of Quality, roll again to determine a different type of Quality table you should select from. If a **QUESTSWORN** model completes a Quest and it already has 3 Qualities, your army gains 1 Requisition point instead.

A Quality is not a Battle Honour and does not count towards the maximum number of Battle Honours a model can have. Each time a model gains a Quality, make a note on its Crusade card and increase its Crusade points by 1 if it is an **ARMIGER-CLASS** model, or by 2 if it is a **IMPERIAL KNIGHTS TITANIC** model.

Each Quality has two associated abilities. The first is an ability that the model with this Quality gains. The second is an Honour Extremis ability.

To use an Honour Extremis ability your army must currently be either Honoured or Virtuous as described in the Code Chivalric ability (pg 118). You can only use 1 Honour Extremis ability per battle round, regardless of how many models in your army have them, and if any models from your army use an Honour Extremis ability during a battle round, then at the end of the battle round you lose 1 Honour point.

QUALITY

D6	TABLE
1-2	Quality of the Sword
3-4	Quality of the Shield
5-6	Quality of the Lance

QUALITY OF THE SWORD

D6 QUALITY

1-2 Close-quarters Fighter

This pilot is a lethal close-range combatant, doing whatever is necessary to destroy their foe, no matter the reputation for recklessness and lack of restraint they might earn.

- Each time this model makes an attack, if the target of that attack is within 12" of this model, the Armour Penetration characteristic of that attack is improved by 1.
- **Honour Extremis:** Once per battle, when this model is selected to shoot or Fight, it can use this ability. If it does, until the end of the phase, each time an attack made by this model is allocated to an enemy model within 12" of this model, that enemy model cannot use any rules to ignore the wounds it loses.

3-4 Superior Duellist

This Knight has challenged the galaxy's most fearsome foes in personal combat and has perfected the art of duelling and parrying, but striking before the proper formalities have been announced is frowned on by the Code Chivalric.

- Each time a melee attack is made against this model, subtract 1 from that attack's hit roll.
- **Honour Extremis:** Once per battle, in the Fight phase, after an enemy unit has fought, if this model is eligible to fight and has not already fought this phase, it can use this ability. If it does, this model fights next.

5-6 The Marksman's Pride

This Knight has honed the art of delivering the killing blow from afar, and prides themselves on their superior aim, feeling strongly that there is little honour to be gained in expending ammunition simply to suppress an unworthy foe.

- Each time this model is selected to shoot, select one ranged weapon it is equipped with. Until the end of the phase, each time this model makes a ranged attack with that weapon, an unmodified hit roll of 6 automatically wounds the target.
- **Honour Extremis:** Once per battle, in your Shooting phase, after this model has resolved its attacks, select one enemy unit that was hit by any of those attacks. Until the start of your next Shooting phase, that enemy unit cannot fire Overwatch or Set to Defend, and each time a model in that enemy unit makes an attack, subtract 1 from that attack's hit roll.

QUALITY OF THE SHIELD

D6	QUALITY

1-2 Exemplar of the Code

This Knight exemplifies the virtues and fighting disciplines espoused by the Code Chivalric, yet on occasion appears to lack humility as they flaunt their prowess.

- When you are determining which Chivalric abilities are active for IMPERIAL KNIGHTS models in your army, if your army is Honoured then this model always counts as if your army was Virtuous. This may mean that different Chivalric abilities are active for different models in your army.
- **Honour Extremis:** Once per battle, When you are determining which Chivalric abilities are active for IMPERIAL KNIGHTS models in your army, select one Oath from the Code Chivalric (pg 118-119) that is not active for your army. Until the start of your next Command phase, that Oath is active for this model and it gains its Honoured and Virtuous Chivalric abilities (it does not gain that Oath's Pledge or Troth). Note that this Oath is active, even if every unit from your army does not have the IMPERIAL KNIGHTS keyword.

3-4 Resolute and Defiant

This Knight is adept at angling their armour plating to deflect the enemy blows, but at what point does a defensive stance become mistaken for cowardice?

- Each time an attack with a Strength characteristic of 8 or less is allocated to this model, subtract 1 from the Damage characteristic of that attack (to a minimum of 1). This is not cumulative with any other rule that reduces the Damage characteristic of an attack.
- **Honour Extremis:** Once per battle, when a saving throw is made for this model, you can use this ability. When you do so, the Damage characteristic of that attack is changed to 0.

5-6 Death Before Dishonour

This Knight always seeks to ensure his foes meet a good death in honourable combat, dying face-to-face with their challenger - for cutting cowards down as they turn and flee is surely to besmirch one's good name.

- Each time an enemy unit that is within Engagement Range of this model is selected to Fall Back, roll off with your opponent. If you win, that unit cannot Fall Back this turn.
- **Honour Extremis:** Once per battle, when an enemy unit that is within Engagement Range of this model is selected to Fall Back, that enemy unit suffers D3+3 mortal wounds.

QUALITY OF THE LANCE

D6	QUALITY

1-2 Master of Lance

This Knight is a formidable warrior, adept in all forms of combat and skilled at ensuring the enemy's defeat, if not outright bloody annihilation.

- Each time this model fights, if it made a charge move, was charged, or performed a Heroic Intervention this turn, then until that fight is resolved, add 1 to the Attacks characteristic of this model.
- **Honour Extremis:** Once per battle, at the end of the Fight phase, if this model has destroyed one or more units during this turn, it can use this ability. If it does, it can fight again.

3-4 Tireless Duty

This Knight dives into the thick of the fray without hesitation, whether honour demands it or not.

- Add 2" to the Move characteristic of this model.
- **Honour Extremis:** Once per battle, at the start of your charge phase, this model can use this ability. If it does, that model is eligible to declare a charge even if it has Fallen Back or Advanced during this turn.

5-6 Run Them Through

This knight is devastating on the charge, their every weapon thrust slaying several foes and scattering a dozen more, but at what point does the thrill of the charge and the skill of the joust turn into wanton, indiscriminate slaughter?

- Each time this model makes a melee attack, if it made a charge move this turn, an unmodified hit roll of 6 scores 1 additional hit.
- **Honour Extremis:** Once per battle, in your Fight phase, the first time this model is selected to fight, if it made a charge move this turn, it can use this ability. If it does, until that fight is resolved, each time this model makes a melee attack, on an unmodified hit roll of 6, one additional hit is scored (this is cumulative with the bullet point above, meaning that for each unmodified hit roll of 6 that is made, 3 hits will be scored).

'Consider the manner in which you slay your foe. We are noble warriors. We are not barbarians. We fight not with the brutish savagery of the greenskin, or the sadistic cruelty of the Drukhari. No, we look our foe in the eye, standing tall, armour and blades polished, our symbols and colours gleaming.'

- Baron Rakashor del Irikthius, House Blackskull

BURDENS

For all their heroic qualities, a Knight must also carry terrible burdens, and it is these unusual martial facets – as much as their chosen panoply of war – that make each warrior's legend distinct.

Each time a model gains a Burden, you can use one of the tables to determine what Burden the model has gained. To do so, first one D6 to determine which of the Burden tables you should select from - Mind, Body or Soul - and then roll another D6 on the appropriate table. Alternatively, just select a Burden from a table that tells the best narrative for your unit. A model can have more than one Burden, but it can only have 1 Burden of the Mind, 1 Burden of the Body and 1 Burden of the Soul – if a **QUESTSWORN** model already has a particular type of Burden, roll again to determine a different Burden table that you should select from. If a **QUESTSWORN** model gains a Burden while it already has 3 Burdens, it loses D6 experience points instead (to a minimum of 0) and its Shame points are reset to 0.

Each time a model gains a Burden, subtract 1 from its Crusade points total if it is an **ARMIGER CLASS** model, or by 2 if it is a **TITANIC IMPERIAL KNIGHTS** model. A Burden is not a Battle Scar and does not count towards the maximum number of Battle Scars a model can have. If a model has the Haunted by Failure or Crippling Damage Burdens, the Battle Scar it gains as a result does not reduce this model's Crusade points total further, as described on page 105 – instead, its Crusade Points are just reduced by virtue of it having a Burden, as described above.

BURDEN

D6	TABLE
1-2	Burden of the Mind
3-4	Burden of the Body
5-6	Burden of the Soul

BURDEN OF THE MIND

D6	BURDEN

1-2 Impetuous Nature

This Knight rarely takes heed when his superiors speak, their wild spirit leading them to make dangerous, irresponsible and unwise choices time and again.

Each time you use a Stratagem to affect this model, and each time you use the Command re-roll Stratagem to re-roll a dice roll made for this model, you must spend 1 additional CP or that Stratagem cannot be used.

3-4 Driven to Slaughter

This Noble pilot and their steed have suffered a traumatising defeat, and now when battle is joined, a blood-mad lunacy consumes them as they lash out at their foes with little skill or finesse.

This model's Weapon Skill characteristic is reduced by 1.

5-6 Obsessed With Vengeance

This Knight's burning desire for retribution can blind them to all else.

- Each time this model wishes to Fall Back, you must first roll 2D6: if the result is greater than this model's Leadership characteristic, it cannot Fall Back.
- Each time this model is selected to shoot, you must first roll 2D6: if the result is greater than this model's Leadership characteristic, until the end of the phase, each time this model makes a ranged attack, unless the target of that attack is the closest eligible enemy unit, subtract 1 from that attack's hit roll.
- Each time this model declares a charge you must first roll 2D6: if the result is greater than this model's Leadership characteristic, you must select the closest enemy unit as one of the targets of that charge.

'So much death have I seen. So many beloved kith and kin broken, their life force spent. So many honoured and ancient steeds shattered and burning. I cannot – will not – see this go unpunished. This I vow to the heretic foe: enjoy these times, for they shall be the last you ever experience. You will face your end at my hands.'

- Freeblade Yenior Pvortis, after the Battle of the Xorehniol Drifts on Armageddon

BURDEN OF THE BODY

D6 BURDEN

1-2 Battle Fatigue

This Knight has fought from one side of the segmentum to the other and grown weary of the ceaseless conflict, their warrior spirit ebbing with the passing years.

Subtract 1 from this model's Attacks characteristic.

3-4 Crippling Damage

This Knight suffered a blow that almost split it in twain. That the Sacristans were able to repair it to even this degree is nothing short of a miracle.

You must immediately generate two Battle Scars from the Knight Suit Battle Scars table (pg 113) that this model does not have and select one of them. This model gains that Battle Scar, it can never be removed from this model, and it does not count towards the maximum number of Battle Scars it can have.

5-6 Reckless Warrior

This Noble throws themselves into battle without pause, heedless of the risk. Though such actions may win the day, their Knight suit often pays a heavy toll for their heroics.

At the end of each battle, if this model was in your Crusade army, it must take an Out of Action test if it lost one or more wounds during that battle, even if it was not destroyed during that battle (if it was destroyed during that battle, that test is failed on a roll of 1-2).

BURDEN OF THE SOUL

D6 BURDEN

1-2 Mark of Dishonour

This Noble bears a mantle of ignominy and shame that they can never set aside.

When you are determining which Chivalric abilities are active for **IMPERIAL KNIGHTS** models in your army, models with this Burden count the number of Honour Points your army currently has as being 1 lower than it actually is (to a minimum of 1). This may mean that different Chivalric abilities are active for models with this tradition than are active for other **IMPERIAL KNIGHTS** models in your army.

3-4 Haunted by Failure

Only once did this Knight fail, but the consequences mean they now constantly second-guess their abilities.

You must immediately generate two Battle Scars from the Knight Pilot Battle Scars table (pg 112) that this model does not have and select one of them. This model gains that Battle Scar, it can never be removed from this model, and it does not count towards the maximum number of Battle Scars it can have.

5-6 Oathbound to the Dead

This Noble has seen many brothers and sisters slain whilst battling at their side. Decades later, and the unquiet ghosts that haunt this Noble are a weighty burden indeed, bearing heavily on their soul.

- Subtract 1 from Advance and charge rolls made for this model.
- Each time this model makes a ranged attack, if the target of that attack is more than 24" away, subtract 1 from that attack's hit roll.

AGENDAS

If your Crusade army includes any **IMPERIAL KNIGHTS** units, you can select one Agenda from the Imperial Knights Agendas listed below. This is a new category of Agendas, and follows all the normal rules for Agendas (for example, when you select Agendas, you cannot choose more than one from each category).

PARAGONS OF HONOUR

Imperial Knights Agenda

Without honour, victory is all but meaningless...

If you select this Agenda, then at the end of the battle:

- If your army is Virtuous, each **IMPERIAL KNIGHTS** unit from your army gains 1 experience point, and you can select one **IMPERIAL KNIGHTS** model from your army – that model loses one Shame point (pg 99), to a minimum of 0.
- If your army is Dishonoured, no **IMPERIAL KNIGHTS** models from your army can be Marked for Greatness after this battle.

HONOUR MUST BE SATISFIED

Imperial Knights Agenda

The noble households do not forget those who have deeply wronged them, and the vengeance of their Nobles can only be tempered in the blood of the hated foe.

If you select this Agenda, then before the battle, after you have deployed armies, you must select one **QUESTSWORN IMPERIAL KNIGHTS** model from your army and then identify the unit in your opponent's army that has the highest points value, and make a note of them on your army roster. A unit's points value includes the points of all weapons and wargear it is equipped with.

At the end of the battle, you gain a number of experience points if that unit has been destroyed by the **QUESTSWORN** model you selected. The number of victory points scored depends on the battle round during which the unit was destroyed, as shown in the table below.

BATTLE ROUND	EXPERIENCE POINTS
1-2	3
3-4	2
5	1

If the enemy unit was destroyed by a melee attack, at the end of the current Battle-round you gain 1 Honour point (pg 118) and at the end of the battle the selected **QUESTSWORN** model gains 2 additional experience points.

At the end of the battle, if the identified enemy unit has not been destroyed, this model gains 1 Shame point (pg 99).

'We fight for many reasons. We fight for family, honour, pride and house. We fight for world, Imperium and Emperor. All of these are worth dying a hundred times a hundred times over. Sometimes we neglect the harder, darker truth. We fight because we must. We fight because to do otherwise is to guarantee extinction.'

- *Aharbius jor Bhelengees, House Blackskull*

MARTIAN PACT

Imperial Knights Agenda

Those noble houses closely aligned to the Adeptus Mechanicus are regularly called upon by the Martian Priesthood to uphold their ancient pacts in return for forge-blessed war materiel.

If you selected this Agenda, then you start the battle with 2 fewer Command points (to a minimum of 0), and after both sides have finished deploying, your opponent must set up one objective marker anywhere on ground level on the battlefield that is not more than 6" from their own deployment zone or any battlefield edge. This objective marker represents an Omnissian Artefact, but does not count as an objective marker for any rules purposes other than for this Agenda.

QUESTOR MECHANICUS models in your army can attempt the following action, as described in the Warhammer 40,000 Core Book:

Secure Omnissian Artefact (Action): At the end of your Movement phase, one **QUESTOR MECHANICUS** model from your army that is within 3" of the Omnissian Artefact objective marker can start to perform this action if no enemy units (excluding **AIRCRAFT** units) are within 3" of that objective marker. The action is completed at the end of your next Command phase, provided that unit is still within 3" of the Omnissian Artefact objective marker. If completed, remove the Omnissian Artefact objective marker from the battlefield.

If an **ARMIGER-CLASS** model successfully completes this action, it gains 3 experience points and your Crusade force gains 2 bonus Requisition points. If a **TITANIC** model successfully completes this action, it gains 4 experience points and your Crusade force gains 2 bonus Requisition points.

SALLY FORTH

Imperial Knights Agenda

The joys of battle are upon you, surging through your systems, firing your blood. With the Code Chivalric as your guide only glory awaits. For the honour of the household! Attack!

If you select this Agenda, keep a Sally Forth tally for each model in your army.

- The first time an **IMPERIAL KNIGHTS** model from your army destroys an enemy unit while that **IMPERIAL KNIGHTS** model is not within either players' deployment zone, add 1 to that model's Sally Forth tally.
- The first time an **IMPERIAL KNIGHTS** model from your army destroys an enemy unit while that **IMPERIAL KNIGHTS** model is within your opponent's deployment zone, add 2 to that model's Sally Forth tally.

Each unit gains a number of experience points equal to their Sally Forth tally.

IMPERIAL PETITION

Imperial Knights Agenda

Whether answering a call for aid from an Imperial commander on campaign, responding to the distress call of some neighbouring world or setting off on a crusade, those noble houses with close ties to the Imperium will not be found wanting in their duty. They march to war with honour in their sights, reclaiming the Emperor's realm one adamantine footfall at a time.

If you selected this Agenda, then you start the battle with 2 fewer Command points (to a minimum of 0), and you must keep a Secure the Realm tally for each **QUESTOR IMPERIALIS** model from your army. If, after both sides have finished deploying, the battlefield has 3 or fewer objective markers on it, your opponent must set up additional objective markers on the ground level of the battlefield until there are 4 objective markers on the battlefield. Each of these additional objective markers must be set up more than 9" from any other objective marker, none can be set up within your deployment zone and only one can be set up within your opponent's deployment zone. These additional objective markers are called Realm objective markers, but they do not count as an objective marker for any rules purposes other than for this Agenda.

QUESTOR IMPERIALIS models in your army can attempt the following action, as described in the Warhammer 40,000 Core Book:

Secure the Realm (Action): One **QUESTOR IMPERIALIS** unit from your army can start to perform this action at the end of your Command phase if it is within range of an objective marker (including a Realm Objective marker) that is not within your deployment zone and which has not already been secured (see below). The action is completed at the start of your Shooting phase. If this action is successfully completed, add 1 to that unit's Secure the Realm tally and that objective marker is said to have been secured (the objective marker loses this status if your opponent controls the objective marker at the start of any phase).

Each **ARMIGER-CLASS** model gains 2 experience points for each mark on its Secure the Realm tally, and each **TITANIC** model gains 3 experience points for each mark on its Secure the Realm tally. At the end of the battle, if 2 or more objective markers (including Realm objective markers) are secured, you gain 2 bonus Requisition points.

SLAYER OF BEASTS

Imperial Knights Agenda

Few Knightly houses do not honour the slaughter of monstrous beasts. Such a deed is not only an impressive feat in its own right, but it harks many back to their earliest days, when they defended their first settlements from predatory creatures.

Keep a Slayer of Beasts tally for each **IMPERIAL KNIGHTS** unit from your army. Add 1 to a unit's Slayer of Beasts tally each time it destroys an enemy **VEHICLE** or **MONSTER** unit with a ranged attack, and add 2 its tally each time it destroys an enemy **VEHICLE** or **MONSTER** unit with a melee attack. If the destroyed unit was **TITANIC**, add an additional 2 to its tally. Each model gains a number of experience points equal to its Slayer of Beasts tally divided by 2 (rounding up).

REQUISITIONS

If your Crusade force includes any **IMPERIAL KNIGHTS** units, you can spend Requisition points (RPs) on any of the following Requisitions in addition to those presented in the Warhammer 40,000 Core Book. Note that the cost of using the Repair and Recuperate Requisition (see the Warhammer 40,000 Core Book) is increased by 1 Requisition point when it is used to remove a Battle Scar from an **IMPERIAL KNIGHTS TITANIC** model.

EXILED — 0RP/1RP

Some Knights forsake their houses to wander alone amongst the stars, or else are cast out as exiles. Such warriors are known as Freeblades, and must carve out their own path to glory.

Purchase this Requisition at any time. Select one **IMPERIAL KNIGHTS** model from your Order of Battle (excluding a **FREEBLADE**). Replace that model's **<NOBLE HOUSEHOLD>** keyword with **FREEBLADE** and select one Martial Tradition for it as described on pages 76-79 (this must be a unique Martial Tradition). If this model has the **EXALTED COURT** keyword, it keeps its upgrade, even though **FREEBLADES** cannot normally have one of the Exalted Court upgrades – replace all instances of the **<NOBLE HOUSEHOLD>** keyword (if any) on its upgraded abilities with **FREEBLADE**. If this model has two or more Knight Pilot Battle Scars (pg 112), this Requisition costs 0RP; otherwise, it costs 1RP.

OATHSWORN BONDSMAN — 1RP

While most Armigers can operate independently, it is common for their Helms Mechanicum to be neurally slaved to the command impulses of a larger Knight, rendering them subordinate. To accept such mental serfdom is to possess the rank of bondsman.

Purchase this Requisition at any time. Select one **<NOBLE HOUSEHOLD> ARMIGER-CLASS** model from your Order of Battle that does not have the **BONDSMAN** keyword and select one **<NOBLE HOUSEHOLD> TITANIC** model from your army that it will be Oathsworn to (no more than 2 models can be Oathsworn to the same model). That **ARMIGER-CLASS** model gains the **OATHSWORN BONDSMAN** keyword and you must make a note on both model's Crusade cards as to which model is Oathsworn to which. Each time you use the Command re-roll Stratagem to re-roll a dice roll made for a **BONDSMAN** model, that Stratagem costs 0CP if it is within 12" of its **OATHSWORN** model when the Stratagem is used. An **OATHSWORN BONDSMAN** model can never be Marked for Greatness.

KNIGHTLY QUEST — 1RP

Imperial Knights often undertake mighty quests, either in the name of the Code Chivalric or else to right an insult to their honour, and so continue their long history of valour and self-sacrifice.

Purchase this Requisition when an **IMPERIAL KNIGHTS** model from your Order of Battle gains a rank or when it gains a Battle Scar. If that model does not have the **QUESTSWORN** keyword, it gains it. If that model does have the **QUESTSWORN** keyword, it gains 1 Glory point.

EXALTED COURT — 1RP

Those Barons who have proved their valour and honour in battle may be elevated to join their household's Exalted Court.

Purchase this Requisition when a **QUESTORIS-CLASS CHARACTER** or **DOMINUS-CLASS CHARACTER** model (excluding **EXALTED COURT** or **FREEBLADE** models) from your Crusade force gains the Battle-hardened, Heroic or Legendary rank. That model is upgraded to the Exalted Court (pg 84-86); increase this model's Power Rating accordingly and make a note on its Crusade card. You cannot purchase this Requisition if doing so would cause your total Power Level to exceed your Crusade force's Supply Limit.

THE ARTS OF WAR — 1RP

When not in battle it is the duty of arms-masters and precepts to train young squires in the skills they will require to pilot a Knight, and to instil the mental fortitude their wards will need to endure the Ritual of Becoming.

Purchase this Requisition either before or after a battle. Select one **MENTOR** model that has a Crusade card from your Order of Battle. You can change what Knightly Teachings (pg 95) that model knows (make a note of the unit's new Knightly Teachings on its Crusade card – all the usual rules for selecting Knightly Teachings apply).

RITUAL OF BECOMING — 1RP

Having completed their training and mastered the teachings of the Code Chivalric, an aspiring pilot must survive the Ritual of Becoming in order to bond with a Throne Mechanicum and command one of the household's venerable Knights.

Purchase this Requisition at any time. Select one **ARMIGER-CLASS** model (excluding **FREEBLADES** and **CHARACTERS**) from your army that has the Battle-hardened, Heroic or Legendary Rank and roll one D6. On a 1, that model gains one Knight Pilot Battle Scar (pg 112) and you can never use this Requisition on that model again. On a 2+, replace that model with a **IMPERIAL KNIGHTS TITANIC** unit with the same **<QUESTOR ALLEGIANCE>** and **<NOBLE HOUSEHOLD>** keywords as the model it replaced. You cannot purchase this Requisition if doing so would cause your total Power Level to exceed your Crusade force's Supply Limit. The new model starts with the same number of experience points as the model it replaced and gains the appropriate number of Battle Honours for its rank. The new unit must have the same Knight Pilot Battle Honours and Knight Pilot Battle Scars (if any) as the unit it replaced. For any remaining Battle Honours, and for any Battle Honour that cannot be applied, select a new Battle Honour to replace it. You can then, if you wish, use the Knightly Quest Requisition (see above) on this model for 0RP.

CRUSADE RELICS

When an **IMPERIAL KNIGHTS CHARACTER** gains a Crusade Relic, you can instead select one of the Relics listed below. All the usual rules for selecting Crusade Relics, as described in the Warhammer 40,000 Core Book, apply. Details on how to give an **IMPERIAL KNIGHTS** model the **CHARACTER** keyword in a Crusade force can be found on page 98.

ARTIFICER RELICS

An **IMPERIAL KNIGHTS CHARACTER** model can be given one of the following Artificer Relics instead of one of the ones presented in the Warhammer 40,000 Core Book.

Electrothaumic Shields

The ion shields projected constantly spit and spark, the machine spirit belligerent and vengeful, and when a foe has the temerity to strike at it, it is roused to wrath – an arc of ionic power lashing out.

- The bearer has a 6+ invulnerable save against melee attacks.
- Each time an attack is made against the bearer, on an unmodified saving throw of 6, the closest enemy unit within 6" suffers 1 mortal wound after all of the attacking unit's attacks have been resolved (to a maximum of 3 mortal wounds).

Oathbreaker Guidance System

The noble houses claim that the machine spirits of their secondary weapons can scent dishonour, hunting out those who would hide behind their thralls and punishing them for their cowardice.

Each time the bearer selects a target for a ranged weapon it is equipped with, if that weapon is a Questor ironhail heavy stubber, a Questor cognis heavy stubber, a Preceptor multi-laser or a heavy flamer, you can ignore the Look Out, Sir rule (see the Warhammer 40,000 Core Book) when selecting targets for that weapon.

The Equerry's Vox

This vox system was installed into the Knight of a trusted vassal to an aloof High Monarch, and so the Noble was able to command the lowly masses without having to sully his own Knight getting too close to the low-born.

ARMIGER-CLASS model only. Each time the bearer is selected to be affected by a Bondsman ability, you can select one other **<NOBLE HOUSEHOLD> ARMIGER-CLASS** model within 9" of it – that model is also affected by the same Bondsman ability.

ANTIQUITY RELIC

An **IMPERIAL KNIGHTS CHARACTER** model of Heroic rank or higher can be given the following Antiquity Relic instead of one of the ones presented in the Warhammer 40,000 Core Book. Add 1 to a unit's total Crusade points for each Antiquity Relic it has – this is in addition to the +1 from gaining a Battle Honour, for a total of +2.

Laurels of Nobility

Awarded only to those Knights who have completed the Seven Trials of Sir Dannother, these laurels proclaim the selfless and virtuous fortitude of the pilot; no matter the burdens they must carry, their true spark of nobility always shines through even if they must act against the Code Chivalric for the betterment of their house.

QUESTSWORN QUESTORIS-CLASS model only.

- At the end of each of your Command phases, if your army is Dishonoured (pg 99), you can select one Honoured Chivalric ability from one of your selected Oaths. Until the end of your next Command phase, that Honoured ability is active for the bearer. This may mean that different Chivalric abilities are active for the bearer than are active for other **IMPERIAL KNIGHTS** models in your army.
- If this model has any Burdens (pg 104-105), at the start of each battle you can select one of them. That Burden does not apply to the bearer during the battle.
- Roll one D6 each time this model gains a Shame point: on a 5+, that Shame point is not gained.

LEGENDARY RELIC

An **IMPERIAL KNIGHTS CHARACTER** model of Legendary rank can be given the following Legendary Relic instead of one of the ones presented in the Warhammer 40,000 Core Book. In addition, in order to give a model a Legendary Relic, you must also pay 1 Requisition point (if you do not have enough Requisition points, you cannot give that model a Legendary Relic). Add an additional 2 to a unit's total Crusade points for each Legendary Relic it has – this is in addition to the +1 from gaining a Battle Honour, for a total of +3.

Honour's Aegis

When the first Knight worlds were rediscovered and brought back into the Imperial fold, the boon to the armies of the Imperium was great. Even amongst those towering warriors though there was rumoured to be a mythical Knight who strode at the head of every lance, their honour so pure they could not be laid low by the enemy's blows.

- While your army is Honoured, the bearer cannot lose more than 8 wounds in the same phase. Any wounds that would be lost after that point are not lost.
- While your army is Virtuous, the bearer cannot lose more than 6 wounds in the same phase. Any wounds that would be lost after that point are not lost.

BATTLE TRAITS

When an **Imperial Knights** model gains a Battle Trait, you can use one of the tables below instead of one of the tables in the Warhammer 40,000 Core Book to determine what Battle Trait the unit has gained. To do so, first roll one D6 to determine which of the Battle Trait tables you should select from, and then roll another D6 on the appropriate table. Alternatively, just select a Battle Trait from the appropriate table that tells the best narrative for your unit. All the normal rules for Battle Traits apply (e.g. a unit cannot have the same Battle Trait more than once). As with any Battle Honour, make a note on the unit's Crusade card when it gains a Battle Trait, as described in the Warhammer 40,000 Core Book, and increase its Crusade points by 1 (if it is an **Armiger-class** model) and by 2 if it is a **Imperial Knights Titanic** model.

BATTLE TRAIT

D6	BATTLE TRAIT TABLE
1-3	**Pilot:** Gain one Battle Trait from the Knight Pilot table. If this model is a **Freeblade**, you can instead choose to gain one Battle Trait from the Freeblade Pilot table.
4-6	**Knight Suit:** If this model is an **Armiger-class** model, gain one Battle Trait from the Armiger table. If this model is a **Dominus-class** model, or if it has a Wound characteristic of 28 or more, gain one Battle Trait from the Dominus table. Otherwise, gain one Battle Trait from the Questoris table.

QUESTORIS BATTLE TRAITS

(**Questoris-class** and **Imperial Knights** models with 20-27 Wounds only)

D6 TRAIT

1-2 Martial Exemplar

Such is this Knight's standing within the household that many young Nobles vie for the honour of fighting beside them.

This model gains the following ability:

Martial Exemplar (Bondsman): In your Command phase, you can select one friendly **<Noble Household> Armiger-class** model within 12" of this model and you can select one Battle Trait or Quality that this model has. Until the start of your next Command phase, that **Armiger-class** model is treated as if it had the same Battle Trait or Quality (duplicated Battle Traits or Qualities have no additional effect).

3-4 Belligerent Machine Spirit

Questoris-class Knights are prone to sudden acts of impulsive pugnacity, especially when wounded and when a foe is threatening their honour.

- Each time an attack is made by this model, if this model has less than half of its starting number of wounds, add 1 to that attack's hit roll.
- While this model has less than half of its starting number of wounds, add 1 to its Attacks characteristic.

5-6 Sanctified Armour

Every immense greave, helm and tilting shield carried by this Knight has been thrice-blessed by a dedicated army of Sacristans against the fell sorceries of witches and daemonkin.

Each time this model suffers a mortal wound, roll one D6, adding 1 to the result if your army is Virtuous: on a 5+, that wound is not lost.

KNIGHT PILOT BATTLE TRAITS

D6 TRAIT

1 Knight of Swords

This pilot is an expert swordmaster, both in and out of their Knight.

Improve the Weapon Skill characteristic of this model by 1 (to a maximum of 2+).

2 Pious Pilot

This pilot's deep wellspring of faith, be it to the Machine God or the immortal Emperor, brings much honour to their household. Fell sorcery cannot easily find a purchase on the soul of such a pious warrior.

Once per turn, this model can attempt to Deny the Witch as if it were a **Psyker**.

3 Warrior Exemplar

This Knight is an exemplar of the martial disciplines of the noble households.

Select one Martial Tradition (pg 76-79) that no model in your army has – this model gains that Martial Tradition in addition to any other Martial Traditions it has. You cannot select the Glorified History or Fealty to the Cog Martial Traditions.

4 Knight Commander

This Knight is a natural leader and is often found at the tip of any lance.

- If this model does not have the **Character** keyword, it gains it.
- Increase the range of any Bondsman abilities and Aura abilities this model has by 3".

5 Stoic Sentinel

When the foe threatens this Knight's battle lines, they ready their blades and unleash a repressive barrage of firepower that cows the enemy before them.

When an enemy unit declares a charge against this model, so long as this model is not within Engagement Range of any enemy units, it can either Hold Steady or it can Set to Defend. If this model Holds Steady, any Overwatch attacks it makes this phase will score hits on rolls of 5+. If this model Sets to Defend, it cannot fire Overwatch this phase, but until the end of the next Fight phase, each time this model makes a melee attack, add 1 to that attack's hit roll.

6 Path of Honour

Even among their peers, this Knight has been noted for their many acts of heroism and honour.

- Each time this model is Marked for Greatness, it gains 2 additional experience points.
- If this model is **Questsworn**, each time this model is Marked for Greatness, it gains 1 Glory point.

ARMIGER BATTLE TRAITS

(**Armiger-class** models only)

D6	TRAIT

1-2 Proficient Learner

This young Noble is a skill learner, not needing a lesson twice.

Each time this model is affected by a Bondsman ability (pg 117), that ability lasts until the end of the battle, or until it is affected by another Bondsman ability (whichever occurs first).

3-4 Shattered Empire Stalker

This Knight is adept at staying one step ahead of the foe.

Each time a ranged attack is made against this model, if the attacker is more than 12" away, then this model is treated as having the benefits of light cover against that attack (see the Warhammer 40,000 Core Book).

5-6 Aggressive Persecution

This eager young Noble is unstinting in ensuring that when the foe is engaged, they are doomed.

In your opponent's Movement phase, when an enemy unit that is within Engagement Range of this model is selected to fall back, if no other enemy units are within engagement range with this model, roll one D6: on a 4+, after the enemy unit has finished making their fall back move, this model can either make a normal move of up to 6" as if it were your Movement phase or it can shoot as if it were your Shooting phase. If this model shoots, when resolving its attacks this phase, it can only select targets that started the phase in engagement range with it.

DOMINUS BATTLE TRAITS

(**Dominus-class** and **Imperial Knights** models with 28+ Wounds only)

D6	TRAIT

1-2 Ionic Shieldwall

This Knight is an unyielding sentinel and a selfless protector.

Once per battle, when you use the Rotate Ion Shields or Ion Aegis Stratagems (pg 83), if you select this model for that Stratagem, it costs 0CP.

3-4 Withering Fire

Lingering in the sights of this Knight is to invite devastation.

- If a ranged attack made by this model destroys an enemy unit, subtract 1 from that unit's Out of Action test at the end of this battle.
- If this model is **Questsworn**, at the end of the battle, if one or more enemy units that were destroyed by this model during that battle failed an Out of Action test, this model gains 1 Glory point.

5-6 Pillar of Honour

This Knight is a beacon of honour, and to fight within its shadow is to be touched by a mote of that valour.

This model has the following ability:

Pillar of Honour (Aura): While a friendly **<Noble Household> Armiger-class** model is within 9" of this model, that model counts the number of Honour points your army currently has as being 1 higher than it actually is. This may mean that different Chivalric abilities are active for models with this tradition than are active for other **Imperial Knights** models in your army.

FREEBLADE PILOT BATTLE TRAITS

(**Freeblade** models only)

D6	TRAIT

1-2 Guardian of the Frontier

Long has this Freeblade fought upon the fringes against innumerable odds and the rapacious hunger that lurks beyond civilisation's borders.

At the start of Fight phase, if this model is within Engagement Range of one or more enemy units that contain 6 or more models, until the end of the phase, add 1 to this model's Strength and Attacks characteristics.

3-4 Exiled Scion

Though this Knight has since departed their household, it was not through any act of dishonour, and their name is still spoken with respect.

When you gain this Battle Trait select the name of one noble household. If this model has the **Questor Imperialis** keyword it must be a noble household that owes its allegiance to the Imperium, and if this model has the **Questor Mechanicus** keyword it must be a noble household that owes its allegiance to the Adeptus Mechanicus.

- This model gains the keyword of that noble household (e.g. **House Terryn**).
- This model can use the Noble Household Warlord Trait and Noble Household Stratagem associated with that noble household.
- This model does not, however, gain the Martial Tradition of that noble household nor access to its Heirloom Relics.

5-6 Renewed Allegiance

Though this pilot's Knight no longer wears the colours of their household, they have not forgotten their oaths of fealty.

- If this model has the **Questor Mechanicus** keyword, add 1 to the Wounds characteristic of this model; if this model is **Titanic**, add 2 to its Wounds characteristic instead.
- If this model has the **Questor Imperialis** keyword, add 1 to Advance and charge rolls made for this model and each time an Advance or charge roll is made for this model, you can ignore any or all modifiers to that Advance or charge roll.

BATTLE SCARS

When an **Imperial Knights** model gains a Battle Scar, you can use one of the tables presented here instead of one of the tables in the Warhammer 40,000 Core Book to determine what Battle Scar the unit has gained. To do so, first one D6 to determine which of the Battle Scar tables you should select from and then roll another D6 on the appropriate table. Alternatively, just select a Battle Scar from the appropriate table that tells the best narrative for your unit. All the normal rules for Battle Scars apply (e.g. a unit cannot have the same Battle Scar more than once). As with any Battle Scar, make a note on the unit's Crusade card when it gains a Battle Scar, as described in the Warhammer 40,000 Core Book, and when it gains one of the Battle Scars from the list below, subtract 1 from its Crusade points if it is an **Armiger-class** model or subtract 2 if it is a **Imperial Knights Titanic** model (to a minimum of 0).

Recall that the cost of using the Repair and Recuperate Requisition (see the Warhammer 40,000 Core Book) is increased by 1 Requisition Point when it is used to remove a Battle Scar from a **Imperial Knights Titanic** model.

BATTLE SCAR

D6	BATTLE SCAR TABLE
1-3	Gain one Battle Scar from the Knight Pilot Battle Scars table.
4-6	Gain one Battle Scar from the Knight Suit Battle Scars table.

A detonation against Madrigal of Vengeance's ion shield slammed Dammas Verenka back hard. The cockpit of the Knight Errant reverberated, metal groaning as giant servos kept the war machine balanced. Ahead, the lurching form of the Ork super-heavy walker she pursued became obscured by roiling clouds of oily fumes. Verenka bared her teeth, noble propriety keeping her from cursing loudly as she registered numerous contact signals. She had been so fixated on her quarry, she had failed to heed the insistent threat chimes. A horde of Ork bikes and transports hurtled towards her, firing a blizzard of shots and more corkscrewing missiles.

Verenka realised she had no choice but to abandon the hunt for now, though the thought galled her. She turned Madrigal of Vengeance towards the onrushing Orks, feeling a nagging slowness in one knee joint. She recognised the sign, feeling neuro-sympathic pain in her own leg. The old hurt the Sacristans had vowed was undone had returned, and she knew the cause. Madrigal of Vengeance felt its prize was denied.

'No,' she willed, 'not now! There is honour yet in culling these vermin. But we will destroy that monstrosity, by my oath.'

Verenka fired her thermal cannon, incinerating a slew of buggies. She piloted forwards in a stiff charge, ploughing into the Orks. She crunched bikers beneath her tread and slammed her gauntlet through the spine of a massive wagon, sweeping its carcass into dozens more Orks. Less than a third survived to run, their parting shots peppering her ion shields which flickered uncertainly, a fact she interpreted as the Knight's irritation.

'Now,' she whispered, a placating hand on the embossed sigil of her house, polished brightly by years of similar gestures, 'Now we hunt down that xenos abomination, I and thee.'

KNIGHT PILOT BATTLE SCARS

D6 BATTLE SCAR

1 Stain of Dishonour

This Knight's failure is a deep personal insult to those who live and die by the Code Chivalric, and their inclusion in the lance caused much political friction before battle, and much time lost that should have been used in war preparations.

At the start of your Command phase, roll one D6 for each model on the battlefield that has this Battle Scar. If any of those rolls are a 5+, you do not receive any Battle-forged CP bonus this phase (note that this means if you had any rules that would mean you gain more than 1CP, they will not apply this turn).

2 Loss of Virtue

Losing a Knight in battle is matched with a loss of standing and respect within a pilot's household.

- This model can never be affected by Virtuous abilities (pg 118-119).
- When you use an Epic Deed Stratagem, you cannot select this model for that Stratagem.

3 Pilot Trauma

This pilot sustained terrible injuries and now they cannot leave the life-sustaining machineries built onto their Throne Mechanicum. Though alive, their near-constant pain interferes with their neural link, making their bond to their Knight sluggish.

In the Fight phase, this model is not eligible to fight until after all other eligible units have fought.

4 Breaker of the Code

This Knight's transgression against the Code Chivalric is almost unforgivable, bringing the entire household's collective honour into question.

If this model is in your Crusade army, you start the battle with 1 less Honour point.

5 Disgrace to the Household

Such is the magnitude of this pilot's failure that they have become a pariah in their own household. They are one failure away from being exiled in shame.

- This model cannot use or be affected by any Bondsman abilities (pg 117).
- This model cannot perform a Heroic Intervention.
- This model cannot be Marked for Greatness.

6 Bonded in Shame

This pilot has been stripped of their right to hold land until such time as they have atoned for their failings.

- If this model has the Objective Secured ability (see the Warhammer 40,000 Core Book), it loses it. Otherwise, this model cannot have the Objective Secured ability.
- This model counts as 3 fewer models when determining control of an objective marker.

KNIGHT SUIT BATTLE SCARS

D6	BATTLE SCAR

1 Weary Machine Spirit

So long has this Knight fought that their suit's machine spirit has become worn down.

This model is considered to have 4 less wounds remaining for the purposes of determining what its characteristics are. If this model has any rule that would let it double the number of wounds it has remaining for the purposes of determining what characteristics on its profile to use (e.g. the Oathkeepers Household Tradition, page 70), after you have doubled those remaining number of wounds, you then subtract 4, and then determine which characteristics to use. This Battle Scar is ignored when determining whether a model with the Belligerent Machine Spirit Battle Trait (pg 110) gets any bonuses.

2 Fractured Hull

The blow that felled this Knight was so devastating that a fractured scar has been left on its internal structures.

- If this model is an **ARMIGER-CLASS** model, reduce its Wounds characteristic by 2.
- If this model is a **QUESTORIS-CLASS** model, reduce its Wounds characteristic by 3.
- If this model is any other **IMPERIAL KNIGHTS** model, reduce its Wounds characteristic by 4.

3 Weakened Servos

This Knight's servo-system is badly damaged and, until this Knight can undergo the rituals of repair, its strength and speed will be hampered.

- Subtract 2 from this model's Strength characteristic.
- This model cannot Advance.

4 Wounded Pride

This Knight's once noble machine spirit is now a sullen, scornful beast full of wounded pride.

- You cannot re-roll any dice rolls made for this model.
- This model can never perform an action.

5 Buckled Armour.

This Knight's armour plating is cracked and buckled beyond the skill of the Sacristans to fully restore.

Each time an attack with an Armour Penetration characteristic of 0 or -1 is allocated to this model, subtract 1 from any armour saving throw made against that attack.

6 Damaged Ion Generator

This Knight's ion generator has become damaged, and despite the ministrations of the Sacristans it has not regained its former might.

This model's Invulnerable saving throws are reduced by 1.

CRUSADE ARMY

This stunning collection of Imperial Knights belongs to James Karch, the Warhammer World Studio Manager. An avid collector of miniatures, James has a much larger, thematically linked, Imperial force of which this is but a small part.

James' ever-growing Imperium collection currently includes eleven Knights of House Taranis. He loves the Knight models and sees them as an iconic part of Warhammer 40,000. Plus, he loves the idea of having lots of big models in his collection!

James chose House Taranis primarily because of the colour scheme – he loves how the black, red and white work together – but also because they are a house aligned with the Adeptus Mechanicus. In fact, House Taranis is based on Mars, and he has painted the Adeptus Mechanicus models in his collection in the colour scheme of the Red Planet. In doing this, James has taken two collections from different codexes and narratively linked them. Thinking about building an army in this way is an excellent method for you to give yourself an even wider variety of miniatures to choose from, whether to give yourself a new painting challenge or to surprise your opponents!

The collection you see here consists of a Knight Valiant known as Ferrum Magnificat, piloted by the Noble Balthazar, an Armiger Warglaive known as Carnivore, piloted by Joscelyn, and two Armiger Helverins, known as Hound Sinistor and Oathkeeper, piloted by the lesser Nobles Mairi and Kenta. Together, they are a balanced force with the means to take on virtually any foe. The largest enemy monsters and battle-tanks stand little chance against the thundercoil harpoon of Ferrum Magnificat, or its twin meltaguns and shieldbreaker missiles. Equally, light vehicles and infantry will be torn to shreds by its twin siegebreaker cannon or turned to puddles of bubbling, molten goo by the raging infernos unleashed by its conflagration cannon. A Knight Valiant, as you can probably tell, is effectively an army in its own right, yet this one is supported by no fewer than three Armigers. Carnivore provides excellent additional anti-armour support with its thermal spear and reaper chain-cleaver. Hound Sinistor and Oathkeeper can provide vast hails of infantry and light-vehicle shredding fire support from their Armiger autocannons. With so much power in one army, not only is there redundancy in the event one Knight is damaged or even destroyed, but it makes it much harder for an opponent to decide what they need to target as a priority.

James takes full advantage of the awesome capabilities of his army in battle, his preferred strategy well-fitting the most honourable of Nobles. With no time for hiding, underhanded tactics or subtlety, he marches his Knights straight towards the foe, in full view, all weapons blazing. This is perfectly in line with the Code Chivalric, a tome which is almost considered holy writ by noble houses across the Imperium. This work tells of the importance of standing tall in the face of the enemy, showing no fear and indicating respect to the foe by not holding back when unleashing firepower or engaging in melee.

DATASHEETS

This section contains the datasheets that you will need to fight battles with your Imperial Knights miniatures, as well as an explanation of the selectable keywords found on those datasheets and details of army specific abilities. You can find out how to use datasheets in the Warhammer 40,000 Core Book.

THE <NOBLE HOUSEHOLD> KEYWORD

Every datasheet in this section has the **<NOBLE HOUSEHOLD>** keyword. This is a keyword that you can select for yourself, as described in the Warhammer 40,000 Core Book, with the guidance detailed below.

All **IMPERIAL KNIGHTS** units (excluding **FREEBLADE** units) are drawn from one of the noble households. When you include a unit with the **<NOBLE HOUSEHOLD>** keyword in your army, you must then do one of the following:

- Declare this unit belongs to a noble household, in which case you must nominate which noble household it is from. You then replace **<NOBLE HOUSEHOLD>** in every instance on its datasheet with the name of your chosen noble household. This could be one of the noble households detailed in a Warhammer 40,000 publication, or one of your own design.
- Declare this unit belongs to no noble household, in which case it is a **FREEBLADE**. You then replace **<NOBLE HOUSEHOLD>** in every instance on its datasheet with **FREEBLADE**.

Example: *If you include a Knight Paladin in your army, and you decide it is from House Hawkshroud, its* **<NOBLE HOUSEHOLD>** *keyword becomes* **HOUSE HAWKSHROUD** *and its Paladin's Duty ability reads 'In your Command phase, you can select one friendly* **HOUSE HAWKSHROUD ARMIGER-CLASS** *model within 12" of this model. Until the start of your next Command phase, each time that* **ARMIGER-CLASS** *model makes an attack, re-roll a hit roll of 1 and re-roll a wound roll of 1.'*

If your army is Battle-forged, you cannot include units drawn from two different noble household in the same Detachment, but it can include any number of **FREEBLADES** in the same Detachment. You can find out more about Battle-forged armies in the Warhammer 40,000 Core Book.

THE <QUESTOR ALLEGIANCE> KEYWORD

Many datasheets in this section have the **<QUESTOR ALLEGIANCE>** keyword. This is another keyword that you can select for yourself, as described in the Warhammer 40,000 Core Book, with the guidance detailed below.

All **IMPERIAL KNIGHTS** units owe allegiance to the Imperium or the Adeptus Mechanicus. When you include a unit with the **<QUESTOR ALLEGIANCE>** keyword in your army, after you have chosen its **<NOBLE HOUSEHOLD>** keyword, you must then do one of the following:

- If your unit is from **HOUSE TERRYN**, **HOUSE HAWKSHROUD**, **HOUSE GRIFFITH**, **HOUSE CADMUS** or **HOUSE MORTAN**, it owes its allegiance to the Imperium, and you must replace the **<QUESTOR ALLEGIANCE>** keyword in every instance on its datasheet with **QUESTOR IMPERIALIS**.
- If your unit is from **HOUSE RAVEN**, **HOUSE TARANIS**, **HOUSE KRAST** or **HOUSE VULKER**, it owes its allegiance to the Adeptus Mechanicus, and you must replace the **<QUESTOR ALLEGIANCE>** keyword in every instance on its datasheet with **QUESTOR MECHANICUS**.
- If your unit is from any other noble house, or if it has the **FREEBLADE** keyword, you must nominate whether it owes allegiance to the Imperium or the Adeptus Mechanicus. You must replace the **<QUESTOR ALLEGIANCE>** keyword in every instance on its datasheet with either **QUESTOR IMPERIALIS** or **QUESTOR MECHANICUS** respectively.

Example: *Continuing the example above, the Knight Paladin comes from* **HOUSE HAWKSHROUD**, *and as such owes allegiance to the Imperium. Its* **<QUESTOR ALLEGIANCE>** *keyword is therefore changed to* **QUESTOR IMPERIALIS**.

Some datasheets already specify whether a unit owes its allegiance to the Imperium or to the Adeptus Mechanicus (e.g. **CANIS REX** has the **QUESTOR IMPERIALIS** keyword, and owes allegiance to the Imperium).

WARGEAR & WEAPON LISTS

The weapon profiles found on a unit's datasheet describe the primary weapons that models in that unit can be equipped with. Some weapons are only referenced on a datasheet; profiles for these, and all other weapons, can be found on pages 132-133.

ABILITIES

A unit's datasheet will list all the abilities it has. Certain abilities that are common to many units are only referenced on the datasheets rather than described in full. These are described below.

ION SHIELDS

Imperial Knights are protected by a powerful directional energy field, able to ward off incoming attacks.

Models in this unit have a 5+ invulnerable save against ranged attacks.

SUPER-HEAVY WALKER

Imperial Knights tower over the battlefield, their footfalls causing the ground to shake as they step over smaller comrades to engage the foe.

This model is eligible to declare a charge in a turn in which it Fell Back. Each time this model makes a Normal Move, Advances or Falls Back, it can be moved across other models (excluding **MONSTER** and **VEHICLE** models) as if they were not there.

BONDSMAN ABILITIES

When an aspiring Knight has the honour of serving a venerated hero, they will refuse to yield while their appointed task remains unfinished, lest they bring shame on their name and that of their household.

Some **IMPERIAL KNIGHTS** have a Bondsman ability, which they can use to affect friendly models. A model can only be affected by 1 Bondsman ability at a time though. If an **IMPERIAL KNIGHTS** model is being affected by a Bondsman ability when it is selected to be affected by another Bondsman ability, the new ability replaces the old one immediately. While an **ARMIGER-CLASS** model is being affected by a Bondsman ability, if your army is either Honoured or Virtuous (see the Code Chivalric, page 118-119), in addition to any other effects, each time an attack is allocated against that model, subtract 1 from the Damage characteristic of that attack (to a minimum of 1).

- Can only be affected by 1 Bondsman ability at the same time.
- While your army is Honoured or Virtuous, subtract 1 from Damage characteristic of attacks made against an **ARMIGER-CLASS** model while it is under the effects of a Bondsman ability.

Code Chivalric

Imperial Knights fight by a stringent set of codes to ensure that in addition to defeating the enemy, honour is always upheld.

If every unit from your army has the **IMPERIAL KNIGHTS** keyword (excluding units with the **AGENTS OF THE IMPERIUM** or **UNALIGNED** keywords) and all of those units (excluding **FREEBLADES**) are from the same noble household, then when you write your army list you must also swear 2 Oaths from those in the following tables, and make a note of them on your army list.

You will start the battle with 1 Honour point. You can gain Honour points during the battle, typically by completing the Pledge of your selected Oaths. You can also lose Honour points during the battle, typically when the Troth of your selected Oaths applies. You can never have less than 0 Honour points, or more than 6. At the start of each battle round, consult the table below to determine your army's current level of Honour.

ARMY HONOUR

NUMBER OF HONOUR POINTS	ARMY'S LEVEL OF HONOUR
0	Dishonoured
1-4	Honoured
5-6	Virtuous

Models with this ability will then gain a number of Chivalric abilities depending on which are active for your army, as follows:

- Whilst your army is Dishonoured, the Honoured and Virtuous Chivalric abilities from your selected Oaths are not active.
- Whilst your army is Honoured, the Honoured Chivalric ability from your selected Oaths are active for all **IMPERIAL KNIGHTS** units in your army, but the Virtuous Chivalric abilities from your selected Oaths are not active.
- Whilst your army is Virtuous, the Honoured and Virtuous Chivalric abilities from your selected Oaths are active for all **IMPERIAL KNIGHTS** units in your army.

Oath
Protect Those in Need

Pledge

If one or both of the following happened during a battle round, then at the end of that battle round, you gain 1 Honour point:

- An **IMPERIAL KNIGHTS** model from your army performed a Heroic Intervention.
- An **IMPERIAL KNIGHTS** model from your army made a charge move against an enemy unit that started the Charge phase within engagement range of another friendly unit.

Troth

If one or both of the following happened during a battle round, at the end of the battle round, you lose 1 Honour point:

- An **IMPERIAL KNIGHTS** model from your army was eligible to declare a Heroic Intervention during your opponent's charge phase, but failed to do so.
- In your charge phase, if one or more **IMPERIAL KNIGHTS** models from your army were eligible to declare a charge against an enemy unit that started the phase within engagement range with another unit from your army, but none of them made a charge move against such an enemy unit during that phase.

Honoured Ability

Selfless Heroes: This model is eligible to perform Heroic Interventions as if it was a **CHARACTER**. If this model is a **CHARACTER**, then it is eligible to perform a Heroic Intervention if it is within 6" horizontally and 5" vertically of any enemy unit, instead of 3" horizontally and 5" vertically, and each time this model makes a Heroic Intervention move, it can move up to 6". All other rules for Heroic Interventions still apply.

Virtuous Ability

Inspiring Heroes: If this model has a Bondsman ability, it can use it one additional time in each of your Command phases.

Oath
Defend the Realm

Pledge

If, at the end of your turn, you control more objective markers than your opponent does, then at the end of that battle round, you gain 1 Honour point.

Troth

If, at the end of your turn, you control less objective markers than you did at the start of your turn, then at the end of the battle round, you lose 1 Honour point.

Honoured Ability

Duty and Wisdom: At the start of your Command phase, the Battle-forged CP bonus grants you 1 additional Command point (this will typically mean you gain 2 CPs, instead of 1).

Virtuous Ability

Duty and Honour: This model has the Objective Secured ability (see the Warhammer 40,000 Core Book). If a model already has this ability, that model instead counts as 3 additional models when determining control of an objective marker.

Oath
Refuse No Challenge

Pledge

At the end of each battle round, if 2 or more enemy units have been destroyed by melee attacks made by IMPERIAL KNIGHTS units from your army during that battle round, then you gain 1 Honour point.

Troth

If any IMPERIAL KNIGHTS units from your army fall back during a battle round, then at the end of that battle round, you lose 1 Honour point.

Honoured Ability

Noble Display: Each time this model makes a melee attack, if it made a charge move, was charged, or performed a Heroic Intervention this turn, add 1 to that attack's hit roll.

Virtuous Ability

Mighty Display: You can re-roll Advance and charge rolls made for this model.

Oath
Lay Low The Tyrants

Pledge

If an IMPERIAL KNIGHTS model from your army destroyed 1 or more WARLORD, CHARACTER, MONSTER or VEHICLE units during a battle round with a melee attack, then at the end of that battle round you gain 1 Honour point.

Troth

If less than 2 enemy units have been destroyed by attacks made by IMPERIAL KNIGHTS units from your army during that battle round, then you lose 1 Honour point.

Honoured Ability

Martial Pride: Each time this model is selected to shoot or fight, you can re-roll one hit roll or one wound roll.

Virtuous Ability

Martial Legacy: Once per battle round, when you make an Advance roll, hit roll, wound roll, or saving throw for one IMPERIAL KNIGHTS model from your army, you can change the result of that roll to a 6.

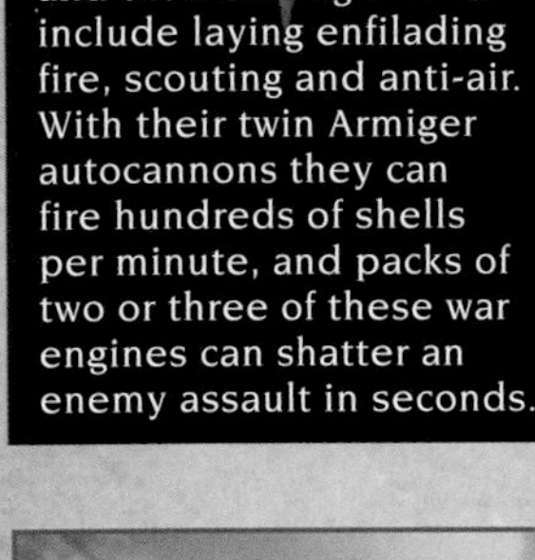

These fast-moving Knights have been designed to lay down hails of heavy fire while running rings around enemy forces, and their strategic roles include laying enfilading fire, scouting and anti-air. With their twin Armiger autocannons they can fire hundreds of shells per minute, and packs of two or three of these war engines can shatter an enemy assault in seconds.

ARMIGER HELVERIN **8** POWER

Some of this model's characteristics change as it suffers damage, as shown below:

No.	Name	M	WS	BS	S	T	W	A	Ld	Sv
1-3	Armiger Helverin (7+ wounds remaining)	12"	3+	3+	6	7	12	4	8	3+
	Armiger Helverin (4-6 wounds remaining)	10"	4+	4+	6	7	N/A	4	8	3+
	Armiger Helverin (1-3 wounds remaining)	8"	5+	5+	6	7	N/A	4	8	3+

If this unit contains 2 models, it has **Power Rating 16**. If this unit contains 3 models, it has **Power Rating 24**. Every model is equipped with: 2 Armiger autocannons; meltagun.

WEAPON	RANGE	TYPE	S	AP	D	ABILITIES
Armiger autocannon	60"	Heavy 2D3	7	-2	3	-
Meltagun	12"	Assault 1	8	-4	D6	Each time an attack made with this weapon targets a unit within half range, that attack has a Damage characteristic of D6+2.

WARGEAR OPTIONS

- If this unit has the **QUESTOR MECHANICUS** keyword, any number of models can each have their meltagun replaced with 1 Questor cognis heavy stubber.
- If this unit has the **QUESTOR IMPERIALIS** keyword, any number of models can each have their meltagun replaced with 1 Questor ironhail heavy stubber.

ABILITIES

Ion Shields, Code Chivalric (pg 117-119)

Armiger Squadron: The first time this unit is set up on the battlefield, if this unit contains more than one model, each model in this unit must be set up within 6" of at least one other model from this unit. From that point onwards, each model operates independently and is treated as a separate unit.

Explodes: When this model is destroyed, roll one D6 before removing it from play. On a 6 it explodes, and each unit within 6" suffers D3 mortal wounds.

FACTION KEYWORDS: **IMPERIUM, IMPERIAL KNIGHTS, <QUESTOR ALLEGIANCE>, <NOBLE HOUSEHOLD>**
KEYWORDS: **VEHICLE, CORE, ARMIGER-CLASS, ARMIGER HELVERIN**

ARMIGER WARGLAIVE

8 POWER

Some of this model's characteristics change as it suffers damage, as shown below:

No.	Name	M	WS	BS	S	T	W	A	Ld	Sv
1-3	Armiger Warglaive (7+ wounds remaining)	12"	3+	3+	6	7	12	4	8	3+
	Armiger Warglaive (4-6 wounds remaining)	10"	4+	4+	6	7	N/A	4	8	3+
	Armiger Warglaive (1-3 wounds remaining)	8"	5+	5+	6	7	N/A	4	8	3+

If this unit contains 2 models, it has **Power Rating 16**. If this unit contains 3 models, it has **Power Rating 24**. Every model is equipped with: meltagun; thermal spear; reaper chain-cleaver.

WEAPON	RANGE	TYPE	S	AP	D	ABILITIES
Meltagun	12"	Assault 1	8	-4	D6	Each time an attack made with this weapon targets a unit within half range, that attack has a Damage characteristic of D6+2.
Thermal spear	30"	Heavy 2	9	-4	D6	Each time an attack made with this weapon targets a unit within half range, that attack has a Damage characteristic of D6+2.
Reaper chain-cleaver	Each time an attack is made with this weapon, select one of the profiles below to make that attack with.					
- Strike	Melee	Melee	+4	-4	3	-
- Sweep	Melee	Melee	User	-3	1	Each time an attack is made with this weapon profile, make 2 hit rolls instead of 1.

WARGEAR OPTIONS

- If this unit has the **QUESTOR MECHANICUS** keyword, any number of models can each have their meltagun replaced with 1 Questor cognis heavy stubber.
- If this unit has the **QUESTOR IMPERIALIS** keyword, any number of models can each have their meltagun replaced with 1 Questor ironhail heavy stubber.

ABILITIES

Ion Shields, Code Chivalric (pg 117-119)

Armiger Squadron: The first time this unit is set up on the battlefield, if this unit contains more than one model, each model in this unit must be set up within 6" of at least one other model from this unit. From that point onwards, each model operates independently and is treated as a separate unit.

Explodes: When this model is destroyed, roll one D6 before removing it from play. On a 6 it explodes, and each unit within 6" suffers D3 mortal wounds.

FACTION KEYWORDS: **IMPERIUM, IMPERIAL KNIGHTS, <QUESTOR ALLEGIANCE>, <NOBLE HOUSEHOLD>**
KEYWORDS: **VEHICLE, CORE, ARMIGER-CLASS, ARMIGER WARGLAIVE**

Armiger Warglaives are nimble and purposeful Knights that possess exceptional speed that allows them to outpace most vehicles. This, in combination with their thermal spears that can melt bunkers and battle-tank armour alike, makes them fearsome hunters of enemy war engines.

KNIGHT ERRANT

23 POWER

Some of this model's characteristics change as it suffers damage, as shown below:

No.	Name	M	WS	BS	S	T	W	A	Ld	Sv
1	Knight Errant (13+ wounds remaining)	10"	3+	3+	8	8	24	4	9	3+
	Knight Errant (7-12 wounds remaining)	8"	4+	4+	8	8	N/A	4	9	3+
	Knight Errant (1-6 wounds remaining)	6"	5+	5+	8	8	N/A	4	9	3+

A Knight Errant is equipped with: meltagun; thermal cannon; reaper chainsword; titanic feet.

WEAPON	RANGE	TYPE	S	AP	D	ABILITIES
Meltagun	12"	Assault 1	8	-4	D6	Each time an attack made with this weapon targets a unit within half range, that attack has a Damage characteristic of D6+2.
Thermal cannon	30"	Heavy 2D3	9	-4	D6+2	Blast. Each time an attack made with this weapon targets a unit within half range, that attack has a Damage characteristic of D6+4.
Reaper chainsword	Each time an attack is made with this weapon, select one of the profiles below to make that attack with.					
- Strike	Melee	Melee	+6	-4	6	-
- Sweep	Melee	Melee	User	-3	2	Each time an attack is made with this weapon profile, make 3 hit rolls instead of 1.
Titanic feet	Melee	Melee	User	-2	2	-

WARGEAR OPTIONS

- If this model has the **QUESTOR MECHANICUS** keyword, its meltagun can be replaced with 1 Questor cognis heavy stubber.
- If this model has the **QUESTOR IMPERIALIS** keyword, its meltagun can be replaced with 1 Questor ironhail heavy stubber.
- This model's reaper chainsword can be replaced with 1 thunderstrike gauntlet.
- This model can be equipped with one of the following: 1 ironstorm missile pod; 1 stormspear rocket pod; 1 twin Icarus autocannon.

ABILITIES

Ion Shields, Super-heavy Walker, Code Chivalric (pg 117-119)

Errant's Duty (Bondsman): In your Command phase, you can select one friendly **<NOBLE HOUSEHOLD> ARMIGER-CLASS** model within 12" of this model. Until the start of your next Command phase, that **ARMIGER-CLASS** model is eligible to declare a charge in a turn in which it advanced, and you add 1 to Advance and Charge rolls made for that **ARMIGER-CLASS** model.

Explodes: When this model is destroyed, roll one D6 before removing it from play. On a 6 it explodes, and each unit within 2D6" suffers D6 mortal wounds.

FACTION KEYWORDS: **IMPERIUM, IMPERIAL KNIGHTS, <QUESTOR ALLEGIANCE>, <NOBLE HOUSEHOLD>**
KEYWORDS: **VEHICLE, TITANIC, QUESTORIS-CLASS, KNIGHT ERRANT**

These aggressive, mid-to-close range assault Knights excel at hunting enemy tanks and monsters thanks to their powerful thermal cannons, reaper chainswords and thunderstrike gauntlets, and typically plunge into the fiercest fighting.

KNIGHT WARDEN

23 POWER

Some of this model's characteristics change as it suffers damage, as shown below:

No.	Name	M	WS	BS	S	T	W	A	Ld	Sv
1	Knight Warden (13+ wounds remaining)	10"	3+	3+	8	8	24	4	9	3+
	Knight Warden (7-12 wounds remaining)	8"	4+	4+	8	8	N/A	4	9	3+
	Knight Warden (1-6 wounds remaining)	6"	5+	5+	8	8	N/A	4	9	3+

A Knight Warden is equipped with: avenger gatling cannon; heavy flamer; meltagun; reaper chainsword; titanic feet.

WEAPON	RANGE	TYPE	S	AP	D	ABILITIES
Avenger gatling cannon	36"	Heavy 12	6	-2	2	-
Heavy flamer	12"	Heavy D6	5	-1	1	Each time an attack is made with this weapon, that attack automatically hits the target.
Meltagun	12"	Assault 1	8	-4	D6	Each time an attack made with this weapon targets a unit within half range, that attack has a Damage characteristic of D6+2.
Reaper chainsword	Each time an attack is made with this weapon, select one of the profiles below to make that attack with.					
- Strike	Melee	Melee	+6	-4	6	-
- Sweep	Melee	Melee	User	-3	2	Each time an attack is made with this weapon profile, make 3 hit rolls instead of 1.
Titanic feet	Melee	Melee	User	-2	2	-

WARGEAR OPTIONS

- If this model has the **QUESTOR MECHANICUS** keyword, its meltagun can be replaced with 1 Questor cognis heavy stubber.
- If this model has the **QUESTOR IMPERIALIS** keyword, its meltagun can be replaced with 1 Questor ironhail heavy stubber.
- This model's reaper chainsword can be replaced with 1 thunderstrike gauntlet.
- This model can be equipped with one of the following: 1 ironstorm missile pod; 1 stormspear rocket pod; 1 twin Icarus autocannon.

ABILITIES

Ion Shields, Super-heavy Walker, Code Chivalric (pg 117-119)

Warden's Duty (Bondsman): In your Command phase, you can select one friendly **<NOBLE HOUSEHOLD> ARMIGER-CLASS** model within 12" of this model. Until the start of your next Command phase, that **ARMIGER-CLASS** model counts as 10 models for the purposes of determining which player controls objective markers.

Explodes: When this model is destroyed, roll one D6 before removing it from play. On a 6 it explodes, and each unit within 2D6" suffers D6 mortal wounds.

FACTION KEYWORDS: **IMPERIUM, IMPERIAL KNIGHTS, <QUESTOR ALLEGIANCE>, <NOBLE HOUSEHOLD>**
KEYWORDS: **VEHICLE, TITANIC, QUESTORIS-CLASS, KNIGHT WARDEN**

With an avenger gatling cannon that spits hundreds of foot-long armour-piercing shells per minute, these Knights are well suited to annihilating enemy infantry, light vehicles and transports. The suits themselves possess strong-willed machine spirits, and it is a great mark of accomplishment for a Noble to pilot one.

Armed with a bristling array of heavy and long-ranged weapons, the Knight Crusader finds key firing positions and unleashes salvo after salvo at the enemy. Pilots will gladly steer their suits even into open ground to find the best place to shoot from, and are regarded as especially dutiful and selfless by their peers.

KNIGHT CRUSADER

26 POWER

Some of this model's characteristics change as it suffers damage, as shown below:

No.	Name	M	WS	BS	S	T	W	A	Ld	Sv
1	Knight Crusader (13+ wounds remaining)	**10"**	**3+**	**3+**	8	8	24	4	9	3+
	Knight Crusader (7-12 wounds remaining)	**8"**	**4+**	**4+**	8	8	N/A	4	9	3+
	Knight Crusader (1-6 wounds remaining)	**6"**	**5+**	**5+**	8	8	N/A	4	9	3+

A Knight Crusader is equipped with: avenger gatling cannon; heavy flamer; meltagun; thermal cannon; titanic feet.

WEAPON	RANGE	TYPE	S	AP	D	ABILITIES
Avenger gatling cannon	36"	Heavy 12	6	-2	2	-
Heavy flamer	12"	Heavy D6	5	-1	1	Each time an attack is made with this weapon, that attack automatically hits the target.
Meltagun	12"	Assault 1	8	-4	D6	Each time an attack made with this weapon targets a unit within half range, that attack has a Damage characteristic of D6+2.
Thermal cannon	30"	Heavy 2D3	9	-4	D6+2	Blast. Each time an attack made with this weapon targets a unit within half range, that attack has a Damage characteristic of D6+4.
Titanic feet	Melee	Melee	User	-2	2	-

WARGEAR OPTIONS

- If this model has the **QUESTOR MECHANICUS** keyword:
  - Its meltagun can be replaced with 1 Questor cognis heavy stubber.
  - Its thermal cannon can be replaced with: 1 rapid-fire battle cannon and 1 Questor cognis heavy stubber.
- If this model has the **QUESTOR IMPERIALIS** keyword:
  - Its meltagun can be replaced with 1 Questor ironhail heavy stubber.
  - Its thermal cannon can be replaced with 1 rapid-fire battle cannon and 1 Questor ironhail heavy stubber.
- This model can be equipped with one of the following: 1 ironstorm missile pod; 1 stormspear rocket pod; 1 twin Icarus autocannon.

ABILITIES

Ion Shields, Super-heavy Walker, Code Chivalric (pg 117-119)

Crusader's Duty (Bondsman): In your Command phase, you can select one friendly **<NOBLE HOUSEHOLD> ARMIGER-CLASS** model within 12" of this model. Until the start of your next Command phase, improve that **ARMIGER-CLASS** model's Ballistic Skill characteristic by 1.

Explodes: When this model is destroyed, roll one D6 before removing it from play. On a 6 it explodes, and each unit within 2D6" suffers D6 mortal wounds.

FACTION KEYWORDS: **IMPERIUM, IMPERIAL KNIGHTS, <QUESTOR ALLEGIANCE>, <NOBLE HOUSEHOLD>**
KEYWORDS: **VEHICLE, TITANIC, QUESTORIS-CLASS, KNIGHT CRUSADER**

KNIGHT GALLANT

21 POWER

Some of this model's characteristics change as it suffers damage, as shown below:

No.	Name	M	WS	BS	S	T	W	A	Ld	Sv
1	Knight Gallant (13+ wounds remaining)	12"	2+	3+	8	8	24	5	9	3+
	Knight Gallant (7-12 wounds remaining)	10"	3+	4+	8	8	N/A	5	9	3+
	Knight Gallant (1-6 wounds remaining)	8"	4+	5+	8	8	N/A	5	9	3+

A Knight Gallant is equipped with: meltagun; reaper chainsword; thunderstrike gauntlet; titanic feet.

WEAPON	RANGE	TYPE	S	AP	D	ABILITIES
Meltagun	12"	Assault 1	8	-4	D6	Each time an attack made with this weapon targets a unit within half range, that attack has a Damage characteristic of D6+2.
Reaper chainsword	Each time an attack is made with this weapon, select one of the profiles below to make that attack with.					
- Strike	Melee	Melee	+6	-4	6	-
- Sweep	Melee	Melee	User	-3	2	Each time an attack is made with this weapon profile, make 3 hit rolls instead of 1.
Thunderstrike gauntlet	Each time an attack is made with this weapon, select one of the profiles below to make that attack with.					
- Strike	Melee	Melee	x2	-3	8	-
- Sweep	Melee	Melee	+2	-2	3	Each time an attack is made with this weapon profile, make 2 hit rolls instead of 1.
Titanic feet	Melee	Melee	User	-2	2	-

WARGEAR OPTIONS

- If this model has the **QUESTOR MECHANICUS** keyword, its meltagun can be replaced with 1 Questor cognis heavy stubber.
- If this model has the **QUESTOR IMPERIALIS** keyword, its meltagun can be replaced with 1 Questor ironhail heavy stubber.
- This model can be equipped with one of the following: 1 ironstorm missile pod; 1 stormspear rocket pod; 1 twin Icarus autocannon.

ABILITIES

Ion Shields, Super-heavy Walker, Code Chivalric (pg 117-119)

Gallant's Duty (Bondsman): In your Command phase, you can select one friendly **<NOBLE HOUSEHOLD> ARMIGER-CLASS** model within 12" of this model. Until the start of your next Command phase, improve that **ARMIGER-CLASS** model's Weapon Skill characteristic by 1.

Explodes: When this model is destroyed, roll one D6 before removing it from play. On a 6 it explodes, and each unit within 2D6" suffers D6 mortal wounds.

FACTION KEYWORDS: **IMPERIUM, IMPERIAL KNIGHTS, <QUESTOR ALLEGIANCE>, <NOBLE HOUSEHOLD>**
KEYWORDS: **VEHICLE, TITANIC, QUESTORIS-CLASS, KNIGHT GALLANT**

Gallants are the most restless and combative of Knights, and have been described as impetuous and beyond bellicose. They are aggressive, bold and difficult to restrain, and their pilots often share these traits. As befitting their nature, they are armed almost exclusively with close combat weapons.

KNIGHT PALADIN

23 POWER

Some of this model's characteristics change as it suffers damage, as shown below:

No.	Name	M	WS	BS	S	T	W	A	Ld	Sv
1	Knight Paladin (13+ wounds remaining)	**10"**	**3+**	**3+**	8	8	24	4	9	3+
	Knight Paladin (7-12 wounds remaining)	**8"**	**4+**	**4+**	8	8	N/A	4	9	3+
	Knight Paladin (1-6 wounds remaining)	**6"**	**5+**	**5+**	8	8	N/A	4	9	3+

A Knight Paladin is equipped with: meltagun; rapid-fire battle cannon; reaper chainsword; titanic feet. If this model has the **QUESTOR MECHANICUS** keyword, is it also equipped with a Questor cognis heavy stubber. If this model has the **QUESTOR IMPERIALIS** keyword, it is also equipped with a Questor ironhail heavy stubber.

WEAPON	RANGE	TYPE	S	AP	D	ABILITIES
Meltagun	12"	Assault 1	8	-4	D6	Each time an attack made with this weapon targets a unit within half range, that attack has a Damage characteristic of D6+2.
Questor cognis heavy stubber	36"	Assault 4	4	0	1	-
Questor ironhail heavy stubber	36"	Heavy 4	4	-1	1	-
Rapid-fire battle cannon	72"	Heavy 2D6	8	-2	3	Blast
Reaper chainsword	Each time an attack is made with this weapon, select one of the profiles below to make that attack with.					
- Strike	Melee	Melee	+6	-4	6	-
- Sweep	Melee	Melee	User	-2	2	Each time an attack is made with this weapon profile, make 3 hit rolls instead of 1.
Titanic feet	Melee	Melee	User	-2	2	-

WARGEAR OPTIONS

- If this model has the **QUESTOR MECHANICUS** keyword, its meltagun can be replaced with 1 Questor cognis heavy stubber.
- If this model has the **QUESTOR IMPERIALIS** keyword, its meltagun can be replaced with 1 Questor ironhail heavy stubber.
- This model's reaper chainsword can be replaced with 1 thunderstrike gauntlet.
- This model can be equipped with one of the following: 1 ironstorm missile pod; 1 stormspear rocket pod; 1 twin Icarus autocannon.

ABILITIES

Ion Shields, Super-heavy Walker, Code Chivalric (pg 117-119)

Paladin's Duty (Bondsman): In your Command phase, you can select one friendly **<NOBLE HOUSEHOLD> ARMIGER-CLASS** model within 12" of this model. Until the start of your next Command phase, each time that **ARMIGER-CLASS** model makes an attack, re-roll a hit roll of 1 and re-roll a wound roll of 1.

Explodes: When this model is destroyed, roll one D6 before removing it from play. On a 6 it explodes, and each unit within 2D6" suffers D6 mortal wounds.

FACTION KEYWORDS: **IMPERIUM, IMPERIAL KNIGHTS, <QUESTOR ALLEGIANCE>, <NOBLE HOUSEHOLD>**
KEYWORDS: **VEHICLE, TITANIC, QUESTORIS-CLASS, KNIGHT PALADIN**

These highly versatile Knights provide strategic backbone to many lances. While not specialised, they are favoured by most houses for their combination rapid-fire battle cannon, a direct-firing artillery gun, and a powerful close combat weapon. Seasoned Nobles prize these suits, and their experience enables them to get the best use from them.

KNIGHT CASTELLAN

31 POWER

Some of this model's characteristics change as it suffers damage, as shown below:

No.	Name	M	WS	BS	S	T	W	A	Ld	Sv
1	Knight Castellan (15+ wounds remaining)	**8"**	**4+**	**3+**	8	8	28	4	9	2+
	Knight Castellan (8-14 wounds remaining)	**6"**	**5+**	**4+**	8	8	N/A	4	9	2+
	Knight Castellan (1-7 wounds remaining)	**4"**	**6+**	**5+**	8	8	N/A	4	9	2+

A Knight Castellan is equipped with: plasma decimator; 4 shieldbreaker missiles; 2 twin meltaguns; twin siegebreaker cannon; volcano lance; titanic feet.

WEAPON	RANGE	TYPE	S	AP	D	ABILITIES
Plasma decimator	Before selecting targets, select one of the profiles below to make attacks with.					
- Standard	48"	Heavy 2D6	8	-4	2	Blast
- Supercharge	48"	Heavy 2D6	9	-4	3	Blast. Each time an unmodified hit roll of 1 is made for an attack with this weapon profile, the bearer suffers 2 mortal wounds after shooting with this weapon profile.
Shieldbreaker missile	48"	Heavy 1	10	-4	D6	Each time the bearer is selected to shoot, it can only make attacks with one shieldbreaker missile, and it can only shoot each shieldbreaker missile it is equipped with once per battle. Each time an attack is made with this weapon, invulnerable saving throws cannot be made against that attack.
Twin meltagun	12"	Assault 2	8	-4	D6	Each time an attack made with this weapon targets a unit within half range, that attack has a Damage characteristic of D6+2.
Twin siegebreaker cannon	36"	Heavy 2D3	7	-1	2	Blast
Volcano lance	80"	Heavy D3	16	-5	D6+8	Blast
Titanic feet	Melee	Melee	User	-2	2	-

WARGEAR OPTIONS

- This model's 4 shieldbreaker missiles and twin siegebreaker cannon can be replaced with 2 shieldbreaker missiles and 2 twin siegebreaker cannons.

ABILITIES

Ion Shields, Super-heavy Walker, Code Chivalric (pg 117-119)

Explodes: When this model is destroyed, roll two D6 before removing it from play. If either of the dice are a 6, it explodes, and each unit within 2D6" suffers D6 mortal wounds (if both of the dice are a 6, each unit within 3D6" suffers D6 mortal wounds instead).

FACTION KEYWORDS: **Imperium, Imperial Knights, <Questor Allegiance>, <Noble Household>**
KEYWORDS: **Vehicle, Titanic, Dominus-class, Knight Castellan**

Based around a Dominus-class chassis, the Knight Castellan is like a towering fortress. Its dual plasma core fuels a frightening array of weapon systems that make it among the foremost artillery Knights of the houses. The combined fire of several of these engines can equal that of an Imperial Navy warship battery, and easily tear the heart out of an enemy army.

KNIGHT VALIANT

30 POWER

Some of this model's characteristics change as it suffers damage, as shown below:

No.	Name	M	WS	BS	S	T	W	A	Ld	Sv
1	Knight Valiant (15+ wounds remaining)	**8"**	**4+**	**3+**	8	8	28	4	9	2+
	Knight Valiant (8-14 wounds remaining)	**6"**	**5+**	**4+**	8	8	N/A	4	9	2+
	Knight Valiant (1-7 wounds remaining)	**4"**	**6+**	**5+**	8	8	N/A	4	9	2+

A Knight Valiant is equipped with: conflagration cannon; 4 shieldbreaker missiles; thundercoil harpoon; 2 twin meltaguns; twin siegebreaker cannon; titanic feet.

WEAPON	RANGE	TYPE	S	AP	D	ABILITIES
Conflagration cannon	18"	Heavy 3D6	7	-2	2	Each time an attack is made with this weapon, that attack automatically hits the target.
Shieldbreaker missile	48"	Heavy 1	10	-4	D6	Each time the bearer is selected to shoot, it can only make attacks with one shieldbreaker missile, and it can only shoot each shieldbreaker missile it is equipped with once per battle. Each time an attack is made with this weapon, invulnerable saving throws cannot be made against that attack.
Thundercoil harpoon	18"	Heavy 1	16	-6	10	Each time an attack is made with this weapon against an **MONSTER** or **VEHICLE** unit (excluding **AIRCRAFT**), add 1 to that attack's hit roll. Each time an attack made with this weapon is allocated to a model, that model's unit suffers 3 mortal wounds in addition to the normal damage.
Twin meltagun	12"	Assault 2	8	-4	D6	Each time an attack made with this weapon targets a unit within half range, that attack has a Damage characteristic of D6+2.
Twin siegebreaker cannon	36"	Heavy 2D3	7	-1	2	Blast
Titanic feet	Melee	Melee	User	-2	2	-

WARGEAR OPTIONS

- This model's 4 shieldbreaker missiles and twin siegebreaker cannon can be replaced with 2 shieldbreaker missiles and 2 twin siegebreaker cannons.

ABILITIES

Ion Shields, Super-heavy Walker, Code Chivalric (pg 117-119)

Explodes: When this model is destroyed, roll two D6 before removing it from play. If either of the dice are a 6, it explodes, and each unit within 2D6" suffers D6 mortal wounds (if both of the dice are a 6, each unit within 3D6" suffers D6 mortal wounds instead).

FACTION KEYWORDS: **IMPERIUM, IMPERIAL KNIGHTS, <QUESTOR ALLEGIANCE>, <NOBLE HOUSEHOLD>**
KEYWORDS: **VEHICLE, TITANIC, DOMINUS-CLASS, KNIGHT VALIANT**

This Dominus-class Knight defeats its enemies through overwhelming firepower at close range. Thanks to its conflagration cannon unleashing a searing, inescapable firestorm, it can easily annihilate incoming hordes or smash through opposing battle lines, and with its thundercoil harpoon it can destroy tanks and monsters with impunity.

KNIGHT PRECEPTOR

22 POWER

Some of this model's characteristics change as it suffers damage, as shown below:

No.	Name	M	WS	BS	S	T	W	A	Ld	Sv
1	Knight Preceptor (13+ wounds remaining)	10"	3+	3+	8	8	24	4	9	3+
	Knight Preceptor (7-12 wounds remaining)	8"	4+	4+	8	8	N/A	4	9	3+
	Knight Preceptor (1-6 wounds remaining)	6"	5+	5+	8	8	N/A	4	9	3+

A Knight Preceptor is equipped with: las-impulsor, Preceptor multi-laser; reaper chainsword; titanic feet.

WEAPON	RANGE	TYPE	S	AP	D	ABILITIES
Las-impulsor	Before selecting targets, select one of the profiles below to make attacks with.					
- Low intensity	36"	Heavy 2D6	6	-2	2	Blast
- High intensity	24"	Heavy D6	12	-4	4	Blast
Preceptor multi-laser	36"	Heavy 4	6	0	1	-
Reaper chainsword	Each time an attack is made with this weapon, select one of the profiles below to make that attack with.					
- Strike	Melee	Melee	+6	-4	6	-
- Sweep	Melee	Melee	User	-3	2	Each time an attack is made with this weapon profile, make 3 hit rolls instead of 1.
Titanic feet	Melee	Melee	User	-2	2	-

WARGEAR OPTIONS

- If this model has the **QUESTOR MECHANICUS** keyword, its Preceptor multi-laser can be replaced with one of the following: 1 meltagun; 1 Questor cognis heavy stubber.
- If this model has the **QUESTOR IMPERIALIS** keyword, its Preceptor multi-laser can be replaced with one of the following: 1 meltagun; 1 Questor ironhail heavy stubber.
- This model's reaper chainsword can be replaced with 1 thunderstrike gauntlet.
- This model can be equipped with one of the following: 1 ironstorm missile pod; 1 stormspear rocket pod; 1 twin Icarus autocannon.

ABILITIES

Ion Shields, Super-heavy Walker, Code Chivalric (pg 117-119)

Explodes: When this model is destroyed, roll one D6 before removing it from play. On a 6 it explodes, and each unit within 2D6" suffers D6 mortal wounds.

MENTOR

This model knows three teachings from the Knightly Teachings (pg 95). In your Command phase, if this model is on the battlefield, it can recount up to two teachings it knows that have not already been recounted by a friendly model this turn. Roll one D6: on a 3+, the recounted teaching is inspiring and takes effect until the start of your next Command phase.

FACTION KEYWORDS: **IMPERIUM, IMPERIAL KNIGHTS, <QUESTOR ALLEGIANCE>, <NOBLE HOUSEHOLD>**
KEYWORDS: **VEHICLE, TITANIC, QUESTORIS-CLASS, MENTOR, KNIGHT PRECEPTOR**

Knight Preceptors are designed to embody the code chivalric. Their pilots close to an honourable range with the foe, engage with enough force to show them respect and kill them cleanly with their las-impulsors. Typically, grizzled veterans pilot these Knights, and set an example for their younger comrades by hunting down the largest and most fearsome enemies.

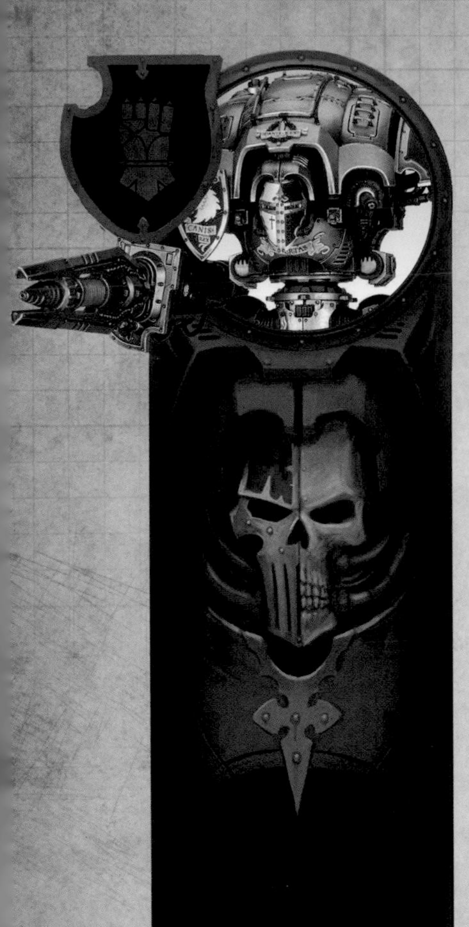

CANIS REX

22 POWER

Some of this model's characteristics change as it suffers damage, as shown below:

No.	Name	M	WS	BS	S	T	W	A	Ld	Sv
1	Canis Rex (13+ wounds remaining)	10"	2+	2+	8	8	24	5	9	3+
	Canis Rex (7-12 wounds remaining)	8"	3+	3+	8	8	N/A	5	9	3+
	Canis Rex (1-6 wounds remaining)	6"	4+	4+	8	8	N/A	5	9	3+
*	Sir Hekhtur	6"	2+	2+	3	3	4	3	9	4+

Canis Rex is equipped with: las-impulsor, Preceptor multi-laser; Freedom's Hand; titanic feet. **Sir Hekhtur** begins the battle piloting **Canis Rex** (see the Sir Hekhtur ability below). Your army can only include 1 **Canis Rex** model.

WEAPON	RANGE	TYPE	S	AP	D	ABILITIES
Hekhtur's pistol	15"	Pistol 1	5	-2	2	-
Las-impulsor	Before selecting targets, select one of the profiles below to make attacks with.					
- Low intensity	36"	Heavy 2D6	6	-2	2	Blast
- High intensity	24"	Heavy D6	12	-4	4	Blast
Preceptor multi-laser	36"	Heavy 4	6	0	1	-
Freedom's Hand	Each time an attack is made with this weapon, select one of the profiles below to make that attack with.					
- Strike	Melee	Melee	x2	-4	8	Each time an attack is made with this weapon profile, an unmodified wound roll of 6 inflicts D3 mortal wounds on the target in addition to the normal damage.
- Sweep	Melee	Melee	+2	-2	3	Each time an attack is made with this weapon profile, make 2 hit rolls instead of 1 and an unmodified wound roll of 6 inflicts 1 mortal wound on the target in addition to the normal damage.
Titanic feet	Melee	Melee	User	-2	2	-

ABILITIES

Ion Shields, Super-heavy Walker, Code Chivalric (pg 117-119)

Sir Hekhtur: If **Canis Rex** is destroyed but does not explode, set up **Sir Hekhtur** within 3" of **Canis Rex** before it is removed. **Sir Hekhtur** is treated as a passenger disembarking from a destroyed **Transport** (see the Warhammer 40,000 Core Book). Assuming he survives, **Sir Hekhtur** then uses his own profile and his own keywords below. He is equipped with Hekhtur's pistol but does not have the Ion Shields or Super-heavy Walker abilities. This unit is not considered to have been destroyed until **Sir Hekhtur** is also destroyed.

Explodes: When **Canis Rex** is destroyed, roll one D6 before removing it from play. On a 6 it explodes, and each unit within 2D6" suffers D6 mortal wounds.

Chainbreaker: Each time **Canis Rex** makes an attack against a non-**Imperium** unit, on an unmodified hit roll of 6, one additional hit is scored.

Legendary Freeblade: Once per battle round, you can re-roll one hit roll, wound roll, charge roll or saving throw made for **Canis Rex**.

MENTOR

Canis Rex knows three teachings from the Knightly Teachings (pg 95). In your Command phase, if this model is on the battlefield, it can recount up to two teachings it knows that have not already been recounted by a friendly model this turn. Roll one D6: on a 3+, the recounted teaching is inspiring and takes effect until the start of your next Command phase.

FACTION KEYWORDS: **Imperium, Imperial Knights, Questor Imperialis, Agent of the Imperium, Freeblade**
KEYWORDS (CANIS REX): **Vehicle, Titanic, Character, Questoris-class, Mentor, Knight Preceptor, Canis Rex**
KEYWORDS (SIR HEKHTUR): **Infantry, Character, Sir Hekhtur**

Once a prisoner of the Iron Warriors, Sir Hekhtur resisted agonising torture and escaped only through sheer faith, determination and honour. Now he travels the galaxy, liberating Imperial citizens enslaved by the forces of the Arch-enemy.

28
CANIS·REX
CANIS REX
CANIS·REX

WEAPON PROFILES

Here you will find the profiles for all the weapons that Imperial Knights models can be equipped with. Note that some weapons have the Blast ability; this ability is detailed in full in the Warhammer 40,000 Core Book.

RANGED WEAPONS	RANGE	TYPE	S	AP	D	ABILITIES
Armiger Autocannon	60"	Heavy 2D3	7	-2	3	-
Avenger gatling cannon	36"	Heavy 12	6	-2	2	-
Conflagration cannon	18"	Heavy 3D6	7	-2	2	Each time an attack is made with this weapon, that attack automatically hits the target.
Heavy flamer	12"	Heavy D6	5	-1	1	Each time an attack is made with this weapon, that attack automatically hits the target.
Hekhtur's pistol	15"	Pistol 1	5	-2	2	-
Ironstorm missile pod	72"	Heavy D6	5	-1	2	Blast. This weapon can target units that are not visible to the bearer.
Las-impulsor	Before selecting targets, select one of the profiles below to make attacks with.					
- Low intensity	36"	Heavy 2D6	6	-2	2	Blast
- High intensity	24"	Heavy D6	12	-4	4	Blast
Meltagun	12"	Assault 1	8	-4	D6	Each time an attack made with this weapon targets a unit within half range, that attack has a Damage characteristic of D6+2.
Questor cognis heavy stubber	36"	Assault 4	4	0	1	-
Questor ironhail heavy stubber	36"	Heavy 4	4	-1	1	-
Plasma decimator	Before selecting targets, select one of the profiles below to make attacks with.					
- Standard	48"	Heavy 2D6	8	-4	2	Blast
- Supercharge	48"	Heavy 2D6	9	-4	3	Blast. Each time an unmodified hit roll of 1 is made for an attack with this weapon profile, the bearer suffers 2 mortal wounds after shooting with this weapon.
Preceptor multi-laser	36"	Heavy 4	6	0	1	-
Rapid-fire battle cannon	72"	Heavy 2D6	8	-2	3	Blast
Shieldbreaker missile	48"	Heavy 1	10	-4	D6	Each time the bearer is selected to shoot, it can only make attacks with one shieldbreaker missile, and it can only shoot each shieldbreaker missile it is equipped with once per battle. Each time an attack is made with this weapon, invulnerable saving throws cannot be made against that attack.
Stormspear rocket pod	48"	Heavy 3	8	-2	D6	-
Thermal cannon	36"	Heavy 2D3	9	-4	D6+2	Blast. Each time an attack made with this weapon targets a unit within half range, that attack has a Damage characteristic of D6+4.
Thermal spear	30"	Heavy 2	9	-4	D6	Each time an attack made with this weapon targets a unit within half range, that attack has a Damage characteristic of D6+2.
Thundercoil harpoon	18"	Heavy 1	16	-6	10	Each time an attack is made with this weapon against an **MONSTER** or **VEHICLE** unit (excluding **AIRCRAFT**), add 1 to that attack's hit roll. Each time an attack made with this profile is allocated to a model, that model's unit suffers 3 mortal wounds in addition to the normal damage.
Twin Icarus autocannon	48"	Heavy 4	7	-1	2	Each time an attack is made with this weapon against an **AIRCRAFT** unit, add 1 to that attack's hit roll.
Twin meltagun	12"	Assault 2	8	-4	D6	Each time an attack made with this weapon targets a unit within half range, that attack has a Damage characteristic of D6+2.
Twin siegebreaker cannon	36"	Heavy 2D3	7	-1	2	Blast
Volcano lance	80"	Heavy D3	16	-5	D6+8	Blast

MELEE WEAPONS	RANGE	TYPE	S	AP	D	ABILITIES
Freedom's Hand	Each time an attack is made with this weapon, select one of the profiles below to make that attack with.					
- Strike	Melee	Melee	x2	-4	8	Each time an attack is made with this weapon, an unmodified wound roll of 6 inflicts D3 mortal wounds on the target in addition to the normal damage.
- Sweep	Melee	Melee	+2	-2	3	Each time an attack is made with this weapon profile, make 2 hit rolls instead of 1 and an unmodified wound roll of 6 inflicts 1 mortal wound on the target in addition to the normal damage.
Reaper chain-cleaver	Each time an attack is made with this weapon, select one of the profiles below to make that attack with.					
- Strike	Melee	Melee	+4	-4	3	-
- Sweep	Melee	Melee	User	-3	1	Each time an attack is made with this weapon profile, make 2 hit rolls instead of 1.
Reaper chainsword	Each time an attack is made with this weapon, select one of the profiles below to make that attack with.					
- Strike	Melee	Melee	+6	-4	6	-
- Sweep	Melee	Melee	User	-3	2	Each time an attack is made with this weapon profile, make 3 hit rolls instead of 1.
Thunderstrike gauntlet	Each time an attack is made with this weapon, select one of the profiles below to make that attack with.					
- Strike	Melee	Melee	x2	-3	8	-
- Sweep	Melee	Melee	+2	-2	3	Each time an attack is made with this weapon profile, make 2 hit rolls instead of 1.
Titanic feet	Melee	Melee	User	-2	2	-

POINTS VALUES

You can use this section to determine the points (pts) value of each unit in your army. Each entry lists the unit's size (i.e. how many models the unit can contain) and how many points the unit costs. If an entry has a unit cost of '*x* pts/model', then the unit costs *x* points for every model in that unit. You must then add points for each weapon, or item of wargear, that is included in that unit if it is listed in that unit's entry (weapons and wargear not listed in a unit's entry cost no additional points to include in that unit).

 LORDS OF WAR

Armiger Helverin (pg 120)

Unit size.......1-3 models
Unit cost.......155 pts/model
- Meltagun.......+5 pts

Armiger Warglaive (pg 121)

Unit size.......1-3 models
Unit cost.......145 pts/model
- Meltagun.......+5 pts

Canis Rex (pg 130)

Unit size.......1 model
Unit cost.......440 pts

EXALTED COURT

Forge Master.......30 pts
Gatekeeper.......35 pts
Herald.......20 pts
High Monarch.......45 pts
Monarchsward.......35 pts
Master of Justice.......30 pts
Master of Lore.......35 pts
Master Tactician.......30 pts
Master of Vox.......20 pts
Princeps.......35 pts

Knight Castellan (pg 127)

Unit size.......1 model
Unit cost.......595 pts
- Twin siegebreaker cannon.......+15 pts

Knight Crusader (pg 124)

Unit size.......1 model
Unit cost.......485pts
- Meltagun.......+5 pts
- Ironstorm missile pod.......+20 pts
- Stormspear rocket pod.......+40 pts
- Twin Icarus autocannon.......+20 pts

Knight Errant (pg 122)

Unit size.......1 model
Unit cost.......425 pts
- Meltagun.......+5 pts
- Ironstorm missile pod.......+20 pts
- Stormspear rocket pod.......+40 pts
- Twin Icarus autocannon.......+20 pts

Knight Gallant (pg 125)

Unit size.......1 model
Unit cost.......400 pts
- Meltagun.......+5 pts
- Ironstorm missile pod.......+20 pts
- Stormspear rocket pod.......+40 pts
- Twin Icarus autocannon.......+20 pts

Knight Paladin (pg 126)

Unit size.......1 model
Unit cost.......425 pts
- Meltagun.......+5 pts
- Ironstorm missile pod.......+20 pts
- Stormspear rocket pod.......+40 pts
- Twin Icarus autocannon.......+20 pts

Knight Preceptor (pg 129)

Unit size.......1 model
Unit cost.......420 pts
- Ironstorm missile pod.......+20 pts
- Stormspear rocket pod.......+40 pts
- Twin Icarus autocannon.......+20 pts

Knight Valiant (pg 128)

Unit size.......1 model
Unit cost.......585 pts
- Twin siegebreaker cannon.......+15 pts

Knight Warden (pg 123)

Unit size.......1 model
Unit cost.......435 pts
- Meltagun.......+5 pts
- Ironstorm missile pod.......+20 pts
- Stormspear rocket pod.......+40 pts
- Twin Icarus autocannon.......+20 pts

GLOSSARY

On this page you will find a glossary that contains a number of terms used in this Codex.

Active Chivalric ability (pg 118-119): The Chivalric abilities that are currently active for your army, or that are active for specified units from your army. Duplicated active Chivalric abilities on the same unit have no additional effect.

Allegiance (pg 66): All IMPERIAL KNIGHTS models owe their allegiance to either the Imperium or the Adeptus Mechanicus. If a model has the QUESTOR IMPERIALIS keyword, it owes its allegiance to the Imperium, and if it has the QUESTOR MECHANICUS keyword, it owes its allegiance to the Adeptus Mechanicus.

Any number of models can each have their Weapon A replaced with 1 Weapon B: When this wargear option is selected for a unit, any number of models in that unit that are equipped with Weapon A can each have its weapon replaced Weapon B. It is possible for only some of the models in that unit to have their weapon replaced and for others not to.

Army of Renown (pg 88): A variant army list for a Faction that can be used in your games of Warhammer 40,000 to represent a specialised force. It must be Battle-forged, cannot include any Specialist Detachments, and will have other specific restrictions that must be adhered to. Doing so, however, will provide you with unique benefits.

Bondsman ability (pg 117): A type of ability that some IMPERIAL KNIGHTS models can have, which they can use to affect other friendly models. A model can only be affected by 1 Bondsman ability at a time; if selected for another Bondsman ability, the new ability's effects replace the previous effects. ARMIGER-CLASS models affected by a Bondsman ability while your army's level of Honour is either Honoured or Virtuous gain a bonus that reduces the Damage characteristic of incoming attacks, in addition to any other effects.

Burden (pg 104): An ability an IMPERIAL KNIGHTS model can acquire in your Crusade games whilst undertaking a Quest. There are three types of Burden: Mind; Body; Soul. Burdens must be gained when you are instructed to do so.

Chivalric ability (pg 118-119): Each Oath contains two types of Chivalric abilities: Honoured and Virtuous. The Chivalric abilities apply when they are active, which is determined by your army's current level of Honour.

Crusade Duty (pg 84): An ability that EXALTED COURT models gain that only applies if that model is part of your Crusade force.

Dishonoured (pg 99): While your army has 0 Honour points, it is said to be Dishonoured.

Drawn from (pg 116): The noble household that a unit belongs to is the noble household they are drawn from. A unit is drawn from a certain noble household if they have that noble household's name listed on its Faction keyword line.

Exalted Court (pg 84-86): An upgrade that can be applied to QUESTORIS-CLASS CHARACTER and DOMINUS-CLASS CHARACTER models from your army. Each upgrade consists of several associated abilities, one of which is the Exalted Court ability, another of which is a Noble Exemplar ability and another of which is a Crusade Duty.

Freeblade (pg 64): A Freeblade has the FREEBLADE keyword instead of the name of a noble household.

Glory points (pg 99): A resource gained by QUESTSWORN models in your Crusade force as part of the Sworn to a Quest rules. Each time the Quest that a model is currently undertaking ends, its Glory points total is reset to 0.

Heirloom Relic (pg 90-93): A type of Relic that can be given to **IMPERIAL KNIGHTS** models.

Honour Extremis (pg 102): A type of ability that an **IMPERIAL KNIGHTS** model from your army can gain in your Crusade games if they have one or more Qualities. Only one Honour Extremis ability can be used by models from your army per battle round, and only if your army's current level of Honour is Honoured or Virtuous. If any models from your army used an Honour Extremis ability, you lose 1 Honour point at the end of the current battle round.

Honour points (pg 118): Part of the Code Chivalric ability. The number of Honour points your army currently has will determine its current level of Honour. Honour points can be gained and lost throughout the battle.

Honoured (pg 99): While your army has between 1 and 4 Honour points, it is said to be Honoured.

Household Tradition (pg 67-75): Detachment ability for **IMPERIAL KNIGHTS** Detachments. An ability gained by a **<NOBLE HOUSEHOLD>** unit (excluding **FREEBLADES**) based on the noble household they are drawn from, if all units in that Detachment (excluding **FREEBLADES**) are drawn from the same noble household.

IMPERIAL KNIGHTS Detachment (pg 64): A Detachment in a Battle-forged army where every model has the **IMPERIAL KNIGHTS** keyword (excluding models with the **AGENT OF THE IMPERIUM** or **UNALIGNED** keywords).

Imperial Knights secondary objectives (pg 96): Additional secondary objectives that can be used in certain matched play mission packs if every Detachment in your army is an **IMPERIAL KNIGHTS** Detachment.

Knightly Deed (pg 100): Each Quest has an associated Knightly Deed. This must be completed by the model undertaking the Quest in order for that Quest to end in success.

Knight Lances (pg 64): Detachment ability for **IMPERIAL KNIGHTS** Detachments.

Level of Honour (pg 99): Your army's level of Honour is based on the number of Honour points you have at the start of a battle round, and can be either Dishonoured, Honoured or Virtuous. If your army includes any **QUESTSWORN** models, you will need to use the Code Chivalric rules on pages 118-119 to determine your army's current level of Honour, even if the other rules described for this ability do not apply (because your army includes non-**IMPERIAL KNIGHTS** models, for example).

Martial Tradition (pg 76-79): Detachment ability for **FREEBLADES** and Noble Household Detachments that are not one of the following: House Terryn; House Griffith; House Cadmus; House Hawkshroud; House Mortan; House Raven; House Vulker; House Krast; House Taranis.

Noble Exemplar ability (pg 84): An ability that **EXALTED COURT** models gain that only applies if that model has one or more Bondsman abilities and your army's level of Honour is Honoured or Virtuous.

Noble Household Detachment (pg 66): An **IMPERIAL KNIGHTS** Detachment in which every **IMPERIAL KNIGHTS** unit that is not a **FREEBLADE** is drawn from the same noble household.

Noble Household Relic (pg 66): An Heirloom Relic associated with one of the noble households. These are only available to **IMPERIAL KNIGHTS** models that are part of a Noble Household Detachment (and only if they, and your **WARLORD**, are drawn from the associated noble household).

Noble Household Stratagem (pg 66): A stratagem associated with one of the noble households. These are only available to **IMPERIAL KNIGHTS** models that are part of a Noble Household Detachment (and only if they are drawn from the associated noble household). All Noble Household Stratagem are considered to also have the Imperial Knights Stratagem label (see below).

Noble Household Warlord Trait (pg 66): A Warlord Trait associated with one of the noble households. These are only available to **IMPERIAL KNIGHTS CHARACTER** models that are part of a Noble Household Detachment (and only if they are drawn from the associated noble household).

Oath (pg 118-119): Part of the Code Chivalric ability. If this ability applies then at the start of the battle you must swear a number of Oaths. Each Oath consists of a Pledge, a Troth and two Chivalric abilities.

Pledge (pg 118-119): Part of an Oath. This is a condition that, if satisfied, will increase the number of Honour points your army has.

Quality (pg 102-103): An bonus an **IMPERIAL KNIGHTS** model can acquire in your Crusade games whilst undertaking a Quest. There are three types of Quality: Sword; Shield; Lance. Qualities must be gained when you are instructed to do so. Each Quality consists of two abilities, one of which is an Honour Extremis ability.

Quest (pg 100-101): **QUESTSWORN** models from your army must undertake Quests. When selecting a new Quest for a model, you cannot select one that another model from your Order of Battle is currently undertaking, unless all the available Quests are currently being undertaken. Each Quest contains a Knightly Deed, which is a condition the model undertaking the Quest must satisfy as part of successfully completing the Quest. That model will also need to have a Glory points total of 3. If both of these conditions are met before the Quest ends in failure, the Quest ends in success and the model undertaking the Quest gains 1 Quality. If a Quest ends in failure, that model instead gains 1 Burden.

Questor Allegiance Oath (pg 65): Detachment ability for **IMPERIAL KNIGHTS** Detachments. An ability gained by **<QUESTOR ALLEGIANCE>** models (excluding a **FREEBLADE**) based on their allegiance, if all models in that Detachment owe their allegiance to the Imperium, or if all models in that Detachment owe their allegiance to the Adeptus Mechanicus.

Shame points (pg 99): A resource gained by **QUESTSWORN** models in your Crusade force as part of the Sworn to a Quest rules. If a model's Shame points total reaches 3, the Quest that a model is currently undertaking ends in failure, and its Shame points and Glory points totals are both reset to 0.

Stratagem label: A Stratagem's labels are written beneath its title and can include: Imperial Knights; Battle Tactic; Epic Deed, Strategic Ploy; Requisition; Wargear. A Stratagem can have more than one label; for example, a Stratagem with 'Imperial Knights – Wargear Stratagem' has both the Imperial Knights and Wargear labels.

Teaching (pg 95): A Knightly Teaching. **MENTORS** can attempt to recount teachings that they know.

Troth (pg 118-119): Part of an Oath. This is a condition that, if satisfied, will decrease the number of Honour points your army has.

Unyielding Knight (pg 64): Detachment ability for **IMPERIAL KNIGHTS** Detachments.

Virtuous (pg 99): While your army has between 5 and 6 Honour points, it is said to be Virtuous.

Wandering Hero (pg 64): Detachment ability for **IMPERIAL KNIGHTS** Detachments.

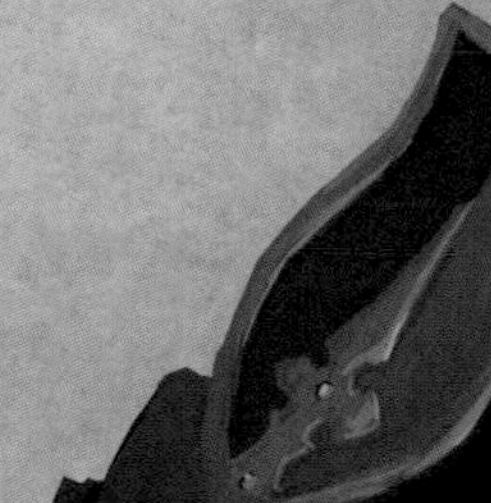

REFERENCE

BONDSMAN ABILITIES (PG 117)

- A model can only be affected by one Bondsman ability at a time
- New Bondsman abilities replace existing ones.
- While an **ARMIGER-CLASS** model is under the effects of a Bondsman ability, if your army is Honoured or Virtuous, each time an attack is allocated to that model, subtract 1 from that attack's Damage characteristic (to a minimum of 1).

CHIVALRIC CODE (PG 118-119)

- Chivalric Code only applies if every model in your army has the **IMPERIAL KNIGHTS** keyword (excluding **UNALIGNED** and **AGENTS OF THE IMPERIUM** models) and all (excluding **FREEBLADES**) are form the same noble household.
- Must select 2 Oaths at the start of the battle, and you start with 1 Honour point.
- Honour points change between 0 and 6 as models satisfy Pledges and Troths.
- Units gain Chivalric abilities depending on army's current level of Honour at start of Battle Round (0 Honour points = Dishonoured; 1-4 Honour points = Honoured; 5-6 Honour points = Virtuous).
- If army Dishonoured, no additional abilities apply.
- If army is Honoured, the Honoured abilities from the selected Oaths apply.
- If army is Virtuous, the Honoured and Virtuous abilities from the selected Oaths apply.

DETACHMENT ABILITIES (PG 64-65)

- **IMPERIAL KNIGHTS** Detachments gain the Knight Lances and Wandering Hero abilities.
- **IMPERIAL KNIGHTS** units in **IMPERIAL KNIGHTS** Detachments gain the Unyielding Knight, Household Tradition and Questor Allegiance Oaths abilities.
- **ARMIGER-CLASS** units in **IMPERIAL KNIGHTS** Detachments gain the Objective Secured ability (this ability is described in the Warhammer 40,000 Core Book).
- **IMPERIAL KNIGHTS** Super-heavy Auxiliary Detachments still get these Detachment abilities.

EXALTED COURT (PG 84-86)

- If Battle-forged, can upgrade **QUESTORIS-CLASS** or **DOMINUS-CLASS** models.
- Doing so increases model's Power Rating and points value.
- Upgraded models will gain new abilities, one of which is a Noble Exemplar ability and one of which is a Crusade Duty.
- Upgraded models also gain the following ability: **Exalted Court:** If this model has a Bondsman ability, it can use it one additional time in each of your Command phases.
- Noble Exemplar ability only applies if army is Honoured or Virtuous and this model has a Bondsman ability.
- Crusade Duty only applies if the model is part of your Crusade force.

HOUSEHOLD TRADITIONS (PG 67-75)

- If every unit in a Detachment (excluding **FREEBLADES**) is from the same noble household, all **<NOBLE HOUSEHOLD>** units in that Detachment gain their noble household's Household Tradition.
- If noble household does not have an associated Household Tradition, select one Martial Tradition from pages 76-79.
- Each **FREEBLADE** unit gains one Martial Tradition that no other unit from your army has.

ION SHIELDS (PG 117)

- 5+ invulnerable save against ranged attacks.

KNIGHT LANCES (PG 64)

- One **ARMIGER-CLASS, QUESTORIS-CLASS** or **DOMINUS-CLASS** model in this Detachment gains the **CHARACTER** keyword.
- Command Benefits on Detachment change if your **WARLORD** is part of that Detachment, depending on the type of Detachment and the number and type of models in that Detachment.

<NOBLE HOUSEHOLD> KEYWORD (PG 66)

- When you include a unit with the **<NOBLE HOUSEHOLD>** keyword, nominate which noble household it is drawn from, or declare if it is a **FREEBLADE**.
- Replace every instance of the **<NOBLE HOUSEHOLD>** keyword on that unit's datasheet with the name of your chosen noble household or **FREEBLADE**.
- A Detachment cannot include units from two different noble households (it can include any number of **FREEBLADES**).

<QUESTOR ALLEGIANCE> KEYWORD (PG 65)

- When you include a unit with the **<QUESTOR ALLEGIANCE>** keyword, nominate if it owes it allegiance to the Imperium or the Adeptus Mechanicus.
- Replace every instance of the **<QUESTOR ALLEGIANCE>** keyword on that unit's datasheet with **QUESTOR IMPERIALIS** or **QUESTOR MECHANICUS** respectively.

QUESTOR ALLEGIANCE OATHS (PG 65)

- If every unit in a Detachment has the same allegiance, all **<QUESTOR ALLEGIANCE>** units in that Detachment (excluding **FREEBLADES**) gain a Questor Allegiance Oath.
- **QUESTOR IMPERIALIS** units gain Vow of Honour: Add 1 to Advance and charge rolls made for this model, and add 1" to its pile-in and consolidation moves. In addition, when making an Advance or charge roll for this model, you can ignore any or all modifiers to that roll.
- **QUESTOR MECHANICUS** units gain Sacristan Pledge: Add 1 to the Wounds characteristic of a this model (add 2 if model is **TITANIC**) and in your Command phase, this model regains 1 lost wound.

SUPER-HEAVY WALKER (PG 117)

- This model can declare a charge in a turn in which it Fell Back.
- When making a Normal Move, Advance or Fall Back move, can move across other models (excluding **MONSTER** and **VEHICLE** models) as if they were not there.

SWORN TO A QUEST (PG 99-105)

- **IMPERIAL KNIGHTS** models in your Crusade force can gain the **QUESTSWORN** keyword.
- **QUESTSWORN** models undertake Quests, each of which has a Knightly Deed, and they gain Glory points and Shame points, depending on that model's rank and your army's level of Honour at the end of the battle.
- Each time a model has both 3 Glory points and has completed its Quest's Knightly Deed, it gains 1 Quality and its Glory points are reset to 0.
- Each time a model has 3 Shame points, it gains 1 Burden and its Glory points and Shame points are both reset to 0.

UNYIELDING KNIGHT (PG 64)

- This model counts as 5 models when determining control of objective markers (or 10, if it is **TITANIC**).

WANDERING HERO (PG 64)

- Only applies to Super-heavy Auxiliary Detachments.
- 1 **FREEBLADE** unit in that Detachment gains the **AGENT OF THE IMPERIUM** keyword (one per army).